Political Parties

Contemporary Trends and Ideas

The CONTEMPORARY ESSAYS Series

GENERAL EDITOR: LEONARD W. LEVY

Political Parties

Contemporary Trends and Ideas

Edited by

Roy C. Macridis

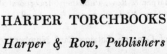

HARPER TORCHBOOKS

Harper & Row, Publishers

New York, Evanston, and London

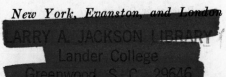

POLITICAL PARTIES

First edition: HARPER TORCHBOOKS, 1967,
Harper & Row, Publishers, Incorporated,
New York, Evanston, and London.

Library of Congress Catalog Card Number: 67-21560.

Designed by Darlene Starr Carbone

Contents

Preface

IN this symposium I have selected some of the most representative recent articles on political parties, with special attention to England and Western Europe. It is not my contention that they are the best ones. It would have been easy to choose another nine essays of equal merit. The essays here, however, were the most representative to me for this reason: they link party development with ideological trends and deal explicitly or implicitly with problems of method and analysis in the study of political phenomena.

I wish to thank the authors of the articles and the editors of the various journals for their permission to reprint these essays. My thanks also to the editor of this series, Dr. Leonard W. Levy, who asked me to prepare this book.

Roy C. Macridis

Waltham, Massachusetts
September 1, 1966

Introduction: The History, Functions, and Typology of Parties

ROY C. MACRIDIS

I. HISTORY

IT is generally taken as axiomatic that no political system can exist without political parties. The exceptions that come to mind are traditional societies, authoritarian systems in which a hereditary monarch relies upon the army or the police to maintain his rule, and some contemporary transitional societies. But the party, an association that activates and mobilizes the people, represents interests, provides for compromise among competing points of view, and becomes the proving ground for political leadership, appears to be the rule today. The party is a ubiquitous phenomenon of contemporary political life. It is an instrument to gain power and to govern. It has been used to defend well-established associations—the Church for example—or to destroy the status quo, as the Bolsheviks did in 1917 when they toppled one of the oldest governmental edifices—the tsarist monarchy. The party, in turn, tamed those who used it to destroy, and has brought into the political process, whose essence is compromise, forces that had rejected democracy.

At the turn of the nineteenth century, the Catholic churches in Europe reconciled themselves to the rule of democracy and to the logic of election, and formed Christian Democratic parties that gradually shed their religious orientation to become undistinguishable in their organization, programs and appeal from "lay" parties. A little later the socialist parties abandoned revolution in favor of reform. After World War II the sharp edge of revolution that typified the Communist parties was blunted. The Italian or the French Communist parties seem to be following the precedent of the Socialist parties in favor of reform

9

within the broad rules of parliamentary government. In many of the new nations the political party appeared to be almost coterminous with politics—in inculcating participation and bringing into the threshold of political awareness the millions who had been discontented or even alienated. The one-party system has been hailed both an instrument of political education and a means to build support for the governing elite. Thus to study political parties is to study one of the most significant and ubiquitous elements of political life. It is often forgotten, however, that it took a long time for the parties to develop and assume the importance that is attributed to them now. It was not until the middle of the nineteenth century that political writers began to refer to them, and it was not until recently that we began to have specific references to and studies on their functions and organization.

If we look at the history of political parties, we shall identify certain stages of development that are common to Western Europe, England, and to some extent to the United States. First, the growth of the party is associated with and generally follows rather than precedes representative government. It is only at the beginning of the nineteenth century that the party emerges as a group consisting of members of representative assemblies in terms that are no longer synonymous with a cabal or as a special relationship to the monarch. It is roughly at the same time that a certain "ideology," often to be traced back to earlier times, is associated with particular party labels—Liberals and Conservatives, Republicans and Democrats, Legitimists, Bonapartists, etc. All parties and the outlook of party leaders are, at this stage, steeped in a liberal philosophy that has a peculiar dialectic. For while the Liberals, particularly James Mill and John Stuart Mill, push their premises to their logical conclusion and argue for "one man, one vote," without which the government may, they claim, become tyrannical, they are both sensitive to Burke's earlier arguments in favor of virtual representation and fearful that the "masses" will use the party as an instrument to gain control and press for the satisfaction of their own interests. Guizot and Benjamin Constans in France, Whigs and Tories alike in England, and, earlier, Madison in the United States, rationalize their fear of the majorities. Some in terms of restricted suffrage or proportional representation, others to defend a middle-class republic, and still others to divide the governmental powers with such skill that no clear-cut majority can ever emerge, let alone govern. Parties are often considered as synonymous with factions, and are distrusted. Their emergence, therefore, is surrounded by many caveats and obstacles. They remain limited in two ways: they are, at first, nothing but labels to identify groupings among the aristocracy and middle classes, and secondly, they are restricted in membership. The political battles—if they can be called that—are limited to the representatives of the well-to-do and the aristocracy.

The second stage in the development of political parties comes after the middle of the nineteenth century. First, the extension of the franchise—by the middle of the thirties in the United States; between 1832 and progressively throughout the nineteenth century in England; in 1848, but for all practical purposes only after the fall of the Second Empire in 1870, in France and at approximately the same time (but with qualifications) in Germany and other countries of Western Europe. It does not change, at first, the character of the parties—it only provides the conditions for change. The leadership and indeed the basis of the party remain the representatives in the assemblies. But support now must come from a wider number of participants. This entails gradual changes in party organization. One of them is the development of permanent central organizations to solicit votes, collect funds, present programs, and to impose, directly or indirectly, the party leaders. First in the United States, and by 1870 in England and in Western Europe, the party becomes a broad organization—something like a pyramid whose apex is always identified in the representative assemblies but whose base is now broad enough to include most of the people. The liberal fears continue to be honored—the organization is not strong, the members cannot control the leaders, the membership is far from massive, the program is a statement of purpose that hardly ever binds the representatives once elected, and finally, the new social classes spawned by the industrial revolution, though increasingly solicited to vote, are left out of the party. Indeed the working class as a whole appears to be disenchanted with parliamentary government—the former preserve of the aristocracy and now of the middle classes. Representative assemblies shied away from the major economic social problems—hours and conditions of work, conditions in employment, education, child labor, housing, compensation for unemployment and for accidents, welfare legislation, etc.—that are of vital concern to the working classes. The nineteenth century was a political century in which political problems, such as suffrage, associational freedoms, relations between Church and state, the development of the instruments of democratic government itself, were the principal issues of controversy and debate.

A third stage in the development of parties occurs in the decades preceding and following the end of the nineteenth century. It is the period that Maurice Duverger aptly associates with the growth of what might be called extra-parliamentary parties. The impetus for organization now comes from sources other than the representatives in Parliament, from persons who are not only uninterested in Parliament, but who often desire to stay out of Parliament and even to do away with it. Their appeal is directed to a specific class—mostly to the working class. The parliamentarian and the notable give place to the organizer; the parliamentary caucus to the territorial federations; and the party leader to the national council or committee. Membership is widely solicited and a member pays dues, participates, agitates, and activates. The party program becomes specific and is generally addressed to the economic and social evils of the industrial revolution—with socialist reformist and revolutionary overtones. The party emerges as a disciplined movement with a vision and mass support. The French Socialists under Jaurès, the German Social Democratic Party under Bebel, the British Labour Party in its first tentative steps under Keir Hardie and the inspiration of the Fabians, are something of a cross between a church and an army—lacking the inspirational devotion of the first and the discipline of the second, yet aspiring to the mystique and the discipline of both.

Faith and rigid discipline will come with the emergence of the Communist parties of Western Europe, founded after World War I. As Isaiah Berlin points out, the Communist Party becomes in essence an army and a church, intransigent, highly disciplined, demanding, and often effectively exacting, the total commitment and loyalty of the individual member. Payment of dues is no longer enough to be a member—individual work and activity must be the rule; participation is not enough either, obedience supersedes debate and endless "chatter"; persuasion is only part of the party work, action is the *mot d'ordre,* and by action we must understand revolutionary action. Membership is drawn not indiscriminately but from among those who show qualities of devotion and discipline. They are usually drawn from their place of work—factories, civil service, universities, high schools, but also from the working-class neighborhoods. They form cells that meet frequently and know only their leader, not fellow members from other cells. Thus protection against detection is insured.

With the development of the Communist Party, the full cycle of party development, curiously enough in the full sense of democratization, is reached. The Socialist parties under the assault of the Communists become increasingly adapted to parliamentary and democratic government; the liberal parties in turn are forced to appeal to the support of the masses wooed by the Socialists and now actively and militantly solicited by the Communists. The Catholic hierarchy becomes fully reconciled to the creation of "Catholic" parties that solicit the support of the citizens in order to stave off the appeal of Socialists and Communists. The full implication of universal suffrage—together with its dangers—is now either put to full use or exploited. Business groups, the middle classes, the Church, the trade unions, all become associated with political parties. In a number of political systems—notably England, the United States, the Scandinavian countries, and in part in France and in the British dominions—the growth of mass parties forces the pace of the democratization of the society. But mass parties and democracy do not always strike a comfortable modus vivendi. In some countries, notably Germany and Italy, the mass potential of the party is exploited, through an imitation of some of the Communist tactics, to overthrow democratic government and establish a one-party rule, to crush all other parties and to make the state an appendage of the party itself. This was the case with the Nazi Party in Germany and the Fascist Party in Italy.

There is perhaps a fifth stage in the development of parties. After World War II, and more notably in the last decade, all political parties of the Western world and of the industrially advanced societies (including of course the Soviet Union and Japan) begin to display some novel characteristics: they begin to lose their ideological character. All parties become brokers of a society that because of progressive industrialization becomes divided into many social, professional, occupational, and interest groups. Therefore, parties become both more representative and reformist; they deal with ad hoc problems and search for ad hoc solutions; that is to say, they become pragmatic. No longer is an attempt made to resolve issues by an appeal to total solutions involving the economic or social structure of the society, but rather by careful compromises and incremental changes. The ideologue recedes in favor of the manipulator and the visionary leader in favor of the cautious representative. Commenting on this situation Jean Paul Sartre, one of the last remaining great ideologues, advised the young men in France to go to Algeria or to Africa to pursue their visions. Western Europe, even France, and the political parties had no ideology to offer!

This brief historical sketch applies to what might be called the "Western world," including the former British dominions and of course the Scandinavian countries. In Japan parties developed only after the turn of the century and it is really only after World War II that a genuine party system seems to have gained a degree of legitimacy. In Russia, after a brief and unsuccessful effort with democracy and parties in the years preceding World War I, the country reverted to tsarist absolutism that was succeeded by the emergence of one-party totalitarian government. Elsewhere parties did not emerge as serious contenders for political power until after World War II. Thus our historical sketch and the stages of development we noted cover only a small part of the world and identify parties with democratic systems. Generally speaking, in all these countries parties developed in terms of a similar background. The issue of national identity had been resolved and in the great majority of cases governmental institutions had gained a certain degree of legitimacy. Wherever the national identity had been made secure and legitimacy of the governmental institutions had gained roots, and wherever participation and representative government had emerged, a party system developed. Where national identity was not secure or where legitimacy was precarious, the development of political parties was impeded. The latter was clearly the case with Germany and Italy (national identity) and with France (legitimacy). But after the middle of the twentieth century, an open and competitive party system seems securely established in these three countries, too.

This historical sketch tells us, therefore, both a great deal and very little about political parties. First, they are the consequences rather than the "causes" of democracy, but once they emerge they reinforce the prior conditions to which they owe their origin. In other words, while an overall acceptance of freedom of association and freedom of participation allows for the formation of parties and the growth of a party system, the parties themselves and the party system as a whole reinforce and sustain the commitment to these basic freedoms. Secondly, in "the West" the industrial revolution had already begun or was in progress when the parties were formed. Their development follows pretty closely the progress of the industrial revolution. Here again we may offer two broad hypotheses: the greater the legitimacy of government and the earlier the impact of the industrial revolution, the more peaceful the development of parties and the greater the attachment to a party system. England is the obvious illustration of this; Russia of the reverse. Thirdly, in what we have called the "Western world" parties evolved to play specific roles—formulate programs, pass legislation, control the government, reconcile conflicts. None of the parties in the Western world, except the Communists, ever had a "total" outlook on life. As a result, the load upon parties was, relatively speaking, never a heavy one. National identity had been realized; a modicum of participation within the system had been attained; the notion that all groups had a right to be heard and to participate had also been accepted, at least in theory; the kind of economic system the society was to have became a matter of violent dispute for only a few decades—to taper off into reformist activities and ultimately to become reconciled with pragmatic and ad hoc rather than ideological and millennial concerns. Thus all parties, with the exception of the Communist Party, evolved and accepted a setting bequeathed to them from the past; they valued and supported participation, national identity, and the government institutions, and they placed certain restraints upon political conflict. Their role in the Western world was specific and instrumental rather than diffuse and total.

Therein, perhaps, lies the reason for the successful development of the parties in the West. They had to decide the manner in which conflict would take place, define the parameter of conflict and concentrate on policy questions. As a result, they have become increasingly pragmatic and when they are ideological, they are only discreetly so—their ideological position relates only to a specific issue and never spills over to challenge the polity as a whole. Lastly, as the Western world evolved, the industrial revolution and the economic prosperity that ensued created a social structure in which new socio-economic groups and occupations emerged, associations proliferated, loyalties multiplied. The party represented them and in doing so secured their support not only to the party but to the system within which the party operated. In Durkheim's sense the social division of labor created an unprecedented multiplicity of groups, roles and occupations with overlapping individual membership. Parties became almost inevitably the agencies that best linked a multigroup social structure with the government. But this in itself was a precondition for compromise and accommodation. A citizen who performs many roles and belongs to many organizations in a modern society becomes open to and tolerant of *all* groups and roles. The same applies to the party that solicits support from the citizens. As a result, Western parties have become increasingly aggregative and comprehensive, rather than sectarian and exclusive. The function of the party became restricted to the training and selection of political leaders to be chosen by the people to run the government over a specific period of time in accord with certain policy pledges. Popular choice was to determine and support the winner and to console the loser with the prospect of future victory. The more pragmatic and the less total the issues dividing the parties, the easier it was to take victory with restraint and defeat without despair or a sense of revolt.

The conditions, then, in which parties come into being and have evolved in the West are vastly different from the emergence of parties in the new nations. Political parties emerged in most of the ex-colonial countries in order to cope with a series of problems with which their

Western counterparts were not directly involved: national emancipation and identity, the creation of a set of values within which political participation would be implemented, the creation of legitimized governmental institutions, the establishment of new norms conducive to industrialization, the creation of governmental institutions to distribute benefits while inculcating support, and last but not least, the management of conflict—i.e., the establishment of procedures to allow for differences, to make compromises between different points of view, and to accommodate conflicting ideologies. The political parties, therefore, were to become, in the Rousseauian sense of the term, legislators—the founders of institutions and procedures, and even more, the founders of new nations! It was an impossible job.

The differences between the West and the new nations are indeed so great that comparison is fairly easy. In the new nations there was no system to support the creation of political parties; no legitimacy of governmental procedures within which the parties could operate and to which they could give their support; there was little, if any, experience with representative government; no sense of citizenship defining even limitatively certain common rights which could in turn give rise to legitimate expectations of participation; finally, the stark and close memory of colonial rule had inculcated a propensity for conflict rather than compromise. The ability to compromise was the major contribution of the political parties in the Western world. It was this exactly that was the first essential to be found wanting as the parties developed in the new nations. Conflict became factional; the parties became intolerant of opposition, and repressive; participation assumed the form of forced mobilization. Without the overall setting of national identity, a modicum of legitimacy and a sense of citizenship, conflict could no longer be managed. With the exception of India and China, this appears to have been the case in the Asian, Southeast Asian and African new states. The Chinese case confirms rather than disproves the argument advanced here since in China there was a sense of national identity, coupled with a relatively higher degree of economic development and organization and a liberal movement at the turn of the century that had given a promise, rather than the reality, of citizenship and representation. Furthermore, the Chinese Communist Party had consolidated its position and strength in many parts of the country and had played an important role in mobilizing national sentiment against the Japanese. It was a ready-made instrument of mobilization and control long before the nationalist forces disintegrated. But it was not strong enough to allow for conflict or to provide for channels of accommodation. It became an instrument of mobilization while remaining a repressive agency. Whether the dialectic between repression and participation will be resolved in favor of the latter, as some think the case to be in the Soviet Union, remains to be seen.

II. THE FUNCTIONS OF PARTIES

Political scientists and sociologists provide us with an impressive listing of the functions of political parties, without always the benefit of the discriminating factors under which certain functions can or cannot be efficiently performed, or a satisfactory conceptualization linking function and structure. Thus among the functions most commonly given we find the following: *representation (and brokerage), conversion and aggregation; integration (participation, socialization, and mobilization); persuasion, repression, recruitment and choice of leaders, deliberation, policy formulation, control of the government.*

By representation (and brokerage) we mean the expression and articulation of interests within the party and through the party. Sometimes the representative function outweighs that of the brokerage—the party is an expression of a given interest, a given class, or a given social grouping. In this sense its major function is to provide a direct political vehicle to the interest it represents—the Church, the farmers, the workers, etc. Brokerage comes into the picture when multiple interests and points of view find themselves for one reason or another within the same party. Then the party as a whole attempts to reach a compromise among them and present an overall point of view that is acceptable to the members and is likely to appeal to the public as a whole.

Conversion and aggregation are only variants of representation and brokerage. By conversion we understand the transformation of what may be called the raw materials of politics—interests and demands—into policy and decisions. As our organisms transform carbohydrates into energy, the party transforms interests into policy. The successful performance of this function, if we continue with our analogy, depends upon a proper balance between intake and output. The function may be impaired by the massive intake of energy material. As we noted earlier with regard to the new nations, a party that attempts to integrate a system without paying attention to the interests involved may finish by destroying itself. A party that attempts to manufacture out of a limited number of demands a set of objectives and policy outputs that go far beyond the expectation of the interests involved, will soon find itself running out of steam in the same way in which an engine will come

to a stop if it tries to go too fast over a long haul with only a limited
supply of fuel. The same may well happen to a party that cannot adjust
its aggregative and conversion engine to new interests and demands.
The motor will be there, but it will not run because the quality of the
fuel has changed.

Participation, socialization and mobilization are variants of essentially
one overall function—integration. Socialization is the process through
which a set of norms about the political system is transmitted to the
younger people; mobilization is the extreme variant of socialization—
the party attempts to bring rapidly large numbers of people who
formerly stood outside the system, either because they were apathetic,
alienated, ignorant, indifferent, or simply afraid, into the system, to
inculcate interest and to secure mass support. Participation stands somewhere between mobilization and socialization—it means that through
the party in all systems a medium of expression of interest and participation in deliberation and choice of policies and leaders is open to
all. A degree of prior socialization and mobilization is a precondition
for participation.

The party by mobilizing and establishing a level of participation
"integrates" the individual into the political system. It establishes both
affective and rational ties between the individual and the political system
and transforms the former into a citizen and the latter into a responsive
government. The manner in which integration takes place and its timing
are of crucial importance. Hypothetically, one might state that the
greater the emphasis upon mobilization, the less open and democratic
the system; the greater the emphasis upon integration, the more repressive the party and the greater the likelihood of a one-party system.

By persuasion we mean those activities of the party that are geared to
the development and the presentation of policy suggestions in order to
gain as widespread support as possible for them. All media of communication are freely used for this purpose with all parties on the same
footing of equality and with guarantees that they will present their
points of view freely. By repression we mean exactly the opposite: the
party, through the government or directly, imposes sanctions upon members and non-members alike, controls the fate of all other associations
and parties, and endeavors to exact obedience and to fashion the minds
and loyalties of the adherents in a manner that not only does not allow
for opposition but penalizes opposition and dissent. Parties that attempt
to integrate and mobilize are generally repressive, but we must remember that there is a constant dialectic that may transform mobilization
into participation and repression into persuasion and brokerage. A totali-

tarian party may move in the direction of persuasion and democracy.

Recruitment is used in the widest possible sense to denote training and preparation for leadership: exposure to the public, the performance of governmental legislative or other functions by members of the party, and of course, successful competition in elections. Few are the leaders in any society, with some notable exceptions, who can attain public office without belonging to and participating actively in a party. The army, the bureaucracy, the university or business may and occasionally do provide "political leaders." The ascension of a charismatic leader, an army officer, or a bureaucrat to a position of political power is often an indication of the weakness or the breakdown of the party system.

The other functions of parties listed were deliberation, policy formulation and control of the government. Party members come to agreement about major objectives and before they do so there is an opportunity for debate. Even in one-party systems the party does this, although Stalin was able through the use of various repressive instruments to dominate and subordinate not only the rank and file but also the leaders of the party. It is equally true that in a one-party system, deliberation remains restricted to the top party echelons and the rank and file is generally expected to give approbation and mobilize in favor of the policy decided at the top. In two- or multi-party systems there is potentially greater room for intra-party discussion and competition between conflicting points of view, so that the deliberative process appears to be open to all. Yet there is evidence that the rank and file does not avail itself of this opportunity and that all parties, as Michels pointed out many years ago, have a propensity towards oligarchy.

By control of the government we generally mean two things. One is the actual function of legislating and governing. This is the case when the party has a majority or controls the legislature and through it, in parliamentary systems or by virtue of direct election as is the case with presidential systems, gets its leader elected either as Prime Minister or as President. We also mean the constant effort on the part of the party to control the government and its activities, either through the day-to-day control that it exercises in parliamentary systems or through its ultimate power to deny nomination and support to a party leader.

One last function of the political party or parties should be mentioned: what we may call the supportive function. The party not only mobilizes and governs, but must create conditions for its own survival and for the survival of the system within which it operates. It must create supports for the system. Socialization, mobilization, participation, grouped here under the heading of integration, have this purpose. The decisions made, the policies formulated and implemented, the degree to which the party listens or fails to listen to its clientele, may strengthen or weaken the support given. No party can afford to ignore pressing demands for too long, and no party can operate for long without attempting to inculcate among the people a pattern of beliefs that sustain it and the political system as a whole. In this sense the parties in the Western world helped, as we noted, to legitimize and strengthen the conditions of freedom and participation that made it possible for them to come into being. In the same sense the one-party system attempts to consolidate and justify the conditions that account for its rule. All parties operate then under the same sociological constraints. In order to sustain the system and enhance its legitimacy, they must perform effectively the conversion function we mentioned. If they do not, their appeals to the legitimacy of the system or to the logic of their own rule will be of no avail.

III. TYPOLOGY

There is a plethora of definitions and typologies of political parties and party systems. Among the first we may list the following: authoritarian and democratic; integrative and representative; ideological and pragmatic; issue-oriented and clientele-oriented; national and regional; religious and secular; democratic and revolutionary; mass and elite; democratic and oligarchic. As for typologies of party systems, the most widely used classification is based upon numbers—one-party, two-party and multi-party; others include closed or competitive; aggregative and ideological; pluralistic or monopolistic; issue-oriented vs. clientele-oriented; integrative and representative. The party system is thus defined in terms of the characteristics of the parties. Confusion and profusion of terms seems to be the rule.

It is a thankless task to attempt to review the literature (the reader will get a taste of the proliferation of terms in the essays that follow), nor is it necessary to despair because of the existence of so many definitions of types. A typology of parties and party systems should be based upon (a) the sources of party support; (b) internal organization; and (c) the functions they perform and their mode of action.

a) *Sources of Party Support:* We suggest one basic distinction: *comprehensive vs. sectarian.* Under the first we shall classify all political parties that are clientele-oriented, i.e., that attempt to get as many votes as possible from each and every citizen. Sectarian parties are those that appeal to a class, a region or an ideology. These two types do not fully correspond to reality. Socialist or religious parties are sectarian, but they are not exclusive. Parties in England and in the United States are comprehensive, but they cannot possibly hope to appeal with equal success to all groups. They have to discriminate somewhat with regard to their clientele, that is, they are to a small degree "exclusive."

(b) *Internal Organization:* The two basic types we propose are *closed* and *open*. Closed parties are those with restricted membership or that impose severe qualifications for membership. Open parties are those that allow anybody to join and impose very light—indeed often hardly any—conditions for membership. "Openness" and "closedness" are associated, however, with other features. Closed parties tend to be authoritarian, i.e., the members are expected to follow the decisions made by the leaders without having easy access to open deliberative procedures; the opposite is the case with open parties. Closed parties tend to stress direct action and to be oriented toward a monopolistic control of government; open parties stress political action and respect political pluralism.

(c) *Modes of Action and Functions:* The two basic types we propose are *diffused* and *specialized*. Specialized parties stress representativeness, aggregation, policy-deliberation and formulation, participation, control of the government for limited purposes and for a limited period of time; diffused parties stress integration, total and permanent control, mobilization and institution-building. As to the mode of action, diffused parties will generally use any means to come to power, while specialized ones will limit their type of action to the accepted procedures.

Taking the three criteria which we have used to classify parties, we shall then distinguish *party systems* as *integrative* and *competitive*. The party system is integrative where the party or parties are sectarian in emphasizing single overriding symbols of political action, closed and diffused. The party system is competitive where the parties are comprehensive, where the party organization is open and where the functions are specialized. Integrative party systems tend to be one-party systems, while competitive party systems tend to have at least two or more parties.

The purpose of this typology is to suggest basic guidelines and landmarks, to provide some order where there appears to be utter confusion, and to simplify where there appears to be such an extraordinary profusion. Our typology ties up very easily with the functional discussion of the preceding section. Thus integrative party systems with the specific characteristics we noted are prevalent among the underdeveloped societies and in great part in China, in the Soviet Union and at least partly so in India. Competitive party systems are prevalent in the Western world and Japan (today) and in great part in India. Some of the Latin American countries have competitive party systems. In others, the party system is in such a state of flux that it is extremely hard to say in what direction it is moving. Cuba, of course, falls in the integrative type. Under specific conditions party systems may appear to have characteristics that partake of both types. Thus the party system in India is to some extent integrative, but is also competitive and both diffused and specialized. The party system in the Soviet Union remains basically integrative, but with noticeable changes in the direction of aggregation and representation.

PARTY SYSTEMS

		INTEGRATIVE	COMPETITIVE
P A R T I E S	SUPPORT	SECTARIAN (Exclusive, regional class, highly ideologic)	COMPREHENSIVE (Clientele-oriented, pragmatic)
	ORGANIZATION	CLOSED (Authoritarian, direct action, repressive)	OPEN (Permissive and pluralistic)
	MODES OF ACTION AND FUNCTIONS	DIFFUSED (National integration, community building, resort to mobilization)	SPECIALIZED (Aggregative and representative)
		ONE-PARTY	TWO OR MULTI-PARTY

The typology I suggest is derived from an overall theory of a political system within which parties, like all other groups and associations, operate. It assumes that a political system is one in which interests (demands) are translated into decisions and that in order for this to take place without resort to violence and coercion, the system as a whole and the decision-making machinery is supported (considered to be legitimate) by the people. The function of the party is, as we have noted, to transform interests and demands into policies, and to gain control of the instrumentalities of government in order to implement them. Integrative party systems operate in order to realize national identity and to legitimize political institutions, including their own role. Competitive party systems, where conditions of legitimacy and national identity already exist, are aggregative, permissive and representative. They have the advantage of operating within a polity which has already been legitimized. They can, therefore, afford to allow for specialization in the tasks of aggregation and representation. The integrative parties have to resort to repression and monopoly control, thus endangering and at times totally undermining their representative function. They become indistinguishable from the government and they equate legitimacy with the values and symbols they wish to impose. Opposition to them becomes opposition to the state and to the government and the result is either recourse to further coercion and repression or the destruction of the party.

∽ 1 ∽

The Place of Parties
in the Study of Politics*

Avery Leiserson

EDITORIAL NOTE: *This article is representative of the methodological debate that is going on in political science. It is also one of the best efforts to develop a comprehensive and consistent typology. The reader will do well to compare it with the typology I suggested in my introduction and refer to the following: Sigmund Neumann, ed., Modern Political Parties. Chicago, 1956; Maurice Duverger, Political Parties. New York, 1954; Samuel H. Eldersveld, Political Parties, A Behavioral Analysis. Ann Arbor, 1964; Joseph La Palombara and Myron Weiner, Political Parties and Political Development. Princeton, 1966; Colin Leys, Models, Theories and the Theory of Political Parties. Political Studies, VII, No. 2 (June 1959), 172-96; H. Eckstein and D. E. Apter, Comparative Politics, A Reader. New York, 1963, Part V; and R. C. Macridis and B. E. Brown, eds., Comparative Politics: Notes and Readings. 2nd edition, Homewood, Ill., 1964, Part II.*

WHEN the beginner approaches the study of politics, one of the most natural questions for him to ask is: what is it that political science studies? This is a way of asking what is the political scientist's conception of reality. More often than not, the teacher finds the student looking for an objective physical structure, simplified yet concrete, like the astronomer's reduced-scale construction of the solar system, the

---

* This article draws on AVERY LEISERSON, *Political Parties and the Study of Politics*. New York: Knopf, 1958.

biologist's photographic reproduction of microscopic cellular organisms, or the physicist's diagram of atomic structure. It is important for the student of human affairs to realize that while individuals, small groups, mass meetings, and even whole cities can be photographed or diagrammed, social scientists have never succeeded in reproducing satisfactory physical models of such concepts as personality, social structure, bureaucratic organization, the price system, or government. Nor do the ends and criteria of government, like order, justice, freedom, welfare or security, lend themselves to analysis in terms of physical or chemical elements like oxygen, carbon, iron, or uranium. Perhaps the closest physical analogy to politics and government is an automobile engine or an electric power plant; but no one would claim that the driver of a car has learned the principles of the engine if all he knows is how to operate it, any more than the power plant engineer understands generation if all he learns is how to read dials and pull switches. Theory is required, and its function is to identify and abstract from total reality the essential minimal concepts and to formulate statements describing the relationships between those concepts whereby the world of experience becomes comprehensible.[1] Theory is never identical with the totality of phenomenal experience; the propositions and principles of theory provide a means by which aspects of reality can be explicitly analyzed and verified, in the hope that some synthesizing minds will make the efforts toward a synthetic reconstruction of reality on the basis of understood principles.

I. PARTIES AND THEORY:
THE PROBLEM OF A LOGICAL MODEL

The classical model of political philosophy was the state, an artificial construct defined as a population occupying a definite territory, rendering habitual obedience to an organized government or body of ruling officials independent of external control, and possessing an attribute called internal sovereignty (supreme legal authority over its citizens). With this model, political analysis consisted of observing and comparing different kinds of states, their forms and processes of government, the relations between government and citizens, and the methods by which states and governmental forms were changed or transformed. States were classified according to the purposes or ends of human nature or

[1] H. REICHENBACH, *The Rise of Scientific Philosophy*. Berkeley, 1951. For non-institutional, mathematical formulations, see H. SIMON and A. NEWELL, Models: Their Uses and Limitations, in L. D. WHITE, ed., *The State of the Social Sciences*. Chicago, 1956, pp. 66-84; D. LERNER and H. D. LASSWELL, eds., *The Policy Sciences* (1951), chs. 1, 8-9.

society assumed by the philosopher, and political specialists were supposed to be experts upon organizational and policy methods, either (a) conducive to establishing or changing governmental institutions to conform to the postulated ends or principles (the idealistic school), or (b) conducive to establishing or maintaining rule by the individual, group, class, or body of persons with whose interests the analyst identified the welfare of the state (the realistic school).

The history of natural science is full of discarded concepts, as of ether and phlogiston, and with cases of complex systems which have been superseded by simpler ones (the Ptolemaic and the Copernican). Something like this appears to be happening to the theory (model) of the state. As an analytical construct, it was not of much help in discriminating or analyzing governmental systems; the concept of sovereignty was defective both for understanding the historical evolution and contemporary distribution of political forces within countries, and it failed to provide any explanation of revolution or governmental transformation. Its principal use was as a justification of political independence and intransigence in international politics, where the term retains its most plausible applicability and most frequent usage. But the history of science, together with the development of logico-experimental reasoning, also suggests that fruitful scientific progress may be made under the influence of quite erroneous and misleading overall models (theories), and that, given the limitations of human understanding it is quite possible that two or more theoretical models may be necessary to provide adequate explanations of experience. The history of political thought provides ample confirmation of the pluralistic, contingent, and hypothetical character of ideals of the state.

Similar considerations are relevant to the famous Aristotelian classification of governmental forms into the rule of one, the few, or the many. The principal utility of these distinctions lies in the opportunity for logical disputation about, and the inquiry they suggest into, the "real" location of political authority, and the "imputed" values and superiorities of each form. When Aristotle himself applied his categories to the empirical analysis of actual Greek city-states (Books IV-VI of the *Politics*), his "best" forms disappeared and he found himself talking almost entirely in terms of two non-ideal categories, oligarchies and democracies. But the most serious defects of the classical distinction between forms of government emerged with the realization (a) that people and politicians under quite inconsistent governmental structures insist that their governments are "true" democracies, and (b) that similarities as well as differences in political behavior and governance can be detected and stated not only between governmental systems but across national complexes or cultures.[2] This does not mean that differences in political ideals and expectations are unreal or unimportant, particularly to people entertaining them. It is quite possible and instructive to develop a typology of political ideologies (liberalism, democracy, fascism, socialism) in terms of aims or preferences about the relative roles of freedom and authority. But this is not the same kind of model, nor is it necessarily an appropriate procedure for analyzing political systems with respect to their bases of political consensus, their methods of choosing and controlling political leaders, and their processes of arriving at authoritative decisions on public policy. In short, there is something wrong with a logical theory, or analytical model, of the state and a classification of governmental systems which is based wholly upon ideals and purposes, and is too far removed from the practices and material interests by which people are also governed. Nevertheless, this is just about the position (the intellectual arsenal) of political science during the last quarter of the nineteenth century, when it first received academic recognition as a discipline separate from moral and practical philosophy, and from schools of law, and abandoned its uneasy liaison with economics under the name "political economy."[3]

The modern reaction from speculative theories of sovereignty and the state may be traced to a series of Anglo-American studies of that period analyzing the political systems of specific countries. None of these studies found it necessary to depend to any observable extent on such concepts in order to show how people governed themselves.[4] On the contrary, the outstanding features of these works were (1) their direct observation and analysis of political processes and governmental institutions in operation, and (2) their sharp differentiation of formal constitutional-legal structure and symbolism from the effective processes of selecting rulers, regulating the relations between the formal branches or parts of government, conducting the business of government, and formulating public policy. So persuasive and brilliant were these books that they almost immediately achieved the status of classics, and were incorporated into

[2] G. A. ALMOND, Comparative Political Systems. *Journal of Politics*, 18 (1956), 391-409.

[3] Some representative works of this period are: J. B. BLUNTSCHLI, *Theory of the State* (1885); J. W. BURGESS, *Political Science and Constitutional Law* (1890); J. R. SEELEY, *Introduction to Political Science* (1893); W. W. WILLOUGHBY, *The Nature of the State* (1896).

[4] J. S. MILL, *Representative Government* (1861); W. BAGEHOT, *The English Constitution* (1872); W. WILSON, *Congressional Government* (1885); J. BRYCE, *The American Commonwealth* (1888); A. L. LOWELL, *Governments and Politics of Continental Europe* (1807); F. J. GOODNOW, *Politics and Administration* (1900).

the literature as a separate branch of the subject, not as a part of political theory or philosophy, but as empirical data for the comparative analysis of governmental institutions and processes. Research and analytical elaboration of governmental systems in terms of *process* (constituent, electoral, legislative, executive, judicial and administrative) proceeded so far that by 1930 their connection with formal political theory was so tenuous as to be highly embarrassing.[5]

But while the empirical scope of political science progressed to the point of recognizing and absorbing the disparate processes of public law and constitutional symbolism, political behavior and organization (public opinion, political parties, pressure groups, legislation) and public administration, by the end of the first third of the twentieth century it had not produced modern counterparts of the classical system-builders of political philosophy. The second third of the century has been occupied with clarifying the connections between the social sciences and grasping the ancient truth that an adequate science of politics cannot be confined to a body of data concerned *solely* with the institutions *conventionally labelled* as political or governmental. The empirical data of politics are interlinked with, and on the analytical level political theorists are explicitly trying to take account of, human personality (which used to be called "human nature"), social structure (groups and classes), economic organization, geography (natural and human resources), and culture (norms, beliefs and technology). Awareness of these linkages compels a re-examination of the analytic focus of political science, unless we are to fall back upon the definition of the scope of political science as government and related phenomena. The principal vehicle of this theoretical shift has been the notion of politics as authority and power relations among people, enforceable by sanctions (rewards or deprivations) of physical force, economic goods, and moral compulsion or persuasion.[6]

Some major variations of the concept of politics as power relationships among people have been the idea of *legitimate authority* (Weber), the act of deliberate social control toward explicitly chosen ends (Catlin),

[5] The dualism appears sharply in the organization of such works as W. F. WILLOUGHBY, *The Government of Modern States* (1918); H. J. LASKI, *A Grammar of Politics* (1925); J. W. GARNER, *Political Science and Government* (1928). Recent efforts to transcend this separation are C. E. MERRIAM, *Systematic Politics* (1945); R. M. MACIVER, *The Web of Government* (1947).

[6] M. WEBER, *Theory of Economic and Social Organization* (1919), trans. Parsons (1947), Part II.; G. CATLIN, *The Principles of Politics* (1930); C. E. MERRIAM, *Political Power* (1943); H. D. LASSWELL, *World Politics and Personal Insecurity* (1935) and, with A. KAPLAN, *Power and Society* (1950); D. EASTON, *The Political System* (1953). But see T. I. COOK, The Methods of Political Science, in *Contemporary Political Science*. Paris: UNESCO, 1950.

the *power situation* (Merriam), the exercise of influence (Lasswell), and the efforts to symbolize politics as the making of important decisions in society (in Easton's phrase, the "authoritative allocation of values"). Robert A. Dahl has suggested a pluralistic model of four overlapping patterns of decision-making in any given society, based on different types of organized relationships between leaders and non-leaders: (1) hierarchy (non-leaders highly controlled by leaders); (2) democracy (formal leaders highly controlled by non-leaders); (3) bargaining (reciprocal control among leaders); (4) the price system (control of leaders by competitive market conditions and by the limits of rational choice).[7] Once again, this conceptual multiplicity of models (theories) should not be misinterpreted by the student as meaning that scientific knowledge is impossible. Rather it should encourage him in the historical conviction of the non-determinism of the great problems facing man-in-society, and of the degree of choice that is possible for man by reflecting about and participating through politics to guile his collective destiny with his fellowmen.[8]

The common residue in all contemporary analytical-empirical theories of politics consists in their agreement that in order to understand the ultimate, perhaps unknowable nature of influence and power relationships among men, it is necessary at least to understand how the major systems of belief operate in respect to relationships between social organization and political authority, how political power is organized and distributed between officials and citizens, how political opinion is generated and shaped in choosing rulers and formulating public policy, and what relationships between public officials and non-governmental leaders affect the determination and execution of public policies. Such empirically based concepts and meaningful hypotheses or propositions as the political scientist is able to formulate concerning the personal relationships of influence and power among men constitute the body of knowledge he has to contribute to the service of his fellowmen in seeking the common values they can agree upon as achievable through institutions of government.

II. THE RELATION OF PARTIES TO PUBLIC OPINION
AND POLITICAL REPRESENTATION

Why theorize about political parties? In the previous section it was observed that thinking about politics implies some basis structural con-

[7] R. A. DAHL and C. E. LINDBLOM, *Politics, Economics and Welfare.* New York: Harper, 1953, Harper Torchbooks, 1963, Part IV; R. A. DAHL, *A Preface to Democratic Theory.* Chicago, 1956.
[8] L. LIPSON, *The Great Issues of Politics.* New York, 1954, esp. ch. 4.

cepts. Whether or not the State is necessary or adequate as one of these, political science starts with the assumption of a community made up of human personalities sharing both common values and conflicting interests, who recognize and accept certain beliefs as legitimizing the authority of a formal organization of rulers and officials to define and carry out these purposes. But while some thinkers may enjoy the game of elaborating the logical (formal) implications of the separation, and consequent relations, between rulers and ruled in a politically organized community,[9] such a game provides the student with little synthetic (factual) knowledge about the functional roles of rulers (politicians), their recruitment and selection, the personal, social and organizational bases of their influence, and how their political organizations affect the making of important public decisions.

If the latter questions indicate the kinds of data we want to get at, and the sort of relationships we want to study, it should be clear that the patterns of interpersonal behavior called "political parties" do not constitute the whole of politics. Yet whether we define parties and party systems as patterns of social interaction, as mass-membership ideological groups, or as historico-legal organizations nominating candidates for public office, we still find that the political party is a strategically critical concept for understanding, in any developed political system,[10] the practices that permit and justify the exercise of political authority, that regulate the effective choice and removal of political rulers, and that prescribe and delimit the authority of the government in power; as well as the processes by which public policy-makers are guided by and subjected to the broad movements of popular sentiment and the balance of inter-group pressures. The political party, or party system, provides the major connective linkage between people and government, between separate, formal agencies and officials of government, and between official and non-official (extra-governmental) holders of power. The political party cuts across, and must be taken into account in, any analysis

---

[9] H. SIMON, On the Observation and Measurement of Political Power. *Journal of Politics*, 15 (1954), 500; J. G. MARCH, An Introduction to the Theory and Measurement of Influence. *The American Political Science Review*, 49 (1955), 431; R. A. DAHL, The Concept of Power. *Behavioral Science*, 2 (1957), 201; F. OPPENHEIM, Control and Causation. *Journal of Politics*, 19 (1958).

[10] The contrast intended here is with political systems based on tribal, kinship, nomadic, agricultural, or primitive, localized communities, where hereditary authority, the persistent resort to violence, religious symbolism and organization, or monolithic mass movements, variously prevent the development of representative government through party politics. See W. C. MACLEOD, *The Origin and History of Politics*. New York, 1931; E. JENKS, *State and Nation*. London, 1919; H. M. CLOKIE, The Modern Party-State. *Canadian Journal of Economics and Political Science*, 15 (1939), 139-57.

of at least four of the conventional processes of government: the electoral, the legislative, the executive, the administrative; and most analysts
would also agree that the appointment of judges is not unrelated to
political beliefs and party affiliation.

Formal governmental structure and symbolism can be understood
without reference to party history and behavior, but the "living constitution," the structure of "effective power in the commonwealth," requires recognition of the organization and distribution of power in
society that is reflected and mobilized in the membership, organization
and customary practices of political parties. One of the most fascinating
and recurrent problems of political science is the relationship of constitutional symbolism and political organization to the distribution of
military force, economic power and social ranking in the community.
Several historic and contemporary ideologies present various *preferred*
answers to the problem, but all of them agree that political authority
and organization are related to the distribution in society of power over
persons, property and prestige. Political organization, whether the
formal, constitutional structure of government or the formal-informal
systems we call interest groups and political parties, is rooted in social
structure; that is to say, political organization *represents* the geographic
and group distribution of social, economic and military power. If power
is unequally distributed, and complicated by the variation of political
opinions within and between the subclasses of each type, this will be
reflected in the units and levels of political organization. In other words,
political organization is not identical with, but functionally related to
(dominated by, superior to, or integrated with) the spatial, functional,
and interpersonal distribution of power in society. It is tempting to assume, and many social theorists have concluded, that political power is
necessarily inferior to and determined by the holders of economic or
military influence:[11] but this is not the only form of the relationship, and
when formulated in this way it rejects too many empirical facts which
complicate the problems of governance through a multiplicity of politically significant organizations.

[11] The most recent formulation of this thesis is c. w. MILLS, *The Power Elite*. New
York, 1956. Although Mills protects himself by presenting facts of personal in-
terpenetration between corporate, military and governmental hierarchies, the whole
weight of his argument reproduces the Marxist and determinist thesis of the
subordination of political to other forms of social power. The more general statement, and more adequate interpretation, goes back to Aristotle, but relevant recent
formulations in terms of the *functional requirements of the political order* may be
found in c. e. MERRIAM, *Systematic Politics*, chs. 1, 6; G. MOSCA, *The Ruling Class*.
New York, 1939; R. K. MERTON, *Social Theory and Social Structure*. Glencoe, Ill.,
1949, ch. 1; F. NEUMANN, Approaches to the Study of Political Power. *Political
Science Quarterly*, 65 (1950), 161.

In addition to their external relations, political parties in their internal organizations present all the phenomena and varieties of centralization-decentralization, coordination-uncoordination, of which complex, large-scale systems of human relationships are capable. Just as the corporation has been labelled the *representative* institution of capitalistic enterprise, so the political party may be designated as the representative institution of *political* enterprise. Again, while some social scientists have committed themselves to a conception of "boss-controlled," tightly organized, hierarchic authority as the prototype of political party organization, systematic and comparative observation indicates that a more flexible, multi-dimensional model is required.[12] What this means for the political analyst is that he should not infer, from the hierarchy and centralization that logically flows from the division of power between leaders and led in political parties, that a wide continuum of alternative forms of political organization is inconceivable or unfeasible.[13]

Finally, the study of political parties is virtually a prerequisite to a realistic understanding of the problems of democracy, both in theory and in action. Since the leaders of almost all independent political systems insist that their governments embody the true principles of democracy and self-government, merely formal definitions of these terms seem somewhat beside the point. Whether or not we try to solve the difficulties by asserting normative or formal criteria of democracy, e.g., popular sovereignty, majority rule, group consultation and minority rights,[14] the student of politics must come to grips with the realities of: (1) power and value-seeking individuals and groups; (2) differentials in human involvement, knowledge and skill in public affairs and self-government; (3) coercive authority and responsibility exercised by voluntary groups, as well as by public representatives and officials; and (4) the establishment and maintenance of conditions whereby such authority is limited and brought into viable, working relationship with group interests and with the common political aspirations or objectives of the whole political community. These are the enduring problems of governance under all

[12] Compare ROBERT MICHELS, *Political Parties*. Glencoe, Ill., 1949, with M. DUVERGER, *Political Parties*. New York, 1954, or S. NEUMANN, ed., *Modern Political Parties*. Chicago, 1956. For an attempt at synthesis of organizational theory ranging from primitive tribes through local communities to industrial factory organization, see G. C. HOMANS, *The Human Group*. New York, 1950.
[13] Historic examples of this reasoning are: Democracy (rule by the majority) implies organization (oligarchy). Organization means control of members (followers) by officers or a minority of leaders. Therefore democracy is impossible (19th century conservatives) or undesirable (20th century fascists).
[14] Examples of these approaches may be found in A. RANNEY and W. KENDALL, *Democracy and the American Party System*. New York, 1956, and R. A. DAHL, *A Preface to Democratic Theory*. Chicago, 1955.

political ideologies and variations in governmental practices. While the study of politics may be approached through other processes besides political parties, notably the judicial or the administrative, the growth and evolution of democracy and rule by public opinion have been uniquely connected with the rise of party government since the seventeenth century. Analytical approaches to the study of politics through political parties will not demonstrate whether democracy according to preferred criteria is possible or desirable, but will inquire, assuming the necessity of multiple political organization through parties and interest groups, what are the requirements and consequences of party government: to what extent and through what processes parties articulate felt public demands, choose political leaders, influence political decisions, shape public opinion and control public officials; and will assess the possibilities of personal and collective choice with respect to political systems for the accomplishment of these functions.

III. THE SIGNIFICANCE OF COMPARATIVE POLITICS

The attainment of knowledge and wisdom through the study of political science seems to proceed through a series of stages:[15] (1) the manipulation of values, goals, ideological systems—what Sigmund Neumann has called "political alchemy"; (2) the empirical description and classification of political forms and process (morphology); and (3) the identification of dynamic political elements (concepts or variables) and the formulation of significant, strategic relationships in differing politico-cultural settings.

Political parties may be analyzed from several points of view. Externally and historically, parties constitute a central institutional link between social and governmental structure in mass-participation political systems. A natural series of hypotheses arises from speculation concerning the mutual effects of formal governmental structure upon party and interest group behavior and organization, as well as of social structure upon the legal framework. Secondly, on the psychological level, party doctrine and perceptions of party membership help the individual to resolve the inner tensions between his several group affiliations and his responsibility for the selection of political-governmental leaders. Thirdly, as organizations, the internal processes of party management and policy-making may be visualized not as closed, self-contained elite groups, but as complex patterns of leader-follower relationships (exhibit-

[15] s. NEUMANN, *Comparative Political Parties* (1956), pp. 1-4, 395-421; Comparative Politics: A Half-Century Appraisal. *Journal of Politics* (August 1957).

ing varying degrees of interpersonal control, rivalry, submission) with other political entities (interest groups, public administrative agencies, mass communications media), with which the parties intersect and overlap in the vital functions of political education, organizing political participation, providing access to and consultation with public officials and coordinating the elective and administrative branches of government.

Finally, we should seek to develop a classification not just of parties, but of political party systems. One such typology may be based upon the variables of: (a) legal-institutional arrangements for political representation, (b) the personal-mass psychological concept of party membership and identification, and (c) the status-and-role relations between party leaders and governmental officials. From these we may derive the following:

Types of Party Systems
1. the Representative-Majority Type
2. the Responsible-Majority Type
3. the Multi-party Coalition
4. Predominant Single-Party

It is not scientifically or logically possible to assert that such a classification is complete and internally consistent, that any one of these types necessarily occurs in connection with a particular type of social structure, or that any one will necessarily recur in any specified conjuncture of political events. Historical research discloses no inevitable historical sequence, cycle, or evolutionary pattern of party development. Furthermore, each category contains sub-categories based upon differing structural arrangements that present varying contexts of equilibrium and strategy to the participant political actors and groups.

For example, the multi-party system operates quite differently in a three-party situation where a rising or declining party-group occupies a balancing role between two major parties, than it does when there are six or more fairly identifiable party groupings, or in a stable, four-party division of the electorate and legislature. Differences also exist within the predominant, single-party category, which may refer to such different situations as: (a) the tradition-bound, caste-divided, pre-industrial society in which the dominance of a single dynasty, ideology, and ruling class is accepted as necessary and inevitable, (b) a social order undergoing rapid, violent transition, characterized by both domestic and foreign ideological competition and organized opposition, (c) a complex, transitional social system in which strong overt intra-party factional struggle exists upon all but one vital issue, upon which political consensus depends. Finally, both types of majority-party systems exhibit internal factional cleavages and relationships with non-party groups which must be taken into account if a majoritarian political system is to be comprehended.

Thus perhaps the basic relevance of comparative party politics is not the mastery of a classification which enables the observer-analyst to label and pigeon-hole a country or community. The classification provides him merely with an analytical framework whereby he can probe more deeply to identify the significant political groupings in different societies, their role structure and functional differentiation, their interplay in the political processes of opinion formation, representation, and decision-making. The instrumental and variable quality of conceptual categories and classifications seems particularly marked when the political scientist turns his attention from the relatively stabilized, developed, differentiated political systems of Western Europe and the United States to the pre-industrial, technologically underdeveloped societies of Asia, Africa and Latin America. In these areas, cultural factors are "being transformed from constants to variables" with explosive ideological effects, the key political groupings are not highly organized and do not recognize the institutional division of political labor characteristic of Western countries (with its high substitutability of roles); and the formal governmental structure is apt to be both alien and misleading as a guide to the repositories and channels of effective political power.[16]

To repeat, the theoretical and comparative analysis of political systems is a basic precondition to self-orientation in the contemporary world. Politics can be and has been studied in a policy-oriented context. To do so, however, implies that the student makes some prior commitment to a concept of national, public or international interest, or identifies himself with an institutional center of political authority. In this context he must cast his findings and recommendations in a framework acceptable to a mass political audience, to the owners or editors of a mass communication medium, to the policy-makers of a political interest or research group, to the higher-level officials of governmental departments or agencies, to legislative committees and chief executives, perhaps even to the bureaucratic and political levels of the U.N. In private and in public,

[16] On these points, see the report of the Committee on Comparative Politics. *The American Political Science Review,* 49 (1955), 1022; D. A. RUSTOW, *The Comparison of Western and Non-Western Political Systems.* Washington: American Political Science Association, 1956; G. A. ALMOND, The Seminar on Comparative Politics. *Items,* 10, No. 4, New York: Social Science Research Council, 1956.

such policy criticism and discussion is vital to a democratic process of opinion formation and representation.

Fundamentally, however, comparative knowledge of the dynamic processes of leadership recruitment, political opinion and policy formation, deserves scientific investigation long before one enters the policy arena of debate over domestic policies of inflation, employment or welfare; foreign policies of national security, diplomacy, trade, aid and stabilization; or programs of international communication and education. Single individuals as well as whole peoples are involved in the process of self-knowledge and clarification of political goals under the challenge of alternative value systems from abroad. As a vehicle both of value conflict and value integration, the political party as no other political institution reaches down, up, across and through the individual, the group, the nation and the cross-national associations of individuals and social classes. The different modes of articulating, through party politics, popular sentiments and group, class, national or international interests constitute a central clue to comprehension, not only of the world-wide ideological struggle between democracy and dictatorship but, beyond ideology, of understanding the requirements, costs and consequences of personal awareness and responsibility for political decision-making, wherever one may live.

IV. INSTITUTIONAL AND BEHAVIORAL ANALYSIS

The conditional and contingent state of political knowledge based upon the classical disciplines of philosophy, history and public law, combined more recently with the empirical study of political and administrative organization, comprises the perceptual and analytical equipment of the main body of modern political science. Collectively, and with its distinctive focus upon government, the oldest tradition in political *science* (as distinct from the philosophical tradition of postulating and elaborating ideal forms of society and government) emerges in what may be called *institutional analysis,* i.e., the historical, legal and logical bases of political institutions, their modes of operation, and their differential effects in terms of broad categories of organizational behavior in operation. Around the beginning of the present century there arose a new emphasis, associated with new developments of anthropology, psychology, and sociology, upon explicit observation and measurement of the perceptions and attitudes in the population at large toward politics, and the effects upon individual perceptions and attitudes of such variables as social group membership, personality, institutions, and events. In recent years, this systematic, social-psychological, methods-oriented approach to politics in terms of people has acquired the label and status of *behavioral analysis,* and through the efforts and writings of such theorists and analysts as Graham Wallas, Charles Merriam, and Harold Lasswell, a process of reconstruction in political theory was set in motion that is not yet completed.[17] A younger generation of political scientists has grown up under the influence of ideas and methods drawn from sociology, psychology and statistics, but applied in a context of investigating specific propositions about behavior in the complex institutional situations of government and politics rather than in the informal, interpersonal relationships of individuals in family, kin, ethnic, religious and work groups.

The principal effects of these influences in the last twenty-five years have been methodological: (1) to sharpen the conceptual focus of political science upon role structures and decision-making processes in power-oriented situations, (2) to improve the training and increase the emphasis of students upon advancing the status-as-knowledge of demonstrable propositions about the behavior of *people,* (3) to encourage the commitment to search for analytical categories capable of ordering the explaining kinds of experimental data that the traditional methods of political analysis ignored or neglected. Not unnaturally, many political scientists resented, resisted and actively fought the incursion of strange methods and odd language, particularly when it was discovered that the advocates of the newer methods had similar motivations and were intrinsically interested in the same phenomena.

In spite of such conflicts it is becoming increasingly evident that the institutional and behavioral approaches are complementary and necessary to each other. The weakness of the institutionalists lies in their inability to identify and measure the factors which produce the variations in personal and mass behavior from the formal requirements and expectations of the political system; hence their emphasis on coercion, moral values and ideologies, and the importance they ascribe to an x-factor of political skill and judgment in supporting their institutional description and prescription. The weakness of the behavioralists lies in an over-emphasis upon methods of data collection and quantitative analysis of minuscular problems of uncertain relevance to the sweeping institutional complexes of politics. But both the macroanalysis of legal, structural, traditional and multi-group institutions and processes of gov-

---

[17] D. B. TRUMAN, The Impact on Political Science of the Revolution in the Behavioral Sciences. The Brookings Institution, *Research Frontiers in Politics and Government.* Washington, 1955, pp. 202-31.

ernment, and the microanalysis of the variables affecting *individual* political attitudes and behavior are essential components of political knowledge. Whatever form the ultimate theoretical integration of the categories of institutional and behavioral analysis may take, the proposition no longer seems seriously in doubt that competent political analysis includes not only the impact of governmental structure and leadership upon behavior but the consequences of group-based personal attitudes, expectations and demands upon the functional operation of the collective processes comprising the political system as a whole.

～ 2 ～

Party Systems and the Representation
of Social Groups

SEYMOUR MARTIN LIPSET

EDITORIAL NOTE: *This is a comprehensive study of the aggregative and representative functions of political parties. As we noted, their role is to transform interest and demands into policy. Institutional factors such as electoral systems may facilitate or impede this task. Depending upon conditions, parties may promote rather than attenuate conflict. But above all, parties both reflect and reinforce the political culture of a given system. The author states succinctly the thesis I attempted to develop in my introduction, according to which the development of a party system presupposes rather than brings about the conditions for democracy. The reader should also consult Seymour Martin Lipset,* Political Man, *New York, 1960; H. Eckstein and D. E. Apter, op. cit., Part IV; Georges E. Lavau,* Partis Politiques et Réalités Sociales, *Paris, 1953; and Samuel H. Beer,* British Politics in the Collectivist Era, *New York, 1965.*

SOCIOLOGISTS and laymen have often seemed to differ over the nature of democracy. Public opinion generally gives prominence to the freedom of citizens to elect representatives, and until recently political scientists devoted most of their attention to the instituted rules which safeguard these rights and make them effective. The socialist's concentration upon elites and social processes must often have seemed, to both layman and political scientist, to blur the distinctions between democracy and totalitarian or aristocratic forms of government. This difference in emphasis sometimes reflects the gap between wish and reality; sometimes, however, it is due to the sociologist's excessive neglect of formal institutions. In this omission, the sociologist is frequently suffering from the undue influence of certain ideas in the sociological tradition, which, when first stated, were salutary correctives of older misconceptions. Thus Max Weber and Joseph Schumpeter stressed, as the distinctive and most valuable feature of democracy, the formation of the political elite in a competitive struggle for the votes of a mainly passive electorate.[1] On account of its heritage of ideas, sociology has yet to create the single theory which will give due weight to the autonomy of legally-constituted elites as well as to the influence of the various other social groups involved in the democratic process.

A step in this direction has been taken by Talcott Parsons.[2] He has argued that the polity can be seen as providing generalized leadership for the larger social system in setting and attaining collective goals, and that this is acknowledged by interested social groups who supply generalized support in the expectation of certain kinds of approved measures. Conversely, a variety of social groups form and advocate the particular policies which eventually result in the specific decisions of public officers, which then become binding on all citizens. The competitive struggle within the elite, for generalized as well as for specific support, gives those outside the authority-structure access to political power.

How much of this interchange takes place through representation? This depends partly upon the breadth of definition of the term, a subject of perpetual dispute.[3] For present purposes it is suggested that most major attempts to influence authoritative decisions fall within a fairly coherent system of action, which may be called the representative system. It receives its structure from those institutional practices which have been developed in democratic societies—notably party systems and interest organizations—to facilitate interchange between authority and the spontaneous groupings of society. This internal differentiation produces its own power-structure and problems of integration.

As a system, the representative structure must have identifiable bound-

[1] See J. SCHUMPETER, *Capitalism, Socialism and Democracy*. New York: Harper and Brothers, 1947, Harper Torchbooks, 1962, p. 269; MAX WEBER, *Essays in Sociology*. New York: Oxford University Press, 1946, p. 226; see also the article by J. PLAMENATZ in R. MCKEON, ed., *Democracy in a World of Tensions*. Chicago: University of Chicago Press, 1951, pp. 302-27; S. M. LIPSET, *Political Man*. New York: Doubleday, 1960, pp. 54-56.

[2] TALCOTT PARSONS, Voting and the Equilibrium of the American Political System; E. BURDICK and A. BRODBECK, eds., *American Voting Behavior*. Glencoe, Ill.: The Free Press, 1959, pp. 80-120.

[3] For a comprehensive summary of definitions, see JOHN A. FAIRLIE, The Nature of Political Representation. *The American Political Science Review*, XXXIV (1940), 236-48, 456-66.

aries with other systems, even if they are rather vague. Most significantly, it is bounded on the one hand by the authority system, wherein binding decisions (legislative, executive and judicial) are reached and implemented, and on the other by the solidary groupings of society. These are the sub-groups with which individuals most readily identify, such as religions, ethnic groups, classes, occupations, regions and other comparable units. There may also be boundaries shared with the economic and cultural systems; here it will only be noted that representative action may embody cultural values in a mediated or an unmediated manner. In the first case values enter into action through the accepted legitimacy of the political community and the regime,[4] or through the institutionalized norms of the representative system itself; the other case is that of ideological commitment, where it is a single idea rather than a number of men that is represented politically. These boundaries are not of course drawn with reference to individual spheres of action, but according to different role-orientations.

It should also be possible to identify inputs and outputs as systemic properties of the representative structure. Inputs from the social base are of two kinds: aspirations or incipient demands for scarce values, and solidarities in the form of diffuse loyalties and specific attachments. Within the system some aspirations are transformed into demands which are then killed, compromised, or magnified into issues, finally to be fed into the authority system as party policies and the detailed recommendations of interest-groups. Inchoate loyalties are turned into organized support. Thus the system provides grist for the political mill and some of the power that drives it, depending upon how far the polity derives its effectiveness and legitimacy from organized support.

This process accounts for most of the "support" in Parsons' equation. It is the merit of the "elitist" view of democracy to have demonstrated how far the representative structure, as well as the authority structure, may be a vehicle of leadership and domination. Therefore two kinds of input from the side of authority can also be identified: information and public policy commitments, which as propaganda shape the demands within the system, and legitimate leadership and domination. This may be generalized (political leadership at various levels and party discipline) or specific (electoral laws, regulation of the lobby, etc.), suppressing some demands, raising others into issues and enforcing compromise. Into the social base the system puts out the political education

---

[4] For this distinction, as well as the conceptual inspiration of this discussion, see DAVID EASTON, An Approach to the Analysis of Political Systems. *World Politics*, IX (1957), 383-400.

of citizens and the political consciousness of groups. Whether or not these consequences are functional for the polity as a whole depends largely upon the form and working of the representative structure.

Viewed like this, representation is neither simply a means of political adjustment to social pressures nor an instrument of manipulation. It may contribute to the maintenance or dissolution of primary ties and to the perception of common interests, to the socialization and security of elites, the effectiveness of the polity in attaining societal goals, and to the political unity or incoherence of society as a whole. With this model in mind, this paper will consider some aspects of the behavior of social groups in politics, taking into account the political alternatives which face the electorates of different countries, with special reference to the ways in which various party systems organize and affect their social bases. It is not primarily concerned with the *differentials* between power wielded by social groups, and economic variables will not be given much prominence. Its aim is to show how certain combinations of relationships between parties and social bases contribute to the possibility of stable and efficient government.

Parties are by far the most important part of the representative structure in complex democratic societies. Such societies show some variation in the salience of particular solidary groupings as the source of demands and support, but generally in contemporary industrial conditions, the stratification system has been the prime source of sustained internal cleavage—classes have been the most important bases of political diversity.[5]

The character and number of the political parties seeking to represent the various groups in a country are perhaps the chief determinants of how far the government acts through a stable system of interchanges between the key solidary groups and the political elite. Discussions of the causes and consequences of diverse party systems often turn upon the question of whether social structure or electoral systems mainly determine their different types. Some argue that the character and number of parties flows almost directly from the social cleavages in a country; others have claimed that the electoral system in use—proportional representation or the single-member district plurality method —has been the main source of stability or instability in democracies. In

[5] They, of course, are far from being the only important such bases. Others such as religious, ethnic or linguistic groups, regions, and rural-urban groupings, have formed the basis for separate parties or differential backings for particular parties. For a detailed discussion of the way in which different groups have varied in support for parties in different democratic countries, see my *Political Man, op. cit.,* pp. 220-82.

general terms this is a sham dispute. There is no reason to believe that
either social cleavage creates political cleavage, or that political cleavages
usually determine the content of social controversies. But, as Maurice
Duverger has said: "The party system and the electoral system are two
realities that are indissolubly linked, and even difficult sometimes to
separate by analysis." [6]

I. SOCIAL STRUCTURE AND THE CHARACTER OF THE PARTY STRUGGLE

The ability of a political system to win or retain the support of different solidary groupings depends largely on whether all the major
parties accept democratic principles. Where some parties reject the
system, it may break down even if democracy is favored by a substantial majority.

It is not possible to present here a detailed analysis of the social
requisites for stable democracy, a task which I have attempted elsewhere.[7] In brief, the evidence seems quite clear that such systems are
to be found in more well-to-do nations, where the greater wealth is
associated with patterns which reduce internal tension: greater equality
of income distribution, of education and of status-enhancing prestige
items, less emphasis on barriers between classes; and a relatively large
middle-class. Secondly, the stability of democratic systems depends upon
how far they have retained or developed legitimacy, a "believed-in title
to rule," for the political elite.[8] Such legitimacy has been most secure
where the society could admit the lower strata to full citizenship, to
rights of participation in the economic and political systems, and at the
same time allow the traditionally privileged strata to keep their high
status whilst yielding power. The constitutional monarchy has been the
most visible symbol of such a process.[9] These two factors—economic development and legitimacy—may operate independently to produce the
conditions for a stable system of representation, as Bagehot has noted:

> There are two kinds of nations which can elect a good Parliament.
> The first is a nation in which the mass of the people are intelligent,

[6] MAURICE DUVERGER, *Political Parties*. London: Methuen, 1954, p. 204. Duverger's
book, however, is the best recent effort to demonstrate the causal effect of electoral
systems. A sophisticated critique of Duverger and the general emphasis on electoral
systems may be found in G. E. LAVAU, *Partis politiques et réalités sociales*. Paris:
Armand Colin, 1953. There is a comprehensive statement of all the arguments for
and against proportional representation in ALFRED DE GRAZIA, *Public and Republic*.
New York: Knopf, 1951. A good general discussion of the theory of electoral systems is D. HOGAN, *Election and Representation*. Cork: Cork University Press, 1945.
[7] See *Political Man, op. cit.*, pp. 45-96, and *passim*.
[8] I am obligated to Carl Friedrich for this definition.
[9] M. WEBER, *op. cit.*, pp. 263-64.

and in which they are comfortable. Where there is no honest poverty, where education is diffused and political intelligence is common, it is easy for the people to elect a fair legislature . . . [Where these conditions are not met, then representative government] is only possible in what I may venture to call *deferential* nations. It has been thought strange but there *are* nations in which the numerous unwiser part wishes to be ruled by the less numerous wise part.[10]

Where traditional legitimacy does not exist, it is not easily developed. It can only be created by prolonged *effectiveness*, that is by government which shows that it can satisfy most of the people most of the time. In fact, those democracies which have lasted through all the strains of this century without suffering any relapse from democratic forms or sustaining a major anti-democratic movement, have possessed either considerable wealth or a traditional monarchy, or both. In Europe, only one republic—Switzerland—has achieved stable democracy, and it is the richest nation on the continent.[11]

But if legitimacy and economic development draw the lines within which political conflict occurs, there remains great variation in the nature of party systems. If democracy is a "translation of the class struggle," why does it take so many different forms? Unfortunately in spite of the extensive literature dealing with social stratification and political behavior, nobody has tried to create a typology of stratification systems which can be related to these variations of party system within Western industrial society. A specification of some of the differences in value systems associated with status differentiation may offer the most promise for future work. However obvious, the basic fact is that the more clear-cut the status demarcation lines in a country, the more likely has been the emergence of explicitly strata-oriented parties.

Although many of the differences in the status systems of various societies may be explained by referring back to conditions of economic development, they are also related to variations in historical circumstances. Democratization and industrialization both occurred within very different social structures, and these initial differences have often left their marks on the new system. For example, one important cause of status rigidity is the inheritance of a hierarchy of status groups from feudalism. The failure of Canada and the United States to develop a major working-class party, and the relative stability of their democratic

[10] w. bagehot, *The English Constitution*. London: Oxford University Press, 1958, pp. 232-35 (emphasis in the original).
[11] See my *Political Man, op. cit.*, pp. 77-79. It should also be noted that Switzerland never had a monarch to overthrow but rather is a historic confederation of small states.

systems, may be partially explained by the difficulty of developing a
working-class political consciousness where no rigid status groups already existed to create a perception of community. On the European
continent, workers were placed in a common class by the value system
of the society, and absorbed a political "consciousness of kind" from
the social structure. Marxists did not have to teach European workers
that they formed a class; the ascriptive values of the society did it for
them.

In the English-speaking parts of the Commonwealth, labor parties
have been class-oriented and class-based, yet much less imbued with
class-feeling than those of continental Europe, as is shown by their
willingness to cooperate with bourgeois parties while still young and
small, and their consistent opposition to Marxist and revolutionary
ideology. The absence of a base for intense class conflict is also affirmed
by the strain towards a two-party system which has characterized their
politics, since inherent in a two-party system is the need for cooperation among diverse strata. In Australia and New Zealand, this pattern
may be explained, as can that in Canada and the United States, by the
absence of feudal tradition. In Britain, the weakness of working-class
extremism is often attributed to the country having borne the early
tensions of industrialization before the rise of modern socialism, and,
after the movement had appeared, to its prosperity. On the other hand,
it may be argued, with Tocqueville, Schumpeter, Mannheim and others,
that the uniquely "open" and "responsible" character of the British
aristocracy enabled it to retain power and influence late into the capitalist
period, thus helping to soften the antagonism of the working classes
to the state and to society. Schumpeter has argued that the aristocracy
served as a "protective stratum" for the workers, helping to enact early
suffrage and various social reform measures.[12] The willingness of the
English upper class to receive the newly rich bourgeois and his children
into their institutions also served to prevent an enduring split between
the old and new upper classes.[13]

The odd political development of Germany is often related to its
relatively late entry on the world scene both as a unified nation and as
an industrial society. Bourgeois economic development, reduction of

[12] J. SCHUMPETER, op. cit., pp. 134-39.
[13] JAMES BRYCE, Modern Democracies. New York: Macmillan, 1921, vol. I, pp. 30-32;
A. BRIGGS, Victorian People. London: Odham's Press, 1954, pp. 153-54, New York:
Harper Colophon Books, 1955. He quotes Matthew Arnold: "It is only in England
that this beneficial salutary intermixture of classes takes place. Look at the bottle-
merchant's son, and the Plantagenet being brought up side by side [. . .]. Very
likely young Bottles will end up by being a lord himself."

ascriptive status lines, and Western political ideas, all were stronger in the western German states than in Prussia; but Prussia ultimately came to dominate unified Germany. Prussia was largely an agrarian, pre-industrial society in which the old Junker nobility retained its landed estates, disliked the dominant classes of commercial and industrial society, and saw no reason to recognize the working class as a legitimate part of the polity. Like the English, the German aristocratic conservatives aspired to serve as "protectors" for the lower strata, and their political representatives—Bismarck especially—did pass an amount of social welfare legislation. They rejected, however, the assumption that the workers should have their own political representatives, and tried for fifteen years in the 1880's and 90's to outlaw the powerful Social-Democratic Party. When this had failed, they still refused an equal suffrage in Prussia until they were overthrown by military defeat and revolution in 1918. This uncompromising attitude, by denying the working class any representation in the political system of Wilhelmine Germany, helped sustain the revolutionary ideology and aims of the socialist movement, which in turn repelled the sympathy of middle-class liberals. Furthermore, it enabled extremists to play leading roles in the largest socialist party of pre-war Europe, in a party which should have been a fairly moderate and bureaucratized labor party.

The great emphasis on status differentiation in Germany may also be responsible for the large number of middle- and upper-class parties, each representing a distinct status group on a national or regional basis, and possessing its own ideology.[14] Similarly, it has been suggested that the relative failure of the German Socialists to gain rural backing, and their weakness among the poorer urban working class, reflected the hostility of the better paid and more skilled workers, who dominated the movement, towards other depressed segments of the population, such as the so-called *Lumpenproletariat*—a hostility which has not existed in other countries.[15] The split within the working class between Socialists and Communists in Weimar Germany was also partly due to this status-consciousness of the skilled workers in the Social-Democratic

[14] SIGMUND NEUMANN, *Die deutschen Parteien: Wesen und Wandel nach dem Kriege.* Berlin: Junker und Dunnhaupt, 1932; THEODOR GEIGER, *Die soziale Schichtung des deutschen Volkes.* Stuttgart: Ferdinand Enke, 1932, p. 79.

[15] See ROBERT MICHELS, Die deutschen Sozialdemokratie, I: Parteimitgliedschaft und soziale Zusammensetzung. *Archiv für Sozialwissenschaft und Sozialpolitik,* XXVI (1906), 512-13; ROBERT LOWIE, *Toward Understanding Germany.* Chicago: University of Chicago Press, 1954, p. 138. For detailed evidence that the contemporary German Social-Democratic party remains weak among the lower-class workers and relatively strong among the more skilled, a pattern which remains almost unique among left parties, see *Political Man, op. cit.,* pp. 240-41.

Party, who left the more depressed sector to be recruited by the Communists. Robert Michels has pointed out how their sense of superiority was reflected in party literature, which attacked the Communists by arguing that their supporters were largely the shiftless *Lumpenproletariat*.[16]

The failure of the multi-party system based on distinct and rigid status-groups to revive in the Federal Republic is the product of a number of causes.[17] Fundamentally, it reflects the fatal weakening of the old status structure during the Nazi and wartime upheavals and the final blow delivered by the end of Prussian domination. Partition removed from view the glaring inequalities of the East and destroyed the stronghold from which the Junkers had dominated the army and defied the Weimar Republic; simultaneously, the greater homogeneity of Western Germany now became a national homogeneity, reinforced by the economic growth which strengthened the achievement values of a profoundly *bourgeois* culture. This homogeneity seems to be expressed in a genuine, if rather skeptical, consensus, rejecting both the Nazi past and the Eastern Communist alternative, and more easily accepted by a generation maturing in an era of expansion where the old ruling groups play little part either as authority or model. Its political manifestation is an interest-group structure much like that of Britain, thoroughly interlaced with the party system, and bringing with it an increasing political professionalism. The former bearers of ideology, the intellectuals, the career judges and bureaucrats, have largely abdicated their special role under the *Rechtsstaat,* and a pragmatic approach has replaced the old emphasis upon the objective rationality of the expert. The SPD has more and more disowned its Marxist heritage, and the interdenominational Christianity of the CDU is more a catchall than an ideology. The accompanying bureaucratization of the two major parties had led to a pattern of occasional, mediated participation by the ordinary citizen in politics, which is generally regarded as a major source of both stability and flexibility in modern democratic electorates.

The general causes were supplemented by the circumstances attending the birth of the present parties. The power to make certain major decisions was retained by the occupying forces until the early 1950's, which restricted the scope of political contention. The parties called into

[16] ROBERT MICHELS, *Sozialismus und Fascismus I*. Karlsruhe: G. Braun, 1925, pp. 78-79.
[17] It is interesting to note that in 1918 Max Weber believed that there were four parties "structurally inherent within German Society: a conservative, a democratic [liberal], a socialist, and a Catholic party." J. P. MAYER, *Max Weber and German Politics*. London: Faber and Faber, 1956, p. 101.

existence by the Allies in 1946 to fill the political vacuum became, as Dolf Sternberger has put it, like "stakes rammed into a swamp," and were able to absorb most of the emerging tendencies. This position was consolidated by the modifications of proportional representation which were adopted, by the legal restrictions upon extremist parties, and by the statesmanship of Adenauer. In particular the stability of the parties has been aided by their ascendancy over the bureaucracy. The acceptance by civil servants of the constitution and the parties as legitimate is largely a product of the social changes mentioned above, and the resulting political stability; it is symbolized, and also advanced, by the practice of staffing top civil service positions below the Minister with political appointees.[18]

The unstable political structure of the major Southern and Latin countries of Europe—France, Italy and Spain—seems to be mainly due to economic and social factors retarding the growth of large-scale, modern industry. This failure has kept alive the tendency of the bourgeoisie to look to the traditional pre-industrial upper classes for models of behavior. Despite considerable social mobility, the status-barrier between the *bourgeoisie* and the *peuple,* and the gradations within the bourgeoisie itself, are meticulously preserved.[19] The business classes often preserve a semi-feudal outlook, emphasizing the stability of family property, and the firm takes the place of land in pre-capitalist society, providing the material basis for family prestige. Traditionalist, noncompetitive norms rather than entrepreneurial policies characterize much of business life, serving to justify a narrowly self-interested politics concerned with protecting many marginal producers, through government regulation and moral pressure to prevent competitive prices and to keep wages low.[20] There is a traditionalist hostility to collective bargain-

---

[18] See OTTO KIRCHHEIMER, The Political Scene in West Germany, *World Politics,* IX (1957), 433-45, and the sources cited there, esp. studies by K. SCHUTZ and G. SCHULZ in M. G. LANGE et al., *Parteien in der Bundesrepublik: Studien zur Entwicklung bis zur Bundestagswahl 1953* [*Schriften des Instituts für politische Wissenschaft,* Bd. VI]. Stuttgart-Düsseldorf: Ring Verlag, 1955; D. STERNBERGER, *Lebende Verfassung: Studien über Koalition und Opposition* [*Parteien-Fraktionen-Regierung,* Bd. I]. Meisenheim: Anton Hain, 1956, p. 86; on the change in bureaucratic attitudes, see K. D. BRACHER, *Die Auflösung der Weimarer Republik* [*Schriften des Instituts für politische Wissenschaft,* Bd. IV]. Stuttgart-Düsseldorf: Ring Verlag, 1955, esp. p. 174; and T. ESCHENBURG, *Staat und Gesellschaft in Deutschland.* Stuttgart: Schwab, 1946, p. 757.
[19] For a detailed discussion of many of these elements see DAVID LANDES, Observations on France: Economy, Society, and Polity. *World Politics,* IX (1957), 329-50.
[20] See DAVID S. LANDES, French Business and the Businessman: A Social and Cultural Analysis, in EDWARD EARLE, ed., *Modern France.* Princeton: Princeton University Press, 1951, pp. 334-53; and JOHN E. SAWYER, Strains in the Social Structure, in *ibid.,* pp. 293-312.

ing, or any form of labor legislation which would acknowledge the equality of the worker in the economic market. The working classes, therefore, unable to build strong, legitimate unions or secure permanent "citizenship" rights within industry, continue to maintain those attitudes of alienation from the body politic which are characteristic of workers in most countries during the period of initial industrialization.[21] They have remained responsive to revolutionary creeds, which in turn reinforce the fear and hostility of the middle and upper classes.

Perhaps the most striking cultural tension in the life of these countries is the cleavage between all those values which are essentially pre-industrial and pre-capitalist—often identified with that other institution of the *ancien régime,* the Catholic Church—and the legitimacy of the tradition of nationalism, democracy, and equality flowing from the Revolution of 1789. The Revolutionary credo is one of achievement and universalism, an open society and equal treatment to all. To some extent, every significant stratum, particularly in France, is divided between support for a modern, secular, industrial society, and preference for the values, if not the fact, of a clerical, non-industrial order. Thus those sections of Latin industrial life where the bourgeoisie have accepted the Revolution because of various historic links with it, or have adopted universalistic values by escaping from the sector of "family capitalism" to that of large, bureaucratized, corporate capitalism, tend to support stable unionism and eschew political extremism.

The discussion so far has sketched some of the conditions under which support will be available for *different* kinds of political leadership. But the number and nature of political parties, the claims they stake out, and the policies they advocate, do not result automatically from underlying social cleavages; political systems possess a certain (varying) autonomy within the larger social system, and it is appropriate to ask how the restraints imposed by the political order itself affect the capacity of parties to provide generalized leadership in different countries.

II. SOCIAL STRUCTURE AND ELECTORAL SYSTEMS

Concern with formal constitutional provisions has generally been outside the province of political sociology. Sociologists tend to see party cleavages as reflections of an underlying structure, and hence, wittingly

---

[21] For a discussion of the strains of industrialization and the ways in which varying patterns of industrialization have affected workers' political behavior in different countries, see *Political Man, op. cit.,* pp. 48-72.

or not, frown on efforts to present the enacted rules of the game as key causal elements of a social structure. The sociologist's image of a social system, all of whose parts are interdependent, is at odds with the view of many political scientists, who believe that such seemingly minor differences in systems as variations in the way in which officials are elected can lead to stability or instability, and account for the success of democracy in one country or its collapse in another. Yet an examination of comparative politics suggests that the political scientists are right, and that electoral laws determine the nature of the *party-system* as much as any other structural variable.

The available evidence gathered together by political scientists such as E. E. Schattschneider, F. A. Hermens, Maurice Duverger and many others indicates that proportional representation encourages the appearance or continuance of more parties of a more equal size than does the plurality system, in which the candidate receiving the most votes in an electoral unit is elected. Wherever we find a two-party system working (wherever the usual situation is the alternating control of government by one of two parties, with an overall majority of representatives) we find also an electoral system which debars from representation in government parties which cannot win a plurality of votes in a geographical election district. On the other hand, every country which uses proportional representation has four or more parties represented in the legislature, and, except in Norway, Sweden and Ireland in recent decades, absolute parliamentary majorities of one party have been extremely rare.

If enough cases existed for analysis, the following rank-order correlation might be found between electoral system and the number of political parties: presidential system with single-member districts and one plurality election, two parties; parliamentary system with single-member districts and one plurality election, tendency to two parties; parliamentary system with single-member districts and alternative ballot or run-off (second) election, tendency to many parties; proportional representation, many parties.

The thesis that the plurality system tends to produce or maintain a two-party system needs some qualification. Groups centered in distinct regions or political units may gain representation, and may sometimes influence policy, within such systems, even where cabinet government is conducted by means of a parliamentary majority. In Great Britain, Parnell's Irish Party was able to hold its own in the House of Commons during the latter part of the nineteenth century through solid regional support. The initial growth of socialist parties in European countries with single-member districts depended on their winning in solidly working-class constituencies, just as various ethnic parties have achieved regional support in India, and from time to time agrarian "third parties" have won considerable backing in the more rural provinces of Canada.

The requirement of ecological isolation limits the type of party which can succeed in a two-party system with single member districts. It must possess a strong appeal to a homogeneous part of the population whose residential areas correspond to electoral units. The problem which this poses is illustrated by the British Liberal Party, which, according to some public opinion studies, would secure as much as 25 per cent of the national vote in a parliamentary election under proportional representation, where every vote counted. The existing single member districts reduce the Liberals to impotence since their appeal is not to groups which dominate electoral districts, but to a large middle-class sector which is usually in a minority in every constituency. This not only keeps the Liberals out of Parliament, but deprives them of most of their votes, since many prospective Liberals prefer to vote for the lesser of two electable evils. To take another case, all efforts to form third parties in the United States have proved futile because the effective constituency in national elections is really the entire country, while in the state it is the entire state. The emphasis on presidential or gubernatorial elections has prevented American third parties from building up local constituency strength as labor, agrarian, religious, or ethnic parties have done in some other single-member constituency systems.[22] As evidence for this view, "third" parties have gained their greatest strength in municipal or occasionally state elections, and have almost invariably lost strength in subsequent presidential elections. The American Socialist Party attained its greatest electoral success in municipal elections and actually captured the government of a number of cities. Its high point as an electoral force was in the municipal elections of 1917 in which it attained an average vote of 20 per cent in a number of major cities.[23] In general, American third parties have been much more successful in Congressional elections conducted in non-presidential election years than in those in which a president was also being elected.

Recognition of the inability to create a new national party has led

[22] The argument and best evidence for this thesis may be found in E. E. SCHATT-SCHNEIDER, *Party Government*. New York: Rinehart and Co., 1942, esp. pp. 65-98.
[23] JAMES WEINSTEIN, Anti-war Sentiment and the Socialist Party, 1917-1918. *Political Science Quarterly*, LXXIV (1959), 223-39; PAUL H. DOUGLAS, The Socialist Vote in the 1917 Municipal Elections. *National Municipal Review*, VII (1918), 131-39.

many American leftists, who would have preferred a new radical party, to operate as factions within one of the old parties, and at different times since 1920 socialist or near-socialist groups have either controlled or greatly influenced one of the two major parties in a large number of states.

The motives underlying the electorate's refusal to sustain third parties in systems where the candidate with the most votes is elected, and third parties are effectively barred from representation, have been analysed in detail in the numerous studies of electoral systems, and I will not discuss them here, Essentially polarization between two parties is maintained by those factors which lead people to see a third party vote as a "wasted vote." [24]

III. PARTY SYSTEMS AND THE BASES OF SOCIAL CLEAVAGE

The interrelated effects of electoral systems and social cleavages may be seen in a comparison of the party systems in different parts of the British Commonwealth, the United States and France.

There is general recognition that stable two-party government works best in Great Britain. Members of Parliament are elected in single-member constituencies in which one factor, class position, is the basic source of political difference.[25] Differences based on regions, religious or ethnic allegiances, urban-rural conflicts or past historical feuds are unimportant or affect groups too small to organize on their own behalf. But if two-party government presents its best and simplest face in Britain, multi-party government has created the most difficult and complicated conditions in France. France currently has at least six important political groupings, in addition to some minor ones. For many decades it has been divided between clericals and anti-clericals, supporters and opponents of a planned economy, and supporters and opponents of parliamentary government, with a few rural-urban and regional cleavages also. These differences have created the following picture of French party life during the period 1955-1960.

[24] See MAURICE DUVERGER, *Political Parties, op. cit.,* pp. 224-28, 246-50; E. E. SCHATT-SCHNEIDER, *op. cit.,* pp. 80-84.
[25] "British politics are almost wholly innocent of those issues which cross the social lines in other lands, for example, race, nationality, religion, town and country interests, regional interest, or the conflict between authoritarian and parliamentary methods." See JOHN BONHAM, *The Middle Class Vote.* London: Faber and Faber, 1954, pp. 194-95; LESLIE LIPSON, The Two-Party System in British Politics. *American Political Science Review,* XLVII (1953), 337-58.

TABLE I. *Overlapping of Cleavages in France**

	CLERICAL		
PLANNED ECONOMY		FREE ECONOMY	
Parliamentary	Anti-Parliamentary	Parliamentary	Anti-Parliamentary
M.R.P. (Catholics)	(left Gaullists)	Independents (conservatives)	U.N.R. (Gaullists)
	ANTI-CLERICAL		
PLANNED ECONOMY		FREE ECONOMY	
Parliamentary	Anti-Parliamentary	Parliamentary	Anti-Parliamentary
Socialists	Communists	Radicals	Poujadists

* Readapted from a somewhat similar diagram in MAURICE DUVERGER, *Political Parties, op. cit.,* p. 232.

France seems to be a country whose social fragmentation has dictated the need for a multi-party system, whatever electoral laws are in force. The fact remains, however, that the various electoral systems in use throughout most of the history of the Third, Fourth, and Fifth Republics, have encouraged the creation or perpetuation of small parties.

The experiences of these two countries, standing near the extremes of stable and unstable government, might suggest that the nature of group differences is the key to the number of parties in a system; yet even for these nations this conclusion may be questioned. Since the development of adult suffrage, Britain has *never* had a pure two-party system. In the late nineteenth century there was a strong Irish third party; before World War I, four parties were represented in the Commons, the Liberals, the Conservatives, the Irish, and Labour; between 1918 and 1931 three major parties were represented; and since then the Liberal party has remained a serious electoral force even though the plurality system minimizes its strength in Parliament.[26]

[26] For a detailed report on the issues and facts involved, see D. E. BUTLER, *The Electoral System in Britain 1918-1951*. London: Oxford University Press, 1953. Though many argue from historical evidence (e.g., LESLIE LIPSON, *op. cit.*) that the British two-party system derives from particular national characteristics, since two parties or tendencies preceded the introduction of the present single-member constituency in the mid-19th century, this argument also may be questioned. Lavau (*op. cit.*) has pointed out that the House of Commons had unstable majorities, with members shifting their support from government to opposition throughout much of the 19th century. Duverger contends that in France itself the contemporary com-

French political history offers striking examples of the way in which formal political institutions may decisively affect political cleavage, and therefore the stability of the democratic system. Despite deep-rooted social tensions and lack of consensus on fundamental political, religious and economic issues, the Third Republic's electoral system diverted considerable support from the anti-democratic extremists. Its double ballot effectively stopped the French Communist party from becoming a major force at this period. For after an auspicious start in 1921, supported by a majority of the former Socialist party and controlling its principal newspaper, *L'Humanité,* it lost ground through being unable to elect members to the Chamber. As a revolutionary party, opposed to constitutional government, it could not combine with other parties for the decisive second ballot, so that many of its potential voters obviously returned to the Socialist fold. Thus in 1928, the Communists secured 11 per cent of the vote in the first ballot, but only 14 out of 600 seats. In the following election of 1932, held in the depths of the depression, the Communist first-ballot vote dropped to 8 per cent, and it elected less than 2 per cent of the representatives. Almost half the Communist first ballot supporters backed candidates of other parties on the second ballot, though the Communists did not withdraw any candidates. Even Communist party discipline and the worst depression in history could not induce many voters to "waste" their ballots. Similarly, Maurice Duverger notes "the complete impossibility" for fascist and right-wing extremist movements "to obtain any representation in parliament," although there were many strong fascist groups during the 1930's.[27]

The Communists only became a major force in French politics after they had pretended to give up their opposition to parliamentary government, and formed the Popular Front coalition with the Radicals and Socialists in 1936. This enabled them to increase their first-ballot per-

---

plex political substructure was built "upon the fundamental conflict which dominated the 19th century, that between conservatives and liberals [. . .]. The principal actors were a landowning aristocracy, bound to monarchical principles [. . .] and, opposed to this aristocracy, an industrial, commercial and intellectual bourgeoisie, attracted to the principles of political liberty.

"The first phase in the moulding of the prevailing spirit in modern Europe ended with the appearance and development of the socialist parties [. . .]. Between 1900 and 1914, the bipartisan tendency which had dominated the preceding century was replaced everywhere by a swing towards tripartisanship; the 'conservative-liberal' duo now changed to a 'conservative-liberal-socialist' trio." MAURICE DUVERGER, Public Opinion and Political Parties in France. *American Political Science Review,* XLVI (1952), 1070.

[27] *Political Parties, op. cit.,* pp. 319-20; see also F. A. HERMENS, *Europe Between Democracy and Anarchy.* Notre Dame: University of Notre Dame Press, 1951, pp. 41-44.

centage to 15.6, and their representation in the Chamber from 11 to 72.[28]

But if the Third Republic demonstrated how electoral rules may punish and inhibit parties which oppose the system, the Fourth Republic showed how different rules may facilitate the ruin of democracy by nourishing such parties.[29] Throughout its history, the Fourth Republic employed different versions of proportional representation. Its last parliament, elected in 1956, was hampered by the presence of 150 Communists and 50 Poujadists. The latter, who secured about 10 per cent of the vote, could probably have elected no candidates under the double ballot, with single-member constituencies. The Fifth Republic, having returned to that system, has only 10 Communists and 1 Poujadist in the Chamber. It remains to be seen whether this change will cause Communist voters to fall away as they come to recognize that their vote is wasted.

Turning to North America, the United States and Canada offer a still more complex picture of the way in which party systems can be affected by the interrelationship between social cleavages and methods of election. For though two-party politics have predominated at the national level in both countries, it is clear that their solidarity structure is in some ways more like that of France than that of Britain. Both are divided along class, ethnic, religious, and regional lines, and while the chief issues for groups like the Southern whites or the French Canadians tend to separate them from the rest of the nation, internally they remain sharply divided over non-ethnic questions.

It seems likely that if the United States had ever adopted proportional representation or even the second ballot run-off, it would have developed several main parties, such as the following: 1) a Labor party, based on urban workers, and perhaps ethnic minorities outside the South; 2) a Northern Conservative party, based on the urban middle class and the higher-status ethnic and religious groups; 3) a Southern Conservative party, based on the strength of the ante-bellum southern

---

[28] For a detailed account of the events leading up to this election as well as an analysis of the vote, see GEORGES DUPEUX, Le Front populaire et les élections de 1936. Paris: Armand Colin, 1959.

[29] "It is especially important, in order to understand what the fundamental political problems of France actually are, to investigate why the state for too many years has seemed so completely powerless to hold the antagonisms and the divisions between the parties within reasonable bounds and to make the divergent forces act in concert for the general welfare. This raises the question of political institutions, the most important problem facing France. *The present difficulties in this sphere stem from the fact that the political institutions that were adopted in 1946 in no way satisfy the requirements of the economic, social, and political situation* [. . .]." FRANÇOIS GOGUEL, France under the Fourth Republic. Ithaca: Cornell University Press, p. 146 (my emphasis).

Whigs and Constitutional Unionists, the urban middle classes and more
well-to-do rural whites; 3) a Southern Populist party, based on the
Southern lower white strata who backed Jackson in 1828, Breckenridge
and the secessionist Democrats in the election of 1860, and various
"populist" parties and agrarian factions of the Democrats in the late
nineteenth century; and 5) a Farmer's party, based on rural elements
outside the South. There would probably also have been a number of
smaller parties from time to time.

Such differentiation has been prevented, not only by the disadvantages
which the American presidential system lays on small parties, as discussed above, but also by the peculiar device of the party primary. This
arrangement, by which different factions within the party may compete
in state-conducted, intra-party contests to determine party candidates
and officials, permits the interests and values of different groups, which
would give rise to separate parties elsewhere, to be expressed within the
major parties. First, the various groups have been forced by the electoral
system to identify with one or the other of the two major blocs on whatever basis of division matters most to them;[30] then their differences
are fought out within each party in the primaries, although they may
often still lead to crossbench alliances in Congress afterwards.

Few observers have been willing to recognize how comparable are
the social bases for multiple parties in France and the United States,
and how far the difference between them in political stability is due to
varying constitutional structures. The French two-ballot system may be
regarded as a functional equivalent to the American primary elections.
In both cases, different tendencies may compete in various ways up to
the decisive final election. Thus, in most elections of the Third Republic,

> at the first ballot few candidates could obtain an absolute majority,
> so that at this stage there was no fear of splitting the vote and no
> deterrent to "splinter parties;" but at the second this fear became as
> effective as in Britain. *Most constituencies then had a straight fight
> between a candidate of the Right and one of the Left.*[31]

[30] The one other country which I know of that has a system akin to the American
primaries is Uruguay, the most stable democracy in Latin America. In ,Uruguay,
the various factions within the two major parties may each nominate a presidential
candidate. On election day, the voters choose the man they prefer. When votes are
counted, the party which has a majority counting the votes of *all* its presidential
candidates wins the election, and the candidate of that party who received more
votes than any other one of the party is elected president. In other words, Uruguay
combines the primary and the final election on the same ballot. For plans to form
a similar system in Brazil, see TAD SZULC, Brazilians Plan Voting Alliance. *The
New York Times,* December 29, 1959.

[31] PHILIP WILLIAMS, *Politics in Post-War France.* London: Longmans, Green and Co.,
1954, p. 310. This book contains an excellent discussion of the nature and effects of

The electoral alliances which, under the Third Republic, gave decisive majorities to the Left or Right, would always break down in parliament; hence the constant reshuffling of cabinets. The common assumption, that these coalitions were so fragile because they tried to harmonize incompatible views and interests—such as those of the Radicals, as the party of small business, with the workers' philosophy of the Socialists—overlooks the fact that these differences have been no sharper than some *within* the American parties. The divergencies on domestic issues between conservative Southern Democrats and left liberal Northern Democrats, or on foreign affairs between petty-bourgeois Republicans from the provincial Midwest and Republicans from the metropolitan centers of the East, with their close ties to international big business, are fully as great. The American party factions have been held together largely by the Presidential system. Thus, the changing Congressional majorities on questions which cut across party lines are comparable to the shifts in the Chamber as new issues were taken up. Since in America this cannot change the party in control of the executive, however, there has been continuity of executive action and also a substantial amount of party loyalty in important Congressional votes, as David Truman has recently demonstrated.[32] It will be interesting to see whether the "American" elements introduced into the French constitution by General de Gaulle will have comparable effects on the party system.[33]

---

the French electoral systems. For a detailed description of the way in which the double ballot worked in the first elections of the Fifth Republic in 1958, see PHILIP WILLIAMS and MARTIN HARRISON, France 1958, in D. E. BUTLER, ed., *Elections Abroad*. London: Macmillan, 1959, pp. 13-90.

[32] DAVID TRUMAN, *The Congressional Party: A Case Study*. New York: John Wiley, 1959. See also DUNCAN MACRAE, JR., *Dimensions of Congressional Voting*. Berkeley: University of California Press, 1958, and V. O. KEY, JR., *Politics, Parties and Pressure Groups*. New York: Crowell, 1958, p. 729.

[33] There is in fact one long-term experiment in Finland with a constitutional system that combines a strong president with a relatively weak cabinet which, as in the Fifth Republic, is responsible to Parliament rather than to the president. This Finnish version of a "Gaullist" constitution has not reduced the number of parties in the country; there are currently seven main groupings, and, on average, there has been a cabinet shake-up every year since 1917. It should be noted that although Finland has a strong presidential system, the president is elected indirectly rather than by the people, and both presidential electors and members of parliament are elected under a system of proportional representation. Consequently, there is little scope for the presidential nature of the system to reduce the number of parties. However, the Finnish sociologist Heikki Waris reports that, "By dividing the power between a stable authority, the president, and a temporary authority, the Cabinet, the Finnish Constitution has considerably lessened, if not eliminated, the apparent instability which is the great weakness of the cabinet system in multiparty countries. The Finnish system [. . .] has assured a certain continuity of policy." HEIKKI WARIS, Fin-

Canada is perhaps an even more interesting case of interaction of the various elements which have been discussed. Its social structure and bases for political division are complex and comparable to the American and French. It retains, however, the British electoral and parliamentary system, which requires disciplined parliamentary action, and does not permit the American practices of cross-party alignments in the House, of ideological divergences between local party machines, or the resolution by public election of differences within the parties. Whenever a Canadian region, class, ethnic group, or province, comes into serious conflict with its party of traditional allegiance, it must either change over to the other party, with which it may be in even greater disagreement on other issues, or form a new "third" party. The result of combining this social diversity with a rigid constitutional structure has been the constant rise and fall of relatively powerful "third" parties. Every single Canadian province, except Prince Edward Island and New Brunswick, has been governed for some time since World War I by a "third" party. At least three such parties, the Progressives in the 1920's, and since 1933, Social Credit (monetary reformers based on farmers and small businessmen) and the socialist Cooperative Commonwealth Federation (C.C.F.) have had significant strength in a *number* of provinces. Nationalist parties, often at odds with one another, have arisen in Quebec, one of which, the *Union Nationale,* has governed the prov-

land, in ARNOLD ROSE, ed., *The Institutions of Advanced Societies.* Minneapolis: University of Minnesota Press, 1958, p. 211.

In European states where local government is highly centralized through the prefectorial system, the argument that strengthening the presidency will stabilize democracy must meet the counter-argument that, by reducing parliamentary control over the state bureaucracy, a strong presidency might weaken still further those local centres of power and responsibility which, ever since Tocqueville, have been regarded as the best foundations for democratic order. The formula for responsible republican government, it seems, must include both a strong, directly elected president and elected local officers possessing real power. Where the local elected officials are the puppets of an appointed prefect, they are in a similar position to that of parliamentary politicians in a weak multi-party system: neither can be held accountable for long-term policies. This evil is greatest when, as often in France, local and national politicians form a single class of men. The liberal and democratic argument against centralized internal authority was forcibly restated as recently as 1944 by Luigi Einaudi, subsequently the first President of the Republic of Italy: "Democracy and the prefect are profoundly repugnant to each other [. . .]. Neither in Italy, nor in France, nor in Spain, nor in Prussia has there ever been, nor will there ever be, democracy so long as there exists a centralized type of government of which the prefect is the symbol." Via col prefetto, in *Il buon governo.* Bari, 1954, p. 52; cited by ROY PRICE, *The Italian Local Elections 1956.* London: Chatto and Windus, 1956, p. 2. It does not seem to have been heeded by any of the countries possessing a prefectorial system, except for some of the German states.

ince almost unbrokenly since 1936. The rise and fall of these parties, mainly at the provincial level, is not the result of any general discontent in Canada, but solely of the interaction between constitutional arrangements and social and economic divisions.[34]

Although the Canadian two-party system has repeatedly broken down, it has never been replaced by a permanent multi-party system. Ultimately, and especially on the national level, the two major parties reabsorb the rebellious elements, since the single-member plurality method of election necessarily represses minorities. They can emerge in homogeneous areas, but in order to become a permanent national force they must oust one of the major parties; otherwise, they will vanish with the crisis that gave them birth, or find their cause successfully captured by one of the dominant parties. At provincial level, however, it has been much easier for them to survive by becoming one of the two major *local* parties.

South Africa, which also combines British constitutional procedure with complex internal bases of cleavage, exhibits the same rapid rise and fall of minor parties as Canada. Within the limits of the dominant ethnic divisions other sources of conflict still exist. Thus for long periods the Afrikaners were divided into two parties; today they are united in the National Party, but the English are split. In addition to the old, but sharply declining Labor Party, a number of parties, mainly English, have come into being in the last decade as splinters from the United Party. All these minor parties have met, in an aggravated form, the same difficulties as the Canadian, being unable to elect candidates on their own.[35]

In New Zealand, the two non-socialist parties merged after Labor had risen to a position in which it seemed able to win a three-cornered fight. Social Credit has shown on at least two occasions that it could get the support of about 10 per cent of the New Zealand electorate, but, being unable to win seats, it has failed to sustain any permanent strength.[36] In Australia, the two major non-socialist parties—the Country and Liberal Parties—have not merged, but generally follow a policy of

---

[34] See SEYMOUR MARTIN LIPSET, Democracy in Alberta. *Canadian Forum,* XXXIV (1954), 175-77 and 196-98. For British Columbia, see H. F. ANGUS, The British Columbia Election, 1952. *Canadian Journal of Economics and Political Science,* XVIII (1952), 518-25; and MARGARET ORMSBY, *British Columbia; A History.* Vancouver: Macmillan, 1958, pp. 477-89.

[35] See GWENDOLEN M. CARTER, *The Politics of Inequality, South Africa since 1948.* New York: Praeger, 1958; for a further report see R. R. FARQUHARSON, South Africa 1958, in D. E. BUTLER, ed., *op. cit.,* pp. 229-75.

[36] PETER CAMPBELL, Politicians, Public Servants, and the People in New Zealand, I. *Political Studies,* III (1955), 196-97.

exchanging seats and refraining from competition.[37] Similar electoral alliances took place in some of the Scandinavian countries before the introduction of proportional representation.

Conversely, in one former dominion of the British Crown, Eire, which has a relatively simple basis for political cleavage, the perpetuation of proportional representation ever since the birth of the Irish Republic in 1922 has meant the continued existence of at least five parties. Only one party, Fianna Fáil, has been able to govern without a coalition under these conditions. The second largest party, Fine Gael, which is somewhat more conservative, can only hope to form a government with the help of minor and often more leftist parties, such as Labour and the Republicans.[38]

No doubt, had Eire adopted the British election system it would now have as stable a two-party system and as responsible cabinets as the United Kingdom. Like many other Irish difficulties, the blame for this failure must be attributed to the English, since, when yielding power in Southern Ireland, they insisted on a system of proportional representation to ensure representation of Protestant and other more pro-Commonwealth minorities. Fianna Fáil, as the dominant party, has tried hard to change the electoral system, but as in other countries the smaller parties oppose such changes for fear that the single-member plurality district system would weaken their electoral position. The result is that the need for "interparty" governments has led to periodic breakdowns in the traditional pattern of responsible Cabinet government.[39]

Similarly, in Israel, another state once governed by Great Britain, independence was followed by the continuance of the system of proportional representation previously used in elections to the council of the Jewish Agency, the dominant pre-independence organ of the Zionist community. Hence, in this immigrant society formed by men from

[37] Although the Country and Liberal parties usually do not run against each other and act, in effect, electorally as the rural and urban wing of the non-socialist party, the continued existence of two such parties is facilitated by the fact that Australia has adopted the preferential ballot system with the single-member constituency. Under this system voters list the order of preference for all candidates on the ballot. Thus when there are Liberal and Country candidates in the same constituency, a Liberal voter will mark the Country candidate as his number two choice, and Country party supporters will do the same for the Liberals. This system has also encouraged occasional splits from the Labor party, since minority Labor party candidates can pick up first votes without these votes being permanently lost to the major party backed by such protest voters. See J. D. B. MILLER, *Australian Government and Politics*. London: Duckworth, 1954, pp. 85-86.

[38] See ENID LAKEMAN and JAMES D. LAMBERT, *Voting in Democracies*. London: Faber and Faber, 1955, pp. 223-30.

[39] BASIL CHUBB, Cabinet Government in Ireland. *Political Studies*, III (1955), 272.

many states and cultures, over 30 different parties have taken part in the elections. There have been at least five different socialist parties, excluding the Communists, represented in the Knesset, and some half dozen religious parties. Basically, however, the Israeli political structure consists of three groups: the socialist parties, the largest of which, the Mapai, has about 40 per cent of the vote, while the others have between 10 and 15 per cent; the non-socialist secular parties, which range from liberal to conservative (in the American sense of the terms), poll about 30 to 35 per cent of the vote; and the religious parties, which poll from 10 to 15 per cent, and are divided fairly equally between pro- and anti-socialist groups. A single-member district plurality system would probably create a two-party system, socialist versus conservative, with each party bidding for the support of the religious. This solution is favored by Mapai, the largest party in the country, but, as in Ireland, it is opposed by the others since none of them feels certain of survival without proportional representation. An Israeli social research institute, in a study of the effects of electoral systems on national life, has strongly urged a change in the Israeli system.

In sum: while the present system of proportional representation aggravates existing social evils in the Israeli society, i.e., absolute rule of central party machines, deepening social divisions and the perpetuation of factional fanaticism, the system of constituency election is designed to counteract and finally to eliminate them, by weakening party power at the centre, placing emphasis on common, integrative, cohesive elements in our society and encouraging the growth of tolerance, fellow-feeling and social compromise [. . .].

The condition for constructive democratic life in the country becomes largely a function of the development of social forces which can combat and counteract these negative features [toward intense destructive conflict]. And the web of social institutions is the most potent, powerful instrument at our disposal to accomplish this end.[40]

Conversely, Maurice Duverger has described the conscious and successful effort made in Belgium to prevent a two-party system reasserting itself when the Socialists rose to second place after the adoption of universal manhood suffrage in 1894, displacing the anticlerical Liberal opposition. By the next election in 1898, the Liberals had declined to parliamentary insignificance with only 13 seats. Rather than see the Liberals disappear, which would have meant, eventually, a Socialist government, the Catholics, who were then in power, introduced pro-

[40] BETH HILLEL [Society for Social Research in Israel], *Electoral Reform in Israel.* Tel Aviv: Beth Hillel Publications, 1953, pp. 24, 26.

portional representation and thus preserved the Liberals as a major third party.[41] The anti-clerical vote has almost always been above 50 per cent, but the Socialists have never reached 40 per cent, while the Liberals have constantly secured between 10 and 15 per cent.[42]

The strain between the institutionalization of specific social cleavages in a multi-party structure and a plurality electoral system is aggravated by the distorted representation which usually results. The major party whose support is most evenly distributed throughout the country tends to be over-represented, and sometimes the largest single party does not win the most seats. In Canada, between 1935 and 1957, the Liberal Party dominated Parliament with overbearing majorities, though it had a majority of the electorate on one occasion only,[43] and the Conservative Party is in a comparable position today. Similarly in India, the Congress Party has over 75 per cent of the seats in the House with less than 50 per cent of the vote, while the Communist Party ruled the Indian state of Kerala for one term with a legislative majority based on 35 per cent of the electorate.[44] In 1945, the British Labour Party took over with an overwhelming majority of 146 seats in the House of Commons, and nationalized a number of industries despite the fact that over half of the electorate had voted for non-socialist candidates. Conversely, the three British Conservative governments since 1951 have governed with parliamentary majorities although the country had given a majority of its votes to Labour and the Liberals.[45]

Essentially, the evidence suggests that whatever potential cleavages exist in the social structure, there is a fundamental incompatibility between a multi-party system and a plurality method of election; where the two co-exist the instability is ultimately resolved by a change to one of the following situations:

1) a change in the electoral system to proportional representation, which preserves declining parties and facilitates the growth of new ones;

2) an arrangement by which different parties continue to exist, but support each other in more or less permanent alliances;

[41] DUVERGER, op. cit., pp. 246-47.
[42] OPPENHEIM, op. cit., p. 167.
[43] GWENDOLEN M. CARTER, The Commonwealth Overseas: Variations on a British Theme, in s. NEUMANN, ed., Modern Political Parties. Chicago: University of Chicago Press, 1956, p. 104.
[44] AVERY LEISERSON, Parties and Politics. New York: Knopf, 1958, p. 286.
[45] Detailed discussion of the relation between votes and seats in the British system in R. B. MCCALLUM, The British General Election of 1945. New York: Oxford University Press, 1947, pp. 277-92; for a table giving votes and seats in British elections since 1900, see s. NEUMANN, ed., Modern Political Parties. Chicago: University of Chicago Press, 1956, p. 57.

3) mergers between parties which recreate a two-party situation, as has occurred a number of times with American third parties; or

4) the elimination over time of the weaker parties and a return to a two-party system, as has occurred in various countries of the Commonwealth and in the United States.

IV. CONSEQUENCES OF THE DIFFERENT SYSTEMS

A number of consequences for the nature of representation and the stability of democracy have been attributed to the two-party and the multi-party systems. Some of these will be briefly discussed here.

In a two-party system, both parties aim at securing a majority. Hence, they must seek support among groups which are preponderantly loyal to their opponents and must avoid accentuating too heavily the interests of their customary supporters. Elections become occasions for seeking the broadest possible base of support by convincing divergent groups of their common interests. The system thus encourages compromise and the incorporation into party values of those general elements of consensus upon which the polity rests. For similar reasons, the system encourages emphasis by both parties upon material interests (concessions and patronage) as against a stress upon ideal interests, thus reducing ideological conflict.[46] Since the "out" party can always realistically aspire to gain office within a few years, this also has the effect of stifling exaggerated commitments to ideal or ideological goals which may gain votes but embarrass office-holders, and reinforces the adherence of the opposition to the "rules of the game." The weakness of ideology inherent in two-party systems has the further consequences of reducing intense concern with particular issues dividing the parties, and sharpening the focus on party leaders. The plebiscitary nature of electoral struggles in two-party systems is largely an effect of the system itself.

In a multi-party system, where parties do not aim at gaining a majority, they usually seek to win the greatest possible electoral support from a limited base. They therefore stress the interests of that base and the cleavages which set it apart from other groups in society. The party's function as a representative of a group is separated from the function of integrating the group in the body politic, which requires a stress on similarities with others and commitments to them.[47] The multi-party

---

[46] See CARL FRIEDRICH, *Constitutional Government and Democracy*. Boston: Ginn and Co., 1950, pp. 416-17; TALCOTT PARSONS, *op. cit.*

[47] See F. A. HERMENS, *The Representative Republic*. Notre Dame: University of Notre Dame Press, 1958, p. 201.

system with proportional representation in fact substitutes the interest group or group of common believers for the territorial unit as the basis of representation, reducing the effect of the local or regional unit as a basis of solidarity which may cut across lines of political affiliation.[48] The small size of many parties and the absence of a need in most multi-party systems for compromise at the electoral level enhances the ideological content of the conflict. This divisiveness encouraged by a multi-party system is perpetuated by the tendency of most parties to attack most virulently those with whom they have most in common and with whom they compete for a similar vote, thus magnifying the differences between them.

The two-party system also helps to maintain the commitment of the entire electorate to the system itself, rather than to a particular party, since it enables the discontented elector to impute responsibility to the governing majority rather than to the regime, and to devote his efforts to the quite legitimate task of replacing the incumbents by their traditional opponents. The necessity for coalition government in most multi-party systems, where the lesser parties wield a disproportionate influence—so that election results may scarcely affect the composition of the government—deprives the elector of the feeling that he is able to turn out leaders who have forfeited his confidence.

There are, however, conditions under which a two-party system is *less* conducive to the preservation of democratic order than a multi-party system. The two-party system works best where it is based on an elaborate, cross-cutting solidarity structure, in which men and groups are pulled in different directions by their diverse roles and interests. Wherever the solidarity structure is polarized by class, race, or religion, and the political lines follow those of social cleavage, a two-party system may intensify internal conflict rather than help integrate the society. For example, the First Austrian Republic (1919-1934) was largely a two-party system, but one which was divided along the interrelated lines of religion, class and region. The parties represented two almost completely separate cultural units and the Civil War which followed was a nearly inevitable consequence of the system.[49] Similarly, in Italy today

[48] "Electoral procedures based on territorial . . . [as distinct from "representation through interest-groups"] is precisely the technique for the organic integration of the whole. As a matter of principle the individual delegate represents the entire area. The ensuing separation into parties according to *political* tendencies implies then only differences of belief concerning the means by which the welfare of the nation is to be achieved." GEORG SIMMEL, *The Web of Group Affiliations*. Glencoe, Ill.: The Free Press, 1955, p. 194.

[49] For a detailed description of the system and an analysis of the events leading to the downfall of the first Austrian republic, see CHARLES GULICK, *Austria: From*

the lines of division between the Christian Democrats and the left Socialist-Communist opposition are such as to reduce consensus rather than increase it. In South Africa, a division into two parties largely based on two ethnic groups, the Afrikaner Nationalists and English United Party, is destructive of national unity and democratic norms.[50] In general, where the class struggle is superimposed upon a conflict between religion and irreligion, or between different ethnic groups— wherever opposing groups see elections as a fight between good and evil, so that conversion from one political faith to another is almost impossible—a two-party system is more destructive of political stability than one in which centre parties can mediate between extreme opponents. Consequently, though it may be validly argued that a two-party system makes for a more stable and effective democratic polity than a multi-party one, this is only true if both actors in the system accord a certain degree of legitimacy to each other; each party must be willing to view the other as an acceptable alternative government.

Considerations such as these have led many to suggest that a system of proportional representation, though making for more parties, may help unify a nation marked by low consensus by forcing all parties to look for votes in every major group and region in the country. A committee of the U.S. Senate urged this view as early as 1869, arguing that the Civil War might have been avoided if the electoral system had permitted minorities in the North and South who agreed with dominant opinion in the other region to elect representatives. The committee argued that the absence of minority representation

in the states of the South when rebellion was plotted, and when open steps were taken to break the Union, was unfortunate, for it would have held the Union men of these states together and have given them a voice . . . Dispersed, unorganized, unrepresented, without

---

Habsburg to Hitler. Berkeley: University of California Press, 1948. A recent study of elections in the first and second republics demonstrates that the second one is genuinely different from the first in that the two major parties, though based on the same groups as before 1934, have much more support today within "opposition strata" than their predecessors did. Thus the conservative People's party is much stronger today among workers, residents of Vienna, Protestants, and irreligious people, than was the pre-1934 Christian Social party. Conversely, the Socialists though weaker in Vienna are much stronger in the outlying provinces than earlier, and they have increased their vote among peasants considerably. Paralleling the growth of the two parties within segments once overwhelmingly opposed to them has been a sharp decline in ideological cleavage. The conservative party is no longer a Christian or Catholic party, and the Socialists have dropped their adherence to Marxist doctrine. See WALTER B. SIMON, Politische Ethik und Politische Struktur. *Kölner Zeitschrift für Soziologie und Sozialpsychologie*, XI (1959), 445-59.
[50] CARTER, *op. cit.*

due voice and power, they could interpose no effectual resistance to secession and to civil war.[51]

John Humphreys suggested that the same system of proportional representation, which is sometimes thought to have prevented stable two-party government in Belgium, has actually reduced the conflict between the Flemish and Walloon groups. Since all parties seek votes in both ethnic groups, the South African pattern of parties representing distinct ethnic and language groups is avoided.[52]

The Swedish political scientist, Herbert Tingsten, has recently suggested, from the experience of his own country, that a multi-party system rooted in proportional representation lowers the vitality of political life by eliminating the slightly spurious dramatics which two-party elections can call forth even among rather homogeneous and satisfied electorates.[53] This is not incompatible with the supposed tendency of the same system to increase the purely numerical participation of the electorate. Thus, when Switzerland changed in 1919 from a plurality system of elections to proportional representation within cantons, not only did the number of significant parties increase, but the average percentage of the eligible electorate who voted jumped from 50 per cent to nearly 80 per cent. The Swiss changeover was extremely revealing, as there were a number of variations among the cantons which permitted some controlled comparisons. For example, in those cantons which had previously been "safe seats" for one party under the plurality system, only 30 to 40 per cent had voted before proportional representation. The vote in these previously "safe" cantons doubled following the change in the system. However, in comparable safe cantons which only elected one member to the national Parliament, so that proportional representation could not be introduced, participation did not increase and remained at about 40 per cent. A somewhat similar situation occurred with comparable results in Norway in 1921.[54] A situation in which every vote "counts"

[51] Cited in JOHN H. HUMPHREYS, *Proportional Representation, A Study in Methods of Election.* London: Methuen, 1911, p. 58.
[52] *Ibid.,* p. 57; a similar point is made by MAURICE DUVERGER in *L'influence des systèmes électoraux sur la vie politique.* Paris: Armand Colin, 1950, pp. 39-40; see also ENID LAKEMAN and JAMES D. LAMBERT, *Voting in Democracies.* London: Faber and Faber, 1945, pp. 63-64. The latter contend also that "An instance of the unifying effect of proportional representation is Czechoslovakia after the first world war, where representation of their respective minorities prevented what might have been a sharp cleavage between Bohemia and Slovakia." *Loc. cit.*
[53] HERBERT TINGSTEN, Stability and Vitality in Swedish Democracy. *The Political Quarterly,* XXVI (1955), 140-51.
[54] HERBERT TINGSTEN, *Political Behaviour.* London: P. S. King, 1937, pp. 219-20, 224-25.

seems to increase both the concern of the voter with the need to participate, and the concern of the parties with the reactions of all voters.

The differences between the two types of party system have thus far
been examined primarily as they affect the voters and the electoral struggle. They also must be tested for their capacity to provide generalized
leadership in return for generalized support, to serve as the interchange
mechanism between the solidary groups of society and the wielders of
power. The experiences of Western industrial society suggest that, in
general, a two-party system is much the better adapted to these needs.

The ability of the two-party system to provide for generalized leadership is closely linked to the fact that one party always represents the
government and actually rules the country, so that the party in power
temporarily becomes identical with the state. Both parties are organized
to be able to take full responsibility, at home and abroad, for the conduct of the nation's affairs; the opposition is always conscious of its role
as the government of tomorrow, and in order to be able to *govern* it
must look beyond electoral victory, to its chance of inspiring at least
some confidence among the supporters of the other party. Insofar as the
party itself overtly represents interests, as does the British Labour party,
they are represented *within* the party and disciplined by the necessity of
being able to govern in the national interest; the same applies to the
party's relationship with pressure-groups. A party is above all a way of
organizing citizens to take part in *public* affairs. It is clearly damaging
to a party, especially to the party in power, if it appears in a light where
its opponents can accuse it of obvious favoritism to a group of party
supporters. Further, since the legitimacy of a party rests ultimately upon
its actual or potential effectiveness as a *national* government, there is
strong pressure on both parties in a two-party system to reduce or
eliminate ideology as a basis for political decision. The access of a given
party to the full power of the state is quite straightforward so long as
everyone is convinced that it will use that power to solve problems from
a practical standpoint.

In contrast to the two-party system, where the party tries to appear
as a plausible representative of the whole society, multiparty systems
have been mainly based upon the premise that a party should consciously
represent the private interests of a section of the population. Only the
state, and no one party, can claim to represent the interests of the
whole. Thus individuals are citizens, and enjoy a public role, only in
relation to the state, and patriotism tends to be found only in action
which "transcends" party, rather than as a value which can infuse the
party in action. As a result, bourgeois and peasant parties have tended

to reflect rather than sublimate the *incivisme* of their constituents, minority working-class parties have often regarded constitutionalism—the basis of any notion of public interest—as a matter of socially irrelevant technicalities, and parties of the right have been tempted to aspire to a position "above parties."

But while almost all minority parties in a multiparty system could ideologically reject responsibility for the political community at large, many have in fact found themselves wielding state power in coalition governments. The consequent divorce between party symbols and party actions for all who participate in coalitions, and the bargaining necessary to fill public offices and obtain parliamentary support may lead to cynicism, or to attitudes resembling that unmediated attachment to abstractions which, as Philip Selznick argues, is a source of irresponsibility, extremism, and manipulability in mass society.[55] These extreme manifestations have, of course, only appeared in some multiparty systems under conditions of stress. It seems likely, however, that multiparty systems accentuate the development of such dangerous traits, while two-party systems are better able to resist political and civil irresponsibility on the part of different solidary groups and their representatives.

While the two-party system has these great advantages, under certain conditions a multiparty system may produce a relatively permanent coalition cabinet which adequately reflects the main groupings of society and can effectively interchange leadership and support. In such systems all parties become, in a sense, "state parties." This development seems to have occurred in Switzerland, and to a certain, lesser degree in the Netherlands, Austria, Uruguay, and the Scandinavian countries. There is some reason to anticipate that the Swiss "solution" to the problem of multiparty government—the inclusion of all democratic parties in the cabinet, so that issues are fought out there as well as in Parliament—may spread to other countries as well.

v. CONCLUSIONS

Political sociologists tend to regard formal political devices as peripheral items, having little effect upon the main features of societies. One purpose of this paper is to distinguish between the more spontaneous elements in the social structure which influence the political process, and the enacted rules which help determine the nature of parties and of representation. Constitutions and electoral systems are the outcome of

[55] PHILIP SELZNICK, *The Organizational Weapon*. New York: McGraw-Hill and Co., 1952, pp. 276-91.

particular decisions which may permanently affect the type of social system which a country develops. It is especially important to emphasize this at a time when men in various "underdeveloped" countries are trying to set up democratic procedures and to foster an open society. For sociologists to treat formal political structures as epiphenomena is not only wrong from a theoretical angle, but may also reinforce the appeal of a vulgar Marxism which would have democracy wait solely upon economic development.

On the other side, it is fairly obvious that a simple change in electoral laws cannot guarantee the transformation of a multiparty system into a two-party one. In multiparty systems, the parties tend to identify closely with class, ethnic, religious, or regional interests and lose the loose structure and flexibility which are needed for the mobilization of mass support and the absorbing of minor parties during a period of transition. In unstable multiparty countries, like France, the alternative to numerous, rather rigid parties has been the *rassemblement* (rally) type of organization, which, while possessing a loose structure, has also just those authoritarian traits which its *raison d'être* demands. For movements of this type arise because parliamentary democracy has failed to produce effective leadership, and since their purpose is to establish a new source of authority in their leader's charisma they are often opposed to democracy itself.

This leads to a consideration of the problem of authority in relation to party systems. Democratic stability requires that the *source* of authority be out of reach of any of the contending parties, which implies that none of them should be committed to a root-and-branch change of political system. Parties should aspire to become the *agents* of authority, not its creators. In all stable democracies we do in fact find an institutionalized separation of the *source* from the *agencies* of authority. In the stable parliamentary monarchies of Northern Europe and the Commonwealth, the monarchy remains the latent source of authority, effectively divorced from its exercise.[56] In the United States and Switzerland, since their systems acquired a traditional legitimacy through pro-

---

[56] See *Political Man, op. cit.,* pp. 77-96; as Walter Bagehot put it almost a century ago: "The functions of [. . .] royalty are for the most part *latent* [. . .]. It seems to order, but it never seems to struggle. It is commonly hidden like a mystery, and sometimes paraded like a pageant, but in neither case is it contentious. The nation is divided into parties, but the crown is of no party. Its apparent separation from business is that which removes it both from enmities and from desecration, which preserves its mystery, which enables it to combine the affection of conflicting parties —to be a visible symbol of unity [. . .]". BAGEHOT, *op. cit.,* p. 40. Bagehot's use of the distinction between manifest and latent activities and functions is, I think, one of the first uses of these concepts in social science.

longed effectiveness, it was the Constitution that became the supreme symbol of authority. And in contrast to France and many other countries, the American and Swiss Constitutions are beyond the direct reach of the elected representatives and are not easily amended. It is unthinkable that they can be abolished or fundamentally revised.

Two-party democracy, therefore, in addition to an electoral system which tends to polarize the electorate, requires that:

1) the groups composing the two potentially dominant parties are not committed to exclusive ideologies which prevent pressuring and manipulating within the parties; and

2) the source and agents of authority be institutionally and legitimately separated, so that neither major party can aspire to become the source of authority.

It would therefore appear that those countries with multiparty systems, in which the possibility of change to a two-party system exists, are in fact those which already have fairly efficient ways of exchanging leadership and support. In none of the chronically unstable democracies are the source and agencies of authority sufficiently separate to insure against a sudden authoritarian turn.

But although too great a faith in the manipulation of electoral laws cannot be justified, some conclusions for action may be drawn: to create democracy it may be necessary to use the legal system to exclude those who would destroy it. Thus the French double ballot, in which the democratic parties could unite for the second ballot against an opponent of the system, limited both the participation and *strength* of the Communists and Fascists in the 1930's.[57] Such a system in Weimar Germany would have obviously kept the Nazis out of the Reichstag in the 1920's, and reduced the parliamentary strength of the Communists to insignificance. It would have guaranteed a large democratic majority in the election of 1930, and even in 1932.[58]

The question is most urgent in the new states of Africa and Asia. There, the source and agencies of authority are not separated. In none of these countries do the underlying structural conditions exist for a stable democratic party system, either two-party or multiparty.[59] Lack

---

[57] Michel Debré, the first Prime Minister of the Fifth Republic, argued in 1947 that the Fourth Republic would *inevitably* collapse because it used proportional representation. See his *La mort de l'État républicain.* Paris: Gallimard, 1947.

[58] DANKWART RUSTOW, Some Observations on Proportional Representation. *The Journal of Politics*, XII (1950), 107-27.

[59] For a general theoretical discussion of how to deal with these problems comparatively, see FRANCIS X. SUTTON, Representation and the Nature of Political Systems. *Contemporary Studies in Society and History*, II (1959), 1-10. For a detailed descrip-

of experience and leadership, illiteracy, poverty, traditional cultures and
status-structures, dependence upon primary products which often provide insufficient resources for expensive government, all militate against
parliamentary rule. These strains are frequently intensified by the lack
of any sense of historical unity, and the conjunction of all the tensions
of rapid industrialization with the opportunities for demagogic licence
afforded by universal suffrage. A further major factor is the differential
impact of Communism, Russian or Chinese, upon these emerging
polities. Whether it appears as an imperialistic threat, as a tempting
solution to urgent and overwhelming problems, or as a source of irresponsible exploitation of discontent, it adds to the already formidable
obstacles to peaceful democratic growth. Under these conditions, the
form of one-party "democratic" government which is emerging in many
of these countries may hold some hope for the future. Such parties tend
to be loosely structured, more like a *rassemblement,* or heterogeneous
movement, than a party of ideology or interest. They combine a number
of interests and strata, either through the charisma of the leader, or
through the original need for unity in the struggle for independence.
This *charisma,* the claim to rule by virtue of what they have been and
are, is necessary if the system is to survive in its early stages, and the
absence of opposition may prove beneficial if it preserves the often frail
mystique upon which authority depends. Such opposition as does exist
must remain factional, even where it has a nominal right of appeal to
the electorate. Other parties may be permitted, as in Ghana, Tunisia, and
Mexico (the model in this pattern for other underdeveloped societies),
but they cannot be allowed a chance of electoral victory. Any failure in
effectiveness—and there are bound to be many—may become grounds
for challenging the entire system if an opposition can hope to gain mass
support and power.

Ever since the rise of Sun Yat-sen in China, many leaders of such
states have spoken of their particular type of government as a "guided"
or a "tutelary" democracy. Unlike Communists or other totalitarians,
these leaders have as their reference group, and their image of the good
society, not a one-party state or a society without internal conflict, but
rather the existing stable Western democracies. They regard the existence of opposition, free elections and public criticism as ideals to be
attained. Turkey, for example, has already developed from a one-party
into a two-party state, and Mexico seems to be gradually moving in the

tion of the party systems and most recent elections in various African states, see
W. J. MACKENZIE and K. E. ROBINSON, *Five Elections in Africa.* Oxford: Clarendon
Press, 1960.

same direction.[60] The dominant parties in both states have tolerated much internal diversity, and acknowledged their opponents' rights to discussion and organization, while at the same time denying them a chance of electoral victory.

Democracy cannot be created by fiat. It grew through many centuries in the West, during which time the concept of representation changed greatly, and the norms regulating the access of different groups to government decisions were slowly modified in the course of great social and political upheavals. As Max Weber pointed out, democracy must be regarded as a *process* rather than as an attribute which a system does or does not possess. In his view *democratization* involves *two* processes:

1) prevention of the development of a closed status group of officials in the interest of a universal accessibility of office, and 2) minimization of the authority of officialdom in the interest of expanding the sphere of influence of 'public opinion' as far as practicable.[61]

In Western societies the absolute power and charismatic authority of the monarch were gradually eroded, mainly through pressure from groups who were consciously loyal to the monarchy. The title of His Majesty's Loyal Opposition echoes this development. Similarly, in some of the dominant charismatic parties of the underdeveloped states, the growth of politically significant solidary groups and of restrictions on the authority of officials has been taking place *within* the party, much as in an earlier age it took place under the shadow of the monarchy. In Mexico, to take the most developed case of this phenomenon, these groups have been brought into the *Partido,* often as formally affiliated groupings, e.g., trade unions, professional associations, and so forth. As in the monarchies of the eighteenth and nineteenth centuries, which were in transition from absolutism to constitutionalism, considerable factionalism exists in many of these parties, which gives the different groups within them access to power. "Insofar as factions develop freely inside a single party this becomes simply a framework which limits political rivalries without destroying them; prohibited outside the single party, pluralism is reborn within the party, and there it can play the

[60] See MAURICE DUVERGER, *Political Parties, op. cit.,* pp. 275-80; ROBERT E. SCOTT, *Mexican Government in Transition.* Urbana: University of Illinois Press, 1959, esp. pp. 145-243; KEMAL H. KARPAT, *Turkey's Politics; The Transition to a Multi-Party System.* Princeton: Princeton University Press, 1959.
[61] MAX WEBER, *op. cit.,* p. 226. These concepts are elaborated in an unpublished paper by PATRICIA RICHMOND, Democracy and Party: The Problem of Political Stability in the Mexican "One-Party" System, which has greatly influenced my thinking on these issues.

same part." [62] An analysis of the political changes in Mexico over the past three decades concludes:

> Intra-party pluralism has produced the following stabilizing consequences in present-day industrial Mexico [. . .]: an increase in the organizational strength of significant secondary groupings; an increase in the legitimacy of the system and of the incumbents; an increase in the representation of all the significant segments in society with a corresponding decrease in the arbitrary power of the president as well as an increase in his resourcefulness; and an increase in the legitimacy and tolerance of opposition groups.[63]

To justify the manipulation of political systems so as to limit the rights of opposition in underdeveloped states, or to deny the rights of anti-democratic forces to equal representation, may seem itself to be a basic denial of democracy. But as the Founding Fathers of the American Republic well recognized, the problem of democracy is not simply to maximize popular influence on government policy; it also involves finding the best way to protect the stability of the political system. They sought to safeguard the infant republic by framing a Constitution which would "prejudice the outcome of democracy," and which would reduce "the likelihood that the majority would decide certain political issues in bad ways." [64]

Wherever democracy has not been institutionalized, whether in the old states of Europe or the new states of Asia and Africa, it is important to recognize that particular political forms will not emerge spontaneously in response to developments in other parts of the social system. Whether these states develop a stable interchange of leadership and support in a democratic framework depends in part on the rules which they adopt for their politics. The study of the social effects of diverse constitutional arrangements should remain a major concern for the student of politics and comparative institutions.

[62] M. DUVERGER, *Political Parties, op. cit.,* p. 278.
[63] PATRICIA RICHMOND, *op. cit.,* p. 29.
[64] MARTIN DIAMOND, Democracy and *The Federalist:* A Reconsideration of the Framers' Intent. *American Political Science Review,* LIII (1959), 56-57.

❧ 3 ❧

Consensus and Cleavage
in British Political Ideology

JAMES B. CHRISTOPH

EDITORIAL NOTE: *The author examines the issue of consensus and cleavage in the British political system. The reader is again referred to Samuel H. Beer's excellent analysis of British contemporary trends in* British Politics in the Collectivist Era. *Also, R. T. McKenzie,* British Political Parties, *London, 1958; Gerhard Loewenberg, The Transformation of the Labor Party Since 1945, Journal of Politics (May 1959), 234-57; Leslie Lipson, Party Systems in the United Kingdom and the Older Commonwealth: Causes, Resemblances and Variations, Political Studies, VII (February 1959), 12-31.*

ONE of the most perplexing questions to students of politics since the mid-1950's has been whether Western societies are now approaching, or have reached, a condition called "the end of ideology." Numerous answers have been propounded, both by those who regard such a development as desirable and by those who view it with disquietude. But difficulties have arisen because exponents of one view or the other have had recourse to markedly different, and often shifting, concepts of the terms "ideology" and "end." If this important controversy is to be saved from sterility, social scientists must both reflect more upon the nature of the terms employed and descend from the level of sweeping cultural generalizations to examine the condition of ideology in particular political settings.

It is my purpose here to try to shed some light on the debate by

surveying the state of political ideology in present-day Britain from
the standpoint of two different uses of the term. My position is that
if we adopt one view of ideology, we find that British politics are profoundly non-ideological; but if we define the concept in different but
still meaningful terms, we discover that in fact it does play an important role in the British system. In other words, by compressing extant
concepts of ideology into two distinct molds we may be able to fashion
tools for judging the ideological condition of countries such as Britain.
These I will designate the *Weltanschauung* and the "attitude structure"
versions of the term.[1]

The first refers to the more traditional meaning of ideology, the
alleged decline of which has occasioned the debate of the past decade.
It has been characterized as a "comprehensive, consistent, closed system
of knowledge, to which its adherents turn to get answers to all their
questions, solutions to all their problems." [2] Its connotations are familiar:
commitment (both intellectual and emotional); orientation toward action; distortion or simplification of reality; hostility to critics and opponents; and goal-orientation (often of the millennial variety). Perhaps its best-known paradigms are classical Christianity and classical
Marxism.

The conception of ideology as attitude structure is more difficult
to set forth because it falls short of the total belief system and tight
logic of a "world view." Like a *Weltanschauung,* it partakes of a generalized view of man; it has moral and normative content; it "places"
the individual in relation to his fellows; and it calls forth commitment
and points to desirable actions. It consists of many separate but related
attitudes which function to relate, and give meaning to, the different
political events experienced by the individual. On the other hand, this
concept of ideology is less apt to provide its holders with a total explanation of life or a full vision of human destiny. It is more earthbound,
culture-bound and diffused, both in its sources and its scope. Ideology
in this sense refers to a more or less institutionalized set of beliefs
about man and society.[3] It is likely to be a composite of prevailing
generalized views of man, the goals that he does and should seek,
the means he uses to achieve them, the outlook for progress under
present or alternative institutions, and so forth. Because such an ideology
may have many sources, it is less likely than the "big" world views to

[1] For discussion of the varieties and uses of the concept, see DAVID W. MINAR,
Ideology and Political Behavior. *Midwest Journal of Political Science,* 5 (November
1961), 317-31, and ROBERT E. LANE, *Political Ideology.* New York, 1962, ch. 1.
[2] HERBERT J. SPIRO, *Government by Constitution.* New York, 1959, p. 180.
[3] MILTON ROKEACH *et al., The Open and Closed Mind.* New York, 1960, p. 35.

be intellectualized, comprehensive, systematic or consistent, and more likely to be fragmentary, limited, even inconsistent. Yet when political man operates with reference to this organized bundle of views, he may derive from it some of the certainty and security that accompany a commitment to fuller, better articulated ideologies. While undoubtedly many would reject this use of the term, it is noteworthy that most of those who have attempted to measure the presence and effects of ideology in the Anglo-American polity have favored this definition, or one similar to it.[4]

Without attempting here to defend my preference for viewing ideology in this two-fold way, I would assert that an awareness of the distinction is necessary for any exploration of the state of ideology in Britain today. In addition, I make two other assumptions that need to be stated explicitly. First, I am assuming that the pertinent kind of ideology for this discussion is one with a fairly direct *political* implication, i.e., one which relates to questions involving the relations of rulers and ruled and the principles of governance. While these aspects of ideology may be torn from a larger context (general belief systems), no attempt will be made to delve into such related problems as the psychological functions served by the holding of ideologies.[5] Second, I proceed on the assumption that a country's ideology is not wholly concentrated among its intellectuals and political leaders, but in a participant political culture like the British also operates in and is expressed by the lives of "average people." For this reason, it will be necessary to examine (in Lane's terms) both *forensic* ideologies—the articulated, differentiated, well developed political arguments put forth consciously by the elite—and *latent* ideologies—the loosely structured and often unreflective statements of the common man—and to see how they relate to each other.

I. THE REJECTION OF TOTAL IDEOLOGY

The kind of ideology associated with a complete world view emerged

---

[4] Among them ANGUS CAMPBELL, PHILIP E. CONVERSE, WARREN E. MILLER, and DONALD E. STOKES, *The American Voter*. New York, 1960, ch. 9; HERBERT MCCLOSKY, Consensus and Ideology in American Politics. *The American Political Science Review*, 58 (June 1964), 361-82; ROBERT E. LANE, *op. cit.*; and S. E. FINER, H. B. BERRINGTON, and D. J. BARTHOLOMEW, *Backbench Opinion in the House of Commons, 1955-59*. Oxford, 1961, chs. 2-3. *Cf.* BERNARD CRICK, *In Defense of Politics*. Chicago, 1962, p. 50: "Politics is an activity and so cannot be reduced to a system of precise beliefs or to a set of fixed goals. Political thinking is to be contrasted to ideological thinking . . . the idea of an ideology of freedom is a contradiction in terms."
[5] For an example, see M. BREWSTER SMITH *et al.*, *Opinions and Personality*. New York, 1956.

and flourished under certain historical and social conditions. Many of these conditions were indeed present during the period from the seventeenth to the nineteenth centuries, the so-called "age of ideology," [6] just as they appear to be present today in a number of the new developing countries.[7] Ideology in this sense seemed to flourish especially in societies that experienced the upheavals of modernization in violent and concerted forms—that pitted classes and religious groups against each other in passionate struggle, that aroused a strong sense of deprivation among underdogs and losers, and that fragmented the community into subcultures alienated from the value patterns of the dominant political system. Put another way, total ideologies were most likely to gain ground in societies with political systems that failed both the test of effectiveness (success in solving the problems put onto them) and the test of legitimacy (widespread agreement on their propriety).[8] Where these conditions are lacking, or disappearing, it has been argued, ideology of this variety cannot really flower. Recent critics have extended the argument to read that when a society achieves modernity (seen as a matter of industrialization, urbanization, secularization, economic prosperity, middle-class expansion and working-class access to political power), then the passionate attachment to total ideology not only subsides, but becames dangerously dysfunctional to the system.[9]

I have no desire to put an oar into the choppy seas of this latter controversy. My point is simply that Britain has not provided the conditions favoring the growth of this kind of ideological thinking. The British have shown a marked disinclination to take up total ideologies for a host of reasons, many of which are familiar and only a few of which can be mentioned here.[10] In the past three hundred years Britain

[6] FREDERICK M. WATKINS, *The Age of Ideology—Political Thought, 1750 to the Present.* Englewood Cliffs, 1964.
[7] PAUL E. SIGMUND, JR., *The Ideologies of the Developing Countries.* New York, 1963.
[8] SEYMOUR MARTIN LIPSET, *Political Man.* Garden City, 1960, chs. 2-3.
[9] Notable examples are DANIEL BELL, *The End of Ideology.* Glencoe, Ill., 1960; S. M. LIPSET, The Changing Class Structure and Contemporary European Politics. *Daedalus,* 93 (Winter 1964), 271-303, and *Political Man,* 403-17; OTTO KIRCHHEIMER, The Waning of Opposition in Parliamentary Regimes. *Social Research,* 24 (1957), 127-56; and MARK ABRAMS, Party Politics After the End of Ideology, in E. ALLARDT and Y. LITTUNEN, *Cleavages, Ideologies and Party Systems.* Helsinki, 1964, pp. 56-63.
[10] "The term 'ideology' is not in very good odour in serious political discussion in this country, except in purely historical or descriptive connections. The grounds of the distaste for the term centre around the feeling, perhaps, that an ideology is something totalitarian in tendency, or at least involves an uncompromising fanaticism inappropriate to liberal democracy of the British type." BERNARD WILLIAMS, Democracy and Ideology. *Political Quarterly,* 32 (Oct.-Dec. 1961), 374.

has avoided, or seriously blunted, the traumatic revolutions that many other countries have undergone, and the main changes in its political, economic and social systems have occurred gradually. The mounting demands of disadvantaged groups have been met in a piecemeal way, with the result that with the exception of the Irish (whose fate was finally settled by truncation) no major group has failed to be integrated in some way into the political system. As is well known, neither the Communists nor the Fascists have gained substantial followings or political leverage. The non-revolutionary character of the British working class is equally well known; and while a distinct working-class sub-culture may exist, as Williams and Hoggart have argued, it does not involve working-class alienation from the values of the *political* system.[11] Social mobility in Britain may not be as great as elsewhere, but it has always been present and visible, and with the postwar changes in the educational system and the rapid expansion of white collar occupations, most Britons see it as increasing.

Another explanation for the lack of enthusiasm for total ideologies is imbedded deep in British political culture: it is the much-cited attachment to precedents and usage in preference to the logic of rational blueprints. In a system where there is widespread agreement on fundamental institutions and on a considerable range of current policies, it is possible to operate without continual reference to eternal verities, large schema, or articulated belief systems. The tendency to settle issues on the basis of accepted usages and through the means of implicit "understandings" is indeed great, to the frustration of those who plump for a fuller rehearsal of arguments or an enlightening confrontation of basic doctrine. Whether the source of this political style is the common law tradition, the evolutionary character of the British constitution, the norms of parliamentary and bureaucratic behavior, or the social homogeneity of the ruling elite is impossible to ascertain, and really beside the point. Political styles develop from many sources. They are bound to be both causes and effects of other phenomena. What can be asserted is that British political leaders have become habituated to thinking in terms of concrete problems and familiar responses; and that this—when coupled with a general complacency toward the outputs of such behavior—serves as a barrier, a disincentive, to the adoption of total ideologies. Thus, however circular the logic may seem, the British tend to be immune to extreme ideological views because they have not been used to

[11] RAYMOND WILLIAMS, *The Long Revolution*. London, 1961, New York: Harper Torchbooks, 1966; RICHARD HOGGART, *The Uses of Literacy*. London, 1957.

thinking along these lines, and they have no strong motivation to abandon the habit.

The point can be put more strongly. Pragmatic norms in Britain have been elevated into something approaching a national cult—so much so, I would argue, that we can speak without sophistry of an ideology of pragmatism, which serves as a foil to the ideology of total ends. For many Britons pragmatism is not simply a descriptive term for the way they approach or grapple with political problems; it is also a particularly British virtue and an object of pride, which they would not trade for what they consider to be the inflexible, irrevocable, and inhumane (in the sense of denying the variety of human nature) qualities of this or that "world view." Thus pragmatism easily becomes imbued with nationalistic affect, and preference for it is supported by other values into which Britons are socialized. The content of this socialization is both positive and negative in character: positive in the sense that Britons learn, both from formal teaching and from informally picking up the views of those around them, that the success and stability of the British parliamentary system is due in large part to the pragmatic frame of mind displayed by its practitioners; and negative in the sense that they also learn that the turbulent, unstable and often grotesque pattern of Continental politics derives from the European habit of looking at the world through the distorting spectacles of total ideologism. What they have learned may be a caricature, but it has had consequences. It has, for example, affected the British Labour Party's relationship with the European socialist movement; it has been partly responsible for the lack of enthusiasm for venturing too fully into experiments in European integration, and undoubtedly it has helped strengthen Britain's relationships with the United States and the older Commonwealth—peoples reputed to be fellow pragmatists under the white skin.

These conditions, and many more, add up to a general climate in which the total ideological structuring of politics is difficult to achieve. The skeptic might counter that the case has yet to be proved, that these generalizations are no more than the accumulated cliches of historians and journalists, who have selected their examples to suit their preconceived case. Fortunately, political scientists have begun to amass more empirical data bearing on the subject and tending to confirm these assertions. Thus far, to be sure, no one has made a comprehensive, systematic exploration of the distribution of ideological propensities among the British people or the political elite. We have, for example, no British counterparts of the extensive surveys of political attitudes made by the Michigan Survey Research Center and by McClosky, Prothro and Grigg, or of the intensive psychoanalytical probing by Lane into the political ideologies of a handful of east coast residents.[12] Nevertheless, in the past several years a small number of rigorous empirical studies of the character and distribution of British political attitudes have appeared, and in an indirect way they offer evidence as to the role of ideology in contemporary British political thinking, both at the mass level and among political activists.

If it can be shown that the mass of Britons are not alienated from the system in which they live, that they look tolerantly on those who hold different political beliefs, and that they tend not to be polarized on policies presumed to be highly charged with ideological affect, then we can reasonably conclude that total ideology has not taken hold of them. And if we can demonstrate further that this same pattern prevails among the political elite as well, we will have further confirmation of the generalization.

Data on Alienation

In an ambitious cross-national survey carried out in 1959, Almond and Verba found that the British ranked comparatively low on social and political alienation and high on willingness to trust and cooperate with other people. For example, 84 per cent of the British sample agreed with the statement, "Human nature is fundamentally cooperative," compared to 80 per cent of the Americans, 58 per cent of the Germans and 55 per cent of the Italians. Another query designed to measure generalized trust ("Most people can be trusted") drew affirmative replies from 49 per cent of the British, 55 per cent of the Americans, 19 per cent of the Germans, and five per cent of the Italians.[13] Almond and Verba not only find in the United States and Britain a widespread belief that people are basically cooperative, trustworthy and helpful; they also show that in these countries social trust is translated into politically relevant trust, thus reducing the alienation of people from the system. From spontaneous and unstructured responses to another survey question designed to test emotional attachment to certain aspects of the nation, the same investigators found that the features mentioned as objects of pride most frequently by Britons were their country's governmental and

[12] CAMPBELL *et al., op. cit.*; HERBERT MCCLOSKY, *op. cit.*; HERBERT MCCLOSKY, PAUL J. HOFFMAN and ROSEMARY O'HARA, Issue Conflict and Consensus Among Party Leaders and Followers. *The American Political Science Review,* 54 (June, 1960), 406-27; JAMES W. PROTHO and CHARLES M. GRIGG, Fundamental Principles of Democracy. *Journal of Politics,* 22 (May 1960), 276-94; Lane, *op. cit.*
[13] GABRIEL A. ALMOND and SIDNEY VERBA, *The Civic Culture.* Princeton, 1963, p. 267, Table 4.

political system (46 per cent), its social legislation (18 per cent), and its position in international affairs (11 per cent). (Only three, one and two per cent, respectively, of the Italians who were asked the same question named these areas as objects of pride. They chose instead the physical attributes of their country [25 per cent], contributions to the arts [16 per cent], and "nothing" [27 per cent].)[14] These are admittedly fragments of indirect evidence, but they seem to point to the presence in Britain of the kind of social and emotional climate in which total ideologies are not apt to flourish.

Intensity of Partisanship

A related consideration is the strength of partisan feeling that runs through a country. If we assume that in the modern state the political party is likely to be a major channel for the expression of ideological thinking, then one would expect to find in countries characterized by *Weltanschauung* politics a high degree of hostility among one party's followers toward rival partisans. Here again, recent surveys of British attitudes show this to be far from the case. While the images of their own and the opposite party's supporters held by Britons are somewhat sharper and more polarized than in the United States, they fall far short of intense hostility. Almond and Verba did find that 28 per cent of Conservative Party supporters, and 29 per cent of Labour Party supporters, believed that "selfish people" support the opposite party; that nearly one-fourth of the Conservative respondents viewed Labourites as "ignorant and misguided," and that 10 per cent of the Labour respondents characterized Conservatives as "militarists and imperialists." On the other hand, almost no followers of either party (three per cent in each case) accepted the view that the followers of the other were "betrayers of freedom and welfare."[15] Furthermore, when asked the hypothetical question, "How would you feel if your son or daughter married a supporter of the Labour (Conservative) Party?", only 12 per cent of Conservatives and three per cent of Labourites expressed displeasure at the thought of intermarriage, and 87 and 97 per cent, respectively, professed indifference.[16]

An even stronger indication of the tolerance of the British electorate toward political opponents is found in the results of the survey made in 1960 by Mark Abrams for *Socialist Commentary* magazine. On the basis of that poll, Abrams reported that

[14] *Ibid.*, p. 102, Table 1.
[15] *Ibid.*, p. 126, Table 2.
[16] *Ibid.*, p. 136, Table 8.

. . . between 40 per cent and 50 per cent of Labour supporters thought that the Conservatives could do as well as their own party in standing for the nation as a whole, in giving fair treatment to all races, in respecting British traditions, and in working for world peace and against nuclear war. Of those who opposed Labour, at least 40 per cent were prepared to describe Labour as equally qualified with the Conservatives in giving fair treatment to all races, working for peace, and opposing nuclear war.[17]

The same survey revealed that supporters of both parties, as well as uncommitted voters, when asked to choose the characteristics they looked for in a good party leader, picked identical traits in the same order and nearly the same degree—the top three being strong leadership, willingness to make unwelcome decisions, and honesty and sincerity.[18]

Policy Attitudes

This tendency toward doctrinal flexibility within the electorate can also be demonstrated by referring to policy attitudes which, in view of their historical importance to the parties, are apt to be imbued with considerable ideological affect. Consider the concept of nationalization, which for many years was linked by the Labour movement with the ideas of economic rationality and social equality, and which was painted by Conservatives as the epitome of economic tyranny and socialist inefficiency. The *Socialist Commentary* poll found "no homogeneous, blanket attitude toward public ownership," and concluded that "views on this subject are apparently not the outcome of either blind faith or blind rejection." [19] When asked to assess the condition of the nationalized industries, Conservative and Labour voters made practically identical judgments, discriminating mainly on the grounds of performance rather than ideology. For example, among Conservatives favorable attitudes toward public ownership exceeded unfavorable ones for four of the industries (electricity, gas, atomic energy and the airlines), while more Labour supporters termed the nationalization of coal and the railways a failure than a success. Eighty-four per cent of Conservatives and 58 per cent of Labourites expressed themselves as opposed to any further nationalization. Finally, when asked more generally how much government regulation of industry they thought was necessary, 10 per cent of the Conservatives and only 18 per cent of the Labourites chose "a good deal," while at the other pole 25 per cent of the Conservatives and 10

[17] MARK ABRAMS, RICHARD ROSE, and RITA HINDEN, *Must Labour Lose?* Harmondsworth, 1960, p. 19.
[18] *Ibid.*, p. 25.
[19] *Ibid.*, p. 31.

per cent of the Labourites replied "practically none." Majorities in both parties accepted the need for a fair amount of regulation, and within each there was goodly support for the "wrong" ideological position on this issue.[20]

Low tension between party supporters also tends to characterize foreign policy attitudes. This is borne out by the analysis made by Davis and Verba of British mass opinions during the period 1947-56 on selected foreign policy issues, many of them presumed to be vested with ideological affect. The polls they examined dealt with respondents' orientations toward the following issues: internationalism, armament, colonialism, the choice between the United States and the Soviet Union, European alliances, the Far Eastern policy.[21] On only 13 per cent of the questions was there a low degree of interparty agreement, as compared with 59 per cent high agreement; and had the Suez crisis not been included, the interparty differences would have virtually disappeared. Davis and Verba conclude that "for the most part adherents to any one political party generally express the same sorts of opinions on international issues as adherents to another party; and a high degree of unity within a party is not so much evidence that the party tends to unify the sentiments of its supporters as that it expresses the sentiments of a highly unified nation." [22]

Insofar, then, as the attitudes of the mass public reveal the extent of ideological modes of thinking, these varied data show not only that a good deal of pragmatism does prevail, but also that the conditions associated with the politics of total ideology—distrust of and hostility to opposing views, a considerable alienation from societal values, and marked polarization on policy questions—are not characteristic of contemporary Britain. It is still conceivable, of course, that these attitudes are not shared by the elite among political activists, and we must now turn briefly to an examination of this possibility.

Again it must be noted that full and systematic data on the basic beliefs of British political leaders are lacking.[23] Nevertheless, several important studies of elite opinion in Britain have appeared recently. They indicate that ideological views at this level too, while more sub-

---

[20] *Ibid.*, pp. 31, 35-36.

[21] MORRIS DAVIS and SIDNEY VERBA, Party Affiliation and International Opinions in Britain and France, 1947-1956. *Public Opinion Quarterly*, 24 (Winter 1960), 590-604.

[22] *Ibid.*, p. 601.

[23] HERBERT MCCLOSKY's studies of the ideological differences between political leaders and the electorate in the United States, for example, have no British counterpart. Consensus and Ideology in American Politics, *loc. cit.*

stantial and coherent than within the general public, are not especially prevalent and tend to keep conflict within manageable bounds. The studies that I shall cite here are those of constituency party attitudes and backbench opinion in the House of Commons.

For some time it has been assumed that the real seat of ideologism in the British political system is the parties' constituency associations. The argument runs something like this: while the top parliamentary leaders of the major parties must blunt any ideological tendencies they might have, for electoral reasons as well as because they are dealing with the realities of governing, the activists who man the local parties are not under these constraints and thus are more likely to be involved in politics for reasons of ideological principle. They work zealously for their party not to advance their own careers, but to further the abstract principles in which they believe passionately. They are more likely to be purists or extremists, more reactionary than the national leadership if they are Conservatives, more radically socialist than the national leadership if they are Labourites. Several demonstrations of this pattern appeared in the 1950's, notably the continuing support for Bevanism in the constituency Labour parties and the stiff punishment meted out to leftward deviating Conservative M.P.s by Conservative associations when their members failed to support the government on issues such as capital punishment and Suez.[24] These gave the impression that the constituency parties are apt to be composed of die-hard, dogmatic, irresponsible ideologues, who are neither representative of grassroots partisan thinking nor, unless they are kept at arm's length from policy-making, assets to responsible party leadership.

This argument has some validity, although a closer look at the local parties shows it to be quite exaggerated. In a painstaking study of resolutions sent by local parties to the annual conferences from 1955 to 1960, Rose has shown that the image of local parties "as a force constantly pressing extremist views upon national leaders" is overdrawn.[25] He found, for example, that the total proportion of resolutions containing ideological elements was 54 per cent, while the remaining 46 per cent dealt with non-partisan questions of little ideological content— expressing mainly views derived from general cultural values or specific interest group demands. Furthermore, most of the resolutions Rose classifies as ideological were simply in line with the standard programs

[24] LEON D. EPSTEIN, *Britain—Uneasy Ally*. Chicago, 1954, chs. 5-7; EPSTEIN, *British Politics in the Suez Crisis*. Urbana, 1964, ch. 6; and NIGEL NICOLSON, *People and Parliament*. London, 1958.
[25] RICHARD ROSE, The Political Ideas of British Party Activists. *The American Political Science Review*, 56 (June 1962), 364.

of the parties (e.g., concerning support for or opposition to the present organization of secondary education, the need for or danger of more economic planning, and so on) and were a far cry from the categories of total ideology. Rose also analyzed the resolutions for their "extremism" content, i.e., whether they deviated markedly from the prevailing doctrine of the party in the direction of purism. He found that in the period in question 66 per cent of Conservative and 38 per cent of Labour associations had submitted no extremist resolutions whatever; while in 11 per cent of Conservative and 18 per cent of Labour associations, over half the submitted resolutions were of this variety.[26] Rather than finding these attitudes to be geographically concentrated in a few constituency parties, however—which might function as party subcultures—Rose determined that they were randomly distributed around the country. So he concluded that there is much less hot partisanship in the local parties than has been thought, and that the supposed doctrinal differences between these parties on the one hand, and either rank-and-file party voters or parliamentary leaders on the other, are really not great.

We have also recently been given a glimpse of the attitude structure of the House of Commons in the research of Finer, Berrington and Bartholomew of Keele University.[27] Recognizing that strict party discipline and caucus decision-making have made it virtually impossible to penetrate behind the unified ranks of the Division List into the real attitudes of individual M.P.s, the Keele group turned instead to an analysis of another expression of parliamentary opinion—the Early Day Motion—which is both publicly available and amenable to statistical treatment. Motions of this type can be made by any M.P. and customarily are signed by those who agree with their expressed sentiments—occasionally as many as 300 Members. They are rarely debated, and support for them is not subject to the party whip. By tradition they are never signed by the government or its whips, and seldom by members of the opposition front bench; hence their description as "spontaneous unwhipped back-bench manifestoes." Obviously any study of these motions is subject to the difficulty that these expressions are often casually made and are not always representative of total parliamentary attitudes. Still, when examined in quantity they afford a rough-and-ready profile of one type of leadership attitudes.

The Keele study focused on nearly 300 Early Day Motions signed by Labour and Conservative M.P.s from 1955 to 1959. They included 111

[26] *Ibid.*, p. 366.
[27] S. E. FINER *et al.*, *Backbench Opinion, op. cit.*

cross-bench motions and 178 motions signed by members of a single party, again revealing the absence of watertight exclusiveness among dedicated partisans. On the Labour side, the study showed—both in the subject of the motions and in the extent of their support—a fairly unified set of concerns and positive correlations between different attitudes. Thus on the seven sets of attitudes which the authors group as "the syndrome of socialism"—humanitarianism, civil liberties, foreign policy, welfare, cost of living, health and education—all attitudes were correlated, on the average, to the degree of .267.[28] But when examined separately, as pairs, these attitudes showed marked differences in their distribution among various types of M.P.s (such as trade-union sponsored, cooperative sponsored, and constituency-party supported Members). In particular, a group of about fifty Labour M.P.s consistently supported all the motions with maximum zeal, forming "the permanent core of the otherwise fluctuating left." In the judgment of the Keele group, the data from the Early Motions bear out the view that British socialism, at least as represented by Labour backbenchers, does not repose on a single coherent universalistic body of doctrine but instead is better described as "a set of propositions or attitudes, which when all or many of them are simultaneously held, constitute socialism." [29]

The Keele group's data for the Conservatives tend to confirm the impression that it is extremely difficult to find clear-cut ideology or even persistent left-center-right factions in this party. While positive correlations were established among a few issues (e.g., attitudes toward Suez policy and penal reform, social progressivism and concern for civil liberties, devotion to national sovereignty and attachment to the Commonwealth), numerous ideological inconsistencies emerged: e.g., many Conservatives displayed enthusiasm for both social reform at home and militant policies abroad, for both world government and intervention in Suez. In contrast to the attitudes of Labour backbenchers, those of the Conservatives did not scale statistically and could only loosely be termed a syndrome. If these data are persuasive, then apparently the average Conservative M.P. does not approach his tasks from a prepared emotional or intellectual position, but rather, as the Keele group has put it, "the Conservative Party acts or thinks as unrelated, *ad hoc* groups of Members, groups whose members join together to contend for one specific objective, and then fall apart once the goal has been attained or has been by-passed by events." [30]

[28] *Ibid.,* pp. 56-58.
[29] *Ibid.,* p. 48.
[30] *Ibid.,* p. 110.

II. THE EQUILIBRIUM OF CONSENSUS AND CLEAVAGE

If Britain lacks the normal concomitants of the politics of total ideology, she is not altogether free of the pull of ideology in the second sense that I have used the term. The British political system manifests certain important beliefs which, though they do not add up to a *Weltanschauung,* nevertheless embody values and principles of action connected to larger views of man, society and the state. These attitudes, however general, affect the functioning of political institutions, and substantial changes in them, when they occur, are likely to be reflected in the balance of the political order. I have mentioned a few of them in the preceding section, in the context of an effort to deny the grip of sterner doctrines on the British people. For example, it seems quite clear that two ideological elements which facilitate democratic politics—a relatively optimistic and trusting view of human nature, and a measure of toleration of political opponents—have a firm place in present British attitudes. In this section I will discuss briefly several more of these elements and show not only some of their consequences for politics, but also some recent additions to more firmly established, historic beliefs. Finally, I will attempt to give the character and flavor of various recent challenges to this bundle of attitudes. No attempt can be made here to present a comprehensive inventory of such beliefs, or to offer empirical evidence of their distribution, salience or intensity.

My argument is not only that certain attitudes in Britain fulfill the functions of an ideology; it is also that they serve as forces making for a balance between consensus and cleavage in the political system. Obviously these attitudes may be deeply held by some Britons and only casually by others. But the overall effect is the maintenance of a moving balance between general agreement on some values and well distributed disagreement on others—the conditions Parsons refers to as a "limited polarization of society." [31]

Consensus

To illustrate both the persistence and changing character of the political belief system, four ideological elements will be cited as fundamentally consensual in nature: the conception of governmental leadership, devotion to procedures, "pragmatism," and the "new feudalism." The first three have been constants in British thinking for many decades, while the last-named has entered the consensual stage only recently.

[31] Voting and the Equilibrium of the American Political System, in E. BURDICK and A. J. BRODBECK, *American Voting Behavior.* Glencoe, Ill., 1959, p. 92.

Britons are widely agreed that the principal duty and task of government is to govern: however important it may be in this age to couple the authority of government with a substantial measure of mass participation, the more populistic elements should not be allowed to paralyze the powers of the Crown. This attitude is a mixture of predemocratic attachment to the notion of a natural ruling class and a recognition that democratic government requires stable and responsible leadership, on the one hand, and a commitment to mass participation and the control of governmental experts and elites by amateurs and non-elites, on the other hand. Its importance as an attitudinal underpinning of political behavior cannot be overestimated. Perhaps the most striking characteristic of the modern British Parliament is its provision and maintenance of a stable majority that permits the government to rule legitimately. Numerous informal institutions which facilitate the conduct of parliamentary business, such as Cabinet hegemony, party discipline and the circumscribed powers of backbench M.P.s, can be linked directly to a general acceptance of the need for strong leadership. This is not simply the ideology of the political elite, for the norm pervades British society in a wider sense. For example, respondents to *Socialist Commentary*'s 1960 poll, when presented with a list of 15 possible characteristics of a good party leader, opted most for "strong leadership" (56 per cent) and "strength to make unwelcome decisions" (47 per cent). Conservative and Labour supporters showed no significant difference in their preference for these qualities.[32] No evidence suggests any weakening in this attitude in recent years; on the contrary, if anything it seems to be increasing in its pervasiveness.

The flavor of ideological commitment attaches also to the place of procedures in the British polity. Whereas they may display flexibility and a willingness to bargain over the content of public policy, the British often show an unbending dogmatism in regard to the process by which policy is established. As Eckstein has aptly observed, ". . . the British invest with very high affect the procedural aspects of their government and with very low affect its substantive aspects; they behave like ideologists in regard to rules and like pragmatists in regard to policies." [33] Numerous examples of this disposition might be cited. The intricate fabric of rules, formal and informal, that bear on the conduct of Parliament has shown amazing resistance to reform, despite the enlarged scope of governmental activity and the agitation for more efficient methods coming from both inside and outside Westminster. Many of them

[32] *Must Labour Lose?*, *op. cit.*, p. 25. These were multiple responses.
[33] HARRY ECKSTEIN, *A Theory of Stable Democracy*. Princeton, 1961, pp. 30-31.

have developed their own mystique and are approached by M.P.s of almost every stripe as akin to absolute values. Interest groups are likely to refuse to accept policies affecting them if they have not been consulted during their formulation. The parties have shown themselves willing to examine critically, and often to abandon, a number of their historic policies; but almost invariably they have held firm in their attachment to time-honored procedures, which are seen as fundamental agencies of legitimation. Thus, the closer it came to actual power, the more the Labour Party divested itself of its radical system-reformers and stressed its adherence to the traditional rules of the game. Conceivably it was their acceptance of the ideology of parliamentarism as much as their growing middle-class character that made Labour leaders palatable to large numbers of non-socialists in the electorate.

When important procedural questions on occasion become mixed with arguments over the substance of policy, the temperature of politics rises appreciably; or, alternatively, disputes over procedure tend to elbow out those over content. The heated Commons debates at the time of the Suez crisis are a case in point. A sitting of the House had to be suspended by the Speaker because of an uproar caused by the refusal of the Prime Minister to answer what Labour M.P.s believed to be a legitimate parliamentary question (whether the country was or was not at war with Egypt),[34] and almost as much criticism was leveled at Eden for allegedly not consulting with his own parliamentary supporters and the leader of the opposition on government plants as was directed against the wisdom of his decision to take military action.[35] A concentration and fixity of dogmatic concern tend to attach to this one aspect of the political system, then, even if they do not carry over into other areas equally.

A third component of this ideological structure, also deeply embedded in British political culture and high in affect, is the concept of pragmatism, already noted. It has come to be shorthand for the belief that sweeping change is unnecessary and dangerous, that effective change is that which comes gradually and builds on, rather than obliterates, previous forms and practices. The test of any institution or any policy, accordingly, is not its esthetic form or logical consistency but its success in performing the fairly immediate task for which it is designed. Anomalies

[34] 558 *House of Commons Debates* 1620-25 (November 1, 1956). For more discussion of the significance of the procedural aspects of the crisis, see RICHARD ROSE, *Politics in England*. Boston, 1964, pp. 232-33.
[35] EPSTEIN, *British Politics in the Suez Crisis, op. cit.*, ch. 5; ROBERT T. MCKENZIE, *British Political Parties*. 2d ed., London, 1963, pp. 585-89.

and loose ends are no problem. The rhetoric of British politics is filled with tributes to this mode of thinking (e.g., "Britain is ruled not by logic but by Parliament" [Disraeli]; "Logic is a poor guide compared with custom" [Churchill]), and no description of the working of basic institutions, from the City of London to the University Grants Committee, seems complete without the proffered explanation that "It may seem odd to you, but it works." [36] Pragmatism is bred into the bones of modern Britons by a self-conscious celebration of its virtues and an insistence that it serve as the most suitable guide to political decision-making.

The attachment to larger principles may often be modified or supplemented by an equally intense belief that translation of these principles into practice should take pragmatic form. The policies adopted by the two major parties toward nationalization and colonialism are illustrative of this tempering. Not only did Labour go slow in implementing the social ideal of public ownership when the party came to power in 1945; it also devoted much of the 1950's to a reappraisal of the place of nationalization in its program, with the resultant de-emphasis—but not extinction—of the older ideal. Conversely, traditional Conservative opposition to nationalization did not prevent the party when in power from retaining in the public sector most of the industries nationalized by its predecessor. Again, though dedicated to ending colonialism and raising the remaining outposts of empire to self-governing status, the Labour government began gradually by concentrating on the Asian flank, and left to succeeding Conservative governments the continuation of the process, step by step, in Africa and the Caribbean. The defense of these actions, as with nationalization, has been largely in terms of the kind of pragmatic outlook that Britons understand and approve.

Pragmatism, then, is closely related to other basic beliefs—in stability, in peaceful solutions, in mixed institutions, and in the legitimating effect of gradual change. It serves as a brake on rapid, root-and-branch societal transformation. In practice, it may also have the effect of reinforcing a preference for amateurs (who are presumed to be more pragmatic in their outlooks) over specialists and technicians (who are thought more likely to be narrow dogmatists—in Keynes's famous jibe, "slaves of some defunct economist"). As I will show very shortly, critics may be found to argue that pragmatism has been raised into a dangerous cult which

[36] ANTHONY SAMPSON, *Anatomy of Britain*. London, 1962. Rev. ed., *Anatomy of Britain Today*. New York: Harper and Row, 1965, Harper Colophon Books, 1966, *passim*.

the country can no longer afford to perpetuate; but of the pervasive hold of pragmatism on British political thinking there can be little doubt.

These three elements of consensus—belief in leadership, attachment to procedures, and pragmatism—have been present in British political culture for many years. Nevertheless, the composition of the blundle of attitudes that comprise the ideology is not static or immutable. As society changes and the role of government is modified, basic attitudes are also likely to undergo transformation. One of the most important recent ideological adjustments involves changing attitudes toward the private and public spheres of British life. These newer attitudes, sometimes referred to as "the new feudalism," parallel ideologically the development of the welfare state and the highly controlled economy. They are attitudinal adjustments to the new balance of social forces created by corporatist developments in the polity, which have given to many private groups what amounts to veto power over public policy. The vast responsibilities now thrown onto government can be carried out only if important affected groups in society agree to go along. By withholding capital, talents or cooperation such groups could make a shambles of any government's program. The requirements of this quasi-corporatism evoke the danger that Britain might reach what Samuel Beer has called the point of "pluralistic stagnation." [37] One reason why this has not yet materialized is that, as Beer has noted, the Keynesian revolution in economics succeeded after World War II in altering popular ideas about the role of government and the pursuit of unlimited private gain. In particular, the almost complete acceptance of the neo-mercantilism associated with Keynesian doctrine, which gives to government the role once played by Adam Smith's "invisible hand," provides new standards for judging group values, demands and behavior. In a sense the ethic of bargaining has displaced what has remained of the ethic of competition, and personal acquisitiveness has given way in large measure to the search for security guaranteed by the community. Put another way, despite the powers of blackmail inherent in the position of interest groups in British society today, the potentialities of this power have generally been held in check by a consensus derived in part from the recognition of governmental responsibility for maintaining the economic equilibrium and in part from the decline of acquisitiveness in favor of the more medieval

---

[37] ". . . the extent of group power . . . means that the country has gone so far as to reach the point of moving with unanimity or not at all." SAMUEL H. BEER, Pressure Groups and Parties in Britain. *The American Political Science Review*, 50 (March 1956), 15-16.

standard of just rewards. The acceptance of a national incomes policy, for example, depends upon the pervasiveness of this attitude.

Cleavage

Along with these consensual elements, other basic attitudes divide the British community and foster some degree of ideological tension. Some of the forces making for cleavage are built into the political party system; others are less organized and function as generalized outside pressures. Broadly speaking, this constitutes the distinction between party competition on the one hand and intellectual criticism on the other. I shall deal first with ideological differences between and within the two main parties and second with the challenges to the prevailing ideology from the outsiders.

In spite of the growing trend toward interparty agreement on many policies, the Conservative and Labour Parties continue to espouse somewhat different conceptions of human nature, society and the state. Their ideological centers of gravity are distinct, and to the extent that activists and supporters are socialized into the historic norms of the parties, significant differences between them will remain. Even when they are forced to support similar programs, it is often for basically different reasons. The ideologies of the parties do not function solely as symbols and myths; they are potentially operative (so long as they have not atrophied completely), and on occasion they fix the boundaries and direction of policy decisions. For Conservatives, the belief in the naturalness and usefulness of inequality, the inevitability of hierarchy, and the positive values of nationalism and empire may have been muted by the necessities of Britain's contemporary situation, but it has not been abandoned in favor of a wholly different value system. Similarly, Labour's attachment to the values of equality, social democracy, classlessness and pacifism, while also tempered by the exigencies of the moment, has remained fairly fixed. As a motivation and a standard for political action, it has not declined to the level of cynical rhetoric. So long as this ideological gap between the parties continues to be perceived by their partisans—and I believe that at the moment it still is—talk of the politics of Tweedledum and Tweedledee is premature.[38]

In addition, each party has within its ranks militant individuals and groups concerned with preserving the party's doctrinal purity and his-

---

[38] One study asserts that only a decided minority of the electorate seems to be able to appraise the ideologies of the parties in any meaningful way. DONALD E. STOKES, Ideological Competition of British Parties, paper given at the annual meeting of the American Political Science Association, September, 1964.

94   JAMES B. CHRISTOPH

toric values. The persistence of such forces, which may or may not take the form of factions, cannot be disregarded as strictly of nuisance value, for they often represent ideological cleavages within the electorate as well. As ideological pressure groups within the party's structure they may serve to set limits beyond which the leadership ventures at its peril. The Labour Party has long been beset by internal doctrinal cleavages, which not only affect the struggle for leadership but create an image with the electorate. During the 1950's and early 1960's, for instance, the party was almost constantly engaged in internecine disputes between left-wing factions and the dominant right-wing leadership. The splits that occurred over the Bevanite view of socialist priorities, over German rearmament, over the status of the commitment to nationalization, and over nuclear disarmament are familiar examples. In each case the disagreement turned at least in part on the question of how strictly the party should adhere to the historic body of doctrine known as "socialism" and "socialist foreign policy." And while the Attlee-Gaitskell forces were usually successful in fending off the left-wing accusations that they had betrayed the fundamental tenets of the Labour movement, the leadership could not afford to be wholly impervious to the substantial body of opinion represented by the Bevanites and their successors. Nor, as the disputes over the party's constitution and over nuclear weapons revealed, was the moderate leadership able to subjugate the radical wing so completely as to foreclose the possibility of a resurgence of doctrinaire opinions within important sections of the party. When Gaitskell attempted after the 1959 election defeat to persuade the party to amend Clause IV of its constitution in the direction of virtually eliminating the commitment to nationalization, he was set upon not only by the left but also the center of the party, and forced to beat a hasty retreat. The controversy over Clause IV showed convincingly that the ideological reflexes of the party are not atrophied, and that electoral calculation has not completely replaced them as the mainspring of Labour's program.[39]

The Conservative Party is much more homogeneous than Labour in its social composition, its relation to outside groups, and its public loyalty to its leadership. But it is not altogether free of ideological dissension. It has its stalwart and reformist elements, who occasionally succeed in moving the party in one direction or the other, often on the basis of very different views of man and society. These forces are apt to take a rather different form from their counterparts on the Labour side. Whereas in the Labour Party the usual instrument of ideological dissension is the

[39] For further examples, see RICHARD ROSE, Parties, Factions and Tendencies in Britain. *Political Studies,* 12 (February 1964), 33-46.

faction, a stable set of politicians organized for political activity, the more common form among the Conservatives is what Rose refers to as a "tendency," a stable set of attitudes expressed in Parliament by less organized, more fluctuating groups of politicians. Thus as the Keele study of backbench opinion made clear, the Conservative leadership has encountered significant internal party opposition on a number of issues invested with ideological affect, such as crime and punishment, colonialism, and the maintenance of free enterprise (e.g., public *vs.* private television). However, the M.P.s who pressed dogmatic views on these issues did not form a stable group but tended to fall apart and regroup along different lines when other controversies arose. Single issues, such as the Suez crisis, may split Conservatives into right, left and center groups, with strong ideological disputation between the extremes; but continuing factionalism, with the risk of intra-party polarization, runs counter to the traditional Conservative belief in loyalty to the chosen leadership. The Conservative Party, like Labour, shows both consensus and cleavage on ideological questions. Unlike the pattern in the Labour Party, the Conservative balance is skewed strongly in the direction of consensus, with ideology generally secondary to more tangible interests.

The overall picture of the condition of ideology in Britain shows, therefore, a continuing mixture of consensus and cleavage, of attitudes making for stability and attitudes fostering change. These attitudes are not distributed uniformly through the population or within the political system; but neither are they polarized in separate groups, and they coexist at almost every important level of political structure. In sum, the process of government rests upon a combination of strong commitment and low-temperature pragmatism. "If too much principle can kill a government," Eckstein has observed, "so can the lack of principle at all . . . what is wanted is 'programmatic' government, and this must of necessity blend principle with pragmatic adjustment." [40] The prevailing distribution of attitudes in Britain goes some distance to satisfy this condition.

Critics

The content of British political attitudes has not escaped criticism, especially in the era of the Common Market. If the 1950's were the heyday of the angry young men of letters, the early 1960's spawned a

[40] HARRY ECKSTEIN, *op. cit.,* p. 33. In a sophisticated analysis bearing on this point, Harvey C. Mansfield, Jr., has distinguished between parties and compromises based upon the concepts of consensus and program. Party Government and the Settlement of 1688, *The American Political Science Review,* 58 (December 1964), 933-46.

number of critics concerned with the condition of the nation's political values. Some of them, notably the so-called "New Left" and the marching and squatting foes of nuclear weapons, are in the long tradition of radical protest in Britain. Although their targets are contemporary, their moral and social values are not markedly different from those of the 1930's.[41] Rather than focusing on this fairly familiar pattern of outgroup protest, I shall concentrate on another group of critics whose concern is less singleminded and whose methods are less spectacular than the "angries" of the traditional left, but whose belief that the nation's values are dangerously outdated is equally strong. I refer to those intellectuals who are devoted to exposing the alleged loss of Britain's *élan vital* and to pleading for the modernization of basic attitudes as well as institutions.

This unorganized group of critics, whom Henry Fairlie has termed disdainfully "State of England" writers, is difficult to fit into ready-made political categories. It numbers, among others, several right-wing Labour M.P.s, a couple of leftish Oxford economists, a few mildly left-of-center journalists, a professor of government known mainly for works on France, the industrial editor of the *Financial Times,* and Arthur Koestler.[42] What they have in common is a reformist outlook, born of disillusionment with the tenacity of certain historic British attitudes in the postwar world. This has led them to strike out without discrimination against left and right alike—in Crosland's phrase, "the conservative enemy," wherever found. Because they share this motivation, their chief ideas can be lumped together for convenience without serious distortion, so long as it is remembered that what follows is a composite of themes scattered in many writings.

Underlying these critics' attack is the non-Marxian assumption that what ails Britain is not so much its material conditions or its new place in the world as its cultural attitudes. "We are faced," Koestler writes, "with a 'functional' rather than a 'structural' disorder. Structural diseases have objective, material causes, functional diseases have subjective,

[41] For the views of these groups see NORMAN BIRNBAUM, Great Britain: The Reactive Revolt, in MORTON A. KAPLAN, ed., *The Revolution in World Politics.* New York, 1962, pp. 55-68, and HENRY J. STECK, The Re-emergence of Ideological Politics in Britain. *Western Political Quarterly,* 18 (March 1965), 87-103.
[42] THOMAS BALOGH, The Apotheosis of the Dilettante, in HUGH THOMAS, ed., *The Establishment.* London, 1962, pp. 72-115; BRIAN CHAPMAN, *British Government Observed.* London, 1963; C. A. R. CROSLAND, *The Conservative Enemy.* London, 1962; Suicide of a Nation? *Encounter* (July 1963), esp. the articles by ALBU, ALTRINCHAM, COLE, SHANKS, and SHONFIELD; ANTHONY SAMPSON, *op. cit.;* MICHAEL SHANKS, *The Stagnant Society.* Harmondsworth, 1961; and JOHN VAIZEY, *Britain in the Sixties: Education for Tomorrow.* Harmondsworth, 1962.

psychological causes." [43] It is a lack of dynamism, of incentives (in more than the pecuniary sense), of social discipline bred by a sense of community, that lies at the root of the *malaise*. The aftermath of empire, the decline of Britain's power in world affairs, the effects of the welfare state, the challenge of new Europe—all are but proximate causes; the real sources of the present difficulties lie deeper, in attitudes toward society and government which stretch back into British history. Paradoxically, it is said, it has been the almost unbroken character of British development, its vaunted evolutionary stability, that now holds back the creation of the types of modern attitudes so badly needed. Having been spared the upheavals of radical social revolution, the interruption of its political regime, the destruction of its land and economy, and the psychological trauma of invasion and alien rule, Britain has not been forced to agonize over, or to reconstruct, its fundamental values. In the view of many of these critics, the very traits so much admired by outside observers—the blending of the pre-industrial and the modern, the conscious preservation of aristocratic institutions, the taste for new wines in old bottles—have unfitted the country for the tasks of survival in a rapidly changing world.

It is hardly surprising that one of the targets of this line of criticism is the alleged historicism of the British, their compulsive fixation, as one writer has put it, on either the glories or the miseries of the past. The consequence in both cases is a retreat into unreality, frustration and passivity. All too many Britons remain, it is asserted, who hanker after the day when Britannia was top-dog and could solve any problem by sending a gunboat. While Suez was supposed to be their lesson, they have refused to hearken to it. More important, others refuse to believe that Britain can learn anything from the rest of the world, in particular from the political and economic experiments now under way in Western Europe. Thus Henry Fairlie:

> I am extremely doubtful whether we have anything to learn from either the Fifth Republic in France or the Federal Republic in West Germany about the manner of ordering and sustaining a free society; I am not even sure whether we have much to learn in the matter from the French and Germans as peoples . . . for the moment, I am prepared to wager fairly heavily that our own social and political arrangements will outlast theirs. Any takers? [44]

Still others, it is maintained, are mesmerized by the ancient rituals and dominant values of Oxford and Cambridge—"fairylands in the heart

[43] ARTHUR KOESTLER, The Lion and the Ostrich. *Encounter* (July 1963), 8.
[44] HENRY FAIRLIE, On the Comforts of Anger. *Ibid.*, 12.

of modern Britain"—the essence of whose magic is that it is pre-industrial.

This satisfied, even complacent, immersion in the British past is coupled, usually at the other end of the social scale, with the equally corrosive tendency of Britons to view the present in terms of the miserable and insecure days of the 1930's, the period when so many leaders of the left came of age. Here the prime target is usually the trade unions: their restrictive practices, their security-mindedness, their suspicion of innovation, their unwillingness to adopt business unionism and provide their leaders with adequate powers, their division of the industrial world into "Them" and "Us," and their "I'm All Right, Jack" response to their own rising affluence. Again, though the causes of this *malaise* are recognized as partly structural, it is argued that at the base of the problem are attitudes derived from situations and days long past. The result of conservatism in this major area of British life is that the unions are proving themselves "the natural allies of the forces of stagnation and conservatism in industry—and not those of expansion and dynamism." [45]

From this target it is but a short step to another: the alleged cult of amateurism and pragmatism. These seemingly valuable traits, it is argued, have been transformed into fetishes in contemporary British usage. The amateur has become not the curious and adaptable all-rounder, but the dilettante; and pragmatism, rather than being synonymous with the experimental outlook, has shrunk to cautious, narrow tinkering. Teleology has given way to functionalism, the spirit of inquiry to the norms of adjustment and conciliation. Not surprisingly, the institutions most under fire for the inculcation of these attitudes are the educational system and the civil service, which at their higher levels are seen as extensions of each other. Hence the claim that the dominant humanist tradition of the top public schools and Oxbridge, while perhaps suitable for the days of laissez-faire and empire, is now hopelessly out of keeping with the requirements of industrial society and positive government. The defense of the prevailing values of British education in terms of training the generalist for the tasks of policy-making is really a deception. In the civil service, as in industry and Parliament, the domination of those possessed of (in Balogh's phrase) the "crossword-puzzle mind, reared on mathematics at Cambridge or Greats at Oxford," is inimical to the kind of rational, comprehensive, long-range planning that British society now requires.

[45] MICHAEL SHANKS, *op. cit.*, p. 93.

The prevailing low esteem for science, technology and business enterprise particularly agitates the critics, who attribute to it much of
Britain's slow economic growth, the "brain drain," and the nervous
ambivalence toward the Common Market. This attitude, they argue, is
one of the negative residues of aristocratic values in a democratic age.
Whereas in the eighteenth and nineteenth centuries the progress of
technology and the promise of economic growth were the special
ideology of the business class in its struggle with the land-owning
aristocracy, over time the ideology faded out as the rising masters of
technology and entrepreneurial power gave in to the tempting possibility
of emulating the life of the landed squire. "The combination of a sharply
divided class society—and the possibility of rising from one class to
another held in greater esteem—meant that the ambition of the sons
of many manufacturers was to leave their family businesses and to
become landowners (or, at least, 'professional men')." [46] Business,
manufacturing and applied science continue to exist, but top creative
talent refused to associate with these activities, and their controllers
became increasingly docile, unadventurous and apologetic. In the view
of the non-socialist wing of this school of critics, the reforms needed to
achieve greater efficiency and expanded production have been stymied
by the unwillingness of Britons to put these values above those of short-
run group security and "fair play." "We are unwilling to advance if it
means that anybody is going to get hurt. . . . This is in many ways an
admirable trait, but it is a sure recipe for national decay." [47] What
these writers call for, then, is a reorientation of basic values in the
direction of recognizing that whatever may have been the contributions
in the past of aristocratic, unspecialized and humanistic standards of
performance, the new Britain requires the upgrading of those attitudes
which will foster technological innovation and organizational efficiency.
Such a reorientation hinges upon the ability of Britons to sublimate, and
finally eliminate, the class-bound attitudes of the past, which have stood
as barriers not only to a democratic life, but also to national growth.

These cries are also echoed by critics of the process of government,
especially those who view with misgivings the increased corporatism of
policy-making. A notable example is Brian Chapman, whose slash-
ing broadside, *British Government Observed*, significantly is subtitled
"Some European Reflections." Although Chapman is critical chiefly of
what he believes to be the archaic, nineteenth century character of the

[46] AUSTEN ALBU, Taboo on Expertise. *Ibid.*, p. 46.
[47] SHANKS, The Comforts of Stagnation. *Encounter* (July 1963), 31.

machinery of government—its "rich Byzantine structure"—he attributes much of this condition to the lack of doctrinal value attached to the concept of public service in Britain. In contrast to the trends in Continental countries, he asserts, British government remains in the grips of the luxuriant amateurism of centuries past and has not developed a genuine pluralism based upon the sentiment that public office carries with it public responsibility. Its pragmatism is a mask for weak-kneed, expensive abdication to whatever pressures happen to be brought to bear. Thus public policy is "simply equated with finding the least controversial course between the conflicting interests of vociferous private groups. It is not a doctrine of government; it is a doctrine of subordination." [48] Other critics sharing these views have added the argument that a system that acts as much on the basis of "understandings"—unarticulated, unstructured, implicit responses to new situations—does not encourage bold solutions or positive action.

This small sample of the expanding literature of discontent testifies to the survival of ideological concern in Britain today. True, these particular critics are not of a single mind, and few of them present fully drawn prescriptions for reform (aside, perhaps, from a common emphasis on the need to reconstruct the educational system). But they do share two strong interests that have influenced their analysis and their prescriptions. First, they are impressed by many of the recent developments occurring on the Continent, and they would shake Britain out of its traditional belief that nothing positive can be learned from that quarter. Thus they would seem to pin their hope of change in part on the prospects of closer union with Europe, if only because this might jolt the country out of its complacent ways. Second, they believe that the primary force making for attitudinal change will be the rising power of the newer, more modern and classless elements in British society— the managers, scientists, technicians and white collar workers—who have reaped the benefits of the 1944 Education Act, and whose occupational skills and roles have removed them from the attitudes of the older England. In this sense, but not in others, these critics would agree with the diagnoses of the "end of ideology" writers.

None of this cluster of critics offers a new "world view" ideology to the British, but most of them are concerned with the reordering of basic political attitudes in the second sense that I have used the term "ideology." While acknowledging the need to retain many of the historic

---

[48] CHAPMAN, op. cit., p. 61. For a challenge to this interpretation, see D. N. CHESTER, British Government Observed. *Public Administration*, 41 (Winter 1963), 375-84.

values associated with the British polity, they would nevertheless adjust the equilibrium of ancient and modern values in the direction of modernity. This can be achieved, they believe, in the best British tradition, without resort to cosmic theories or to the intolerance of closed systems.

4

Parties, Factions, and Tendencies in Britain

RICHARD ROSE

EDITORIAL NOTE: *A more recent appraisal of the party configuration and party trends in England is given in this essay by Richard Rose. The reader should do well to consult also his* Politics in England, *Boston, 1964.*

IN studies of party politics, Britain is often cited as the leading example of a two-party system. The purpose of this essay is to challenge the utility of labeling the whole of party politics by a term which describes only one aspect of national party politics—electoral competition. British parties have many functions beside that of supporting competing teams of leaders at general elections. The most salient characteristics of the entities called "parties" shift as functions change and attempts are made to reconcile the conflicting pressures arising from the bundle of roles, individuals and institutions normally lumped together under one omnibus heading. Distinguishing between parties as electoral institutions and as policy institutions may reduce some of the confusion caused by use of the broader term, as well as explaining how parties place restraints upon government today.

I. THE FUNCTIONS OF PARTIES

Definitions of party systems usually emphasize the function of parties *qua* electoral institutions. In consequence, systems are distinguished by

102

the number of parties competing at the polls: this provides a means of classifying parties, although it hardly provides a "systematic" description of the workings of parties within a political society, as the term "system" is now used by political sociologists.[1] Parties function only intermittently as electoral institutions, and much of the long-term work of attending to elections is delegated to relatively unimportant bureaucrats. This is particularly true in Britain where elections occur only once in every four or five years. Electoral considerations are usually in the middle distance. In the short run, the parties, especially the governing party, are confronted with national problems upon which positions must be taken in Parliament. Most policy decisions cannot be taken on the basis of electoral preferences, because of the narrow range of electoral concerns and the vagueness of preferences. Public opinion polls may show that voters want peace and prosperity; such information is virtually worthless to ministers and potential ministers attempting to choose between alternative economic and international policies concerned with means to these ends. Elitist traditions in the political culture emphasize the duty of governors to be unpopular in the short run, if they think they are right, and most party leaders are sophisticated enough to appreciate that temporarily unpopular policies may produce popular consequences by the date which the governing party chooses for the general election.

In terms of shaping public policy, the party *qua* government is much more significant than, and significantly different from, an electoral party. Politicians in office have both party and government roles, and the claims of these roles are not always identical. Priority out of office can be given to the demands of groups within the extra-parliamentary party. In office, priority must usually be given to administrative exigencies and to intractable dilemmas which cannot be glossed over simply by means of a party conference resolution. Civil servants are ever present, proffering administrative objections to policies which are acceptable or desired by sections of the party outside its ministerial membership. The goodwill of pressure groups is important to the success of some government policies, even when these groups may be supporting the opposition party at elections. Duties of a departmental nature reduce the time politicians have for meeting partisans outside government. In so far as role conflicts lead to transparent differences between previous party policy and the policy of the party as government, then party members excluded from the government may follow their principles and ambitions and

---

[1] Cf. the sociologically systematic discussion of parties in R. K. MERTON, *Social Theory and Social Structure*. Glencoe, Ill.: Free Press, rev. ed., 1957, pp. 71 ff., and the approach of MAURICE DUVERGER, *Political Parties*. London: Methuen, 1954.

make an issue of such discrepancies. Since the leaders of the governing party can give immediate effect to their decisions, differences within the party can be intensified. Behind the façade of unity maintained by the conventions of parliamentary government, M.P.s can differ privately with each other and with ministers, and ministers may differ with each other. Conflicts in personalities or in personal ambitions can stimulate or intensify differences arising either from conflicts on party principles or conflicts based upon contrasting departmental concerns.

The party *qua* opposition is organized differently and subjected to other pressures. An opposition leader, immediately after an electoral defeat, in theory may be a potential Prime Minister, although only three times in this century has a new Prime Minister stepped directly from a position as leader of the opposition. Normally, a new Prime Minister comes into office between elections after a long apprenticeship in Cabinet. The opposition leader is after defeat a potential scapegoat for the disappointed within his party, lacking the resources of a Prime Minister for stifling public controversy. *Ex hypothesi,* a party as opposition concentrates upon victory at the next general election, however distant. But in practice, there are often disagreements as to what are the best means to this end, and in the Labour Party there have always been some who have rejected electoral success as an irrelevant standard by which to determine party actions. And it is the Labour Party which has usually provided the opposition in the past forty years.

Perhaps the greatest degree of cohesiveness can be found in the party *qua* organization.[2] Both major parties have stable, hierarchical institutions which deploy full-time bureaucrats at all levels from constituencies to national headquarters. Party employees enjoy pensions and may refer to themselves as civil servants. Their status as pensionable party servants depends in part upon their ability to serve the leadership while keeping free from identification with factions inside the party. Much of the day-to-day work of party bureaucrats is free from controversy. When policy statements are required, the officials can draft them so as to concentrate fire upon the electoral opponent, thus avoiding factional disputes. This, for instance, has normally been the tactic of the international secretary of the Labour Party, even though this makes such statements ineffectual with regard to the long and important dispute about foreign affairs within the electoral party.

The foregoing sketch of the structures and functions of political parties is illustrative, not exhaustive. Political parties are also instruments of pressure groups, vehicles of men seeking power and status, centers of

[2] See RICHARD ROSE, The Professionals of Politics. *New Society* (August 8, 1963).

social activity, vehicles for individuals seeking to reduce psychological tensions and agencies involved in local government and local life. Parties are all these things at once, and these many functions are not always harmoniously combined. That is why it is necessary to use modifying terms with the word "party" in order to avoid confusion.

II. PARTIES IN THE POLICY PROCESS

The focus of this essay is upon the party *qua* government and the party *qua* opposition, that is, upon parties as policy parties, participating with pressure groups, civil servants and others in the making of public policy. From this perspective, it is important not only to ask which electoral party has a parliamentary majority, but also, which policy party predominates in the victorious electoral party? In this way recognition is given both to the differences *between* electoral parties and to the differences *within* electoral parties. The latter differences are at least as important as the former, because most general elections since 1900 have not resulted in a formal change in party government, but in a confirmation of the combination in office. Often differences within electoral parties are treated as much less significant than differences between electoral parties. For instance, Austin Ranney and Willmoore Kendall define a party as "a large-scale organization whose purpose is to control the personnel and policies *of the government*" and a faction as "an element inside a party whose purpose is to control the personnel and policies *of the party*." [3] But when a faction attempts to control the governing party, then it is, by this definition, both a party and a faction.

In modern British political history, the realignment of policy groups within and across electoral lines has been as significant, if not more significant, than shifts in government caused by general elections. Since 1885, only the elections of 1906 and 1945 may be said to have directly precipitated major realignments in government policy. More often, major changes have arisen from divisions within electoral parties: the Liberal Unionists split from the Liberals in 1886; the Conservatives divided on tariff reform after 1900; the Lloyd George Coalition was formed, by a split in 1916 and ended in one in 1922; the Labour Party split in 1931, the Conservatives divided in 1940, and Labour split in 1951. The Conservatives' unwillingness to divide in public has not sustained continuous harmony in private. The Labour Party is federal or confederal in policy as in structure; since its origins it has combined groups in basic dis-

[3] *Democracy and the American Party System.* New York: Harcourt, Brace, 1956, p. 126. Italics in the original.

agreement on policy.[4] The Liberals have split, split and split again since 1886.

Contemporary evidence of divisions within the electoral parties may be drawn from many sources, and from many sections of parties. The government of Harold Macmillan experienced the resignation of three senior ministers on policy grounds; one can only speculate about how many resignations have been threatened and forestalled in the course of dividing, then coalescing on policy. Hugh Dalton's memoirs document divisions on Cabinet policy in the 1945-51 Labour government. The volumes of Hansard are full of expressions of differences between M.P.s nominally in the same party. Signatures to parliamentary motions offer additional substantiation. Of the resolutions sent by activists to annual party conferences, about half of those which are overtly partisan stress internally divisive policies. Among voters, disagreements on policy among those supporting the same party cover a wide range of issues.[5]

Policy parties emerge between elections and concentrate attention upon the literal and metaphorical centers of policy-making, the Cabinet and Shadow Cabinet. Policy parties do not seek absolute control of government; a realistic aim is predominance. Because questions of policy usually do not affect the nomination of parliamentary candidates, there is little scope for policy factions to operate within the electoral process. Studying them involves both conceptual and empirical problems. In analyzing parties as policy institutions, three elements are of special importance—factions, tendencies and non-aligned partisans.[6] These three elements have been of importance over a very long period of time. Clarity can be gained by analyzing these three elements separately, although actual policy parties mix the three elements. The difference in the proportions mixed remains of major operational significance.

A political *faction* may be defined as a group of individuals based on representatives in Parliament who seek to further a broad range of policies through consciously organized political activity. Factions are thus distinguished from other influence groups by having membership based in Parliament, rather than in the civil service or elsewhere.

[4] See e.g., R. T. MCKENZIE, *British Political Parties*. London: Heinemann, 1955, ch. 3; and HENRY PELLING, *The Origins of the Labour Party, 1880-1900*. London: Macmillan, 1954.
[5] See especially S. E. FINER, H. B. BERRINGTON and D. J. BARTHOLOMEW, *Backbench Opinion in the House of Commons, 1955-59*. London: Pergamon, 1961; RICHARD ROSE, The Political Ideas of English Party Activists. *American Political Science Review*, 56, No. 2 (1962); R. S. MILNE and H. C. MACKENZIE, *Marginal Seat, 1955*. London: Hansard Society, 1958, ch. 8.
[6] The author is indebted to S. H. Beer for the formulation of the difference between a faction and a tendency.

Because they persist through time, factions can be distinguished from *ad hoc* combinations of politicians in agreement upon one particular issue or at one moment in time. Factions may be distinguished from pressure groups because the former are concerned with a wide range of political issues, including foreign affairs, colonial policy and defense, as well as economics and social welfare. Factions may be distinguished from exponents of a political tendency because factions are self-consciously organized as a body, with a measure of discipline and cohesion thus resulting. Identification with a faction usually increases an individual's commitment to a program, as well as creating the expectation that the politician will consistently take the same side in quarrels within an electoral party. These expectations are a form of discipline operating socially and internalized by an individual. To abandon a faction is to risk appearing publicly as a renegade, as well as causing tension in the personal relations of the defector with his political associates. The existence of recognized lines of conflict can become the cause of policy disagreements, as factional opponents transfer old enmities to new issues.[7]

By contrast, a political *tendency* is a stable set of attitudes, rather than a stable group of politicians. It may be defined as a body of attitudes expressed in Parliament about a broad range of problems; the attitudes are held together by a more or less coherent political ideology. One may speak of right-wing and left-wing tendencies within both British parties because of the extent to which political differences in this country may be placed along a single left-right axis. The number of M.P.s who adhere to a tendency varies from issue to issue. Adherents are often not self-consciously organized in support of a single policy and they do not expect, nor are they expected, to continue to operate as a group supporting the same tendency through a period of time. This makes it easier for M.P.s to shift positions from tendency to tendency. Individuals may be attached to conflicting tendencies, resolving the resulting cross pressures in different ways in differing contexts. For instance, many M.P.s will at some time or another show a reform tendency with regard to a particular measure. But this will not make them all members of a reform faction, supporting a wide range of changes. In so far as an electoral party is primarily characterized by factionalism, then cleavages within the party tend to be stable and follow predictable lines. In so far as groups of politicians do not self-consciously band together, then party divisions are fluid and less easy to anticipate.

[7] See on this point, J. S. COLEMAN, *Community Conflict*. Glencoe, Ill.: Free Press, 1957, ch. 2.

Non-alignment is identification with positions supported by the whole of the electoral party, rather than with factions or tendencies. This is a real and important alternative for M.P.s and activists.[8] Non-alignment may result from an active concern with only the gross differences between electoral parties, from a passive attitude towards policy issues, or from a calculated desire to avoid identification with particular tendencies or factions in order to gain popularity within the whole electoral party. At times of intense differences on policy within an electoral party, non-aligned partisans represent a slack resource which disputants attempt to mobilize in order to shift the balance.

Policy parties are not pure factions, tendencies or collections of non-aligned partisans. For instance, the Bevanites combined the stable core of a faction with occasional support from those supporting a left-wing tendency on one issue. The right-wing of the Conservative Party, by contrast, has in recent years been unorganized; a few Conservatives frequently follow right-wing tendencies, but many come and go in accordance with circumstances and issues. The complex nature of this scheme of analysis, juxtaposing groups of individual politicians and analytic categories, is intended to correct the over-simplifications arising from concentration on electoral parties. Yet it is in turn an over-simplification. Groups and categories could be further divided and sub-divided until one was left only with individual politicians—each divided within himself and divided in his sympathies with others. But then, a process of building up patterns would have to be begun again.

III. POLICY PARTIES IN ELECTORAL PARTIES

The policy parties formed by an amalgam of factions, tendencies and non-aligned partisans have a relatively simple and somewhat fluid structure, which may operate only intermittently within the electoral parties, as the cohesiveness of the electoral party and its salience varies. The chief features of a policy party, particularly a consciously organized faction, appear to be an ideology, leadership, limited technical expertise, *cadres,* a communications network, and rewards, whether material or psychological.

Ideology is important in so far as a common adherence to shared political values may cause politicians to act together. Adherence to ideological principles, presented as the essence of the electoral party's beliefs, can be used by factions to justify activities which might be judged to

[8] Cf. the analysis of constituency party resolutions in RICHARD ROSE, The Political Ideas of English Party Activists, *op. cit.,* pp. 362 ff.

harm the party electorally. Whether the principles have much intellectual content, or are purely symbolic, they can none the less cause shifts within an electoral party, as the dispute within the Labour Party on repealing Clause IV demonstrated in 1960-61. Leadership gives a recognized focus and stature to what may otherwise be a collection of second-string politicians. With a leader of national stature, disputes are no longer between front bench and back bench, but are fought out within the ranks of front bench M.P.s. The resignation of Aneurin Bevan from the Labour Government in 1951 provides a classic illustration of how the emergence of a leader can help a tendency to crystallize into a recognized faction. But, as Bevan's *rapprochement* with Hugh Gaitskell in 1957 demonstrated, factional leaders, if they are not to become intransigents and politically isolated, face the difficult task of leading a faction and acting as a broker in negotiations with opposing political groups.[9] Technical expertise is important in so far as a faction is pressing detailed proposals. But the various parliamentary elements often appear less concerned with matters of detail than with general principles, seeking to influence the evaluation of detailed claims and counter-claims, rather than to originate proposals based upon expert knowledge. For instance, the development of opinion among M.P.s on the European Common Market appears to have far outpaced the assimilation of expert and detailed knowledge on the Market. *Cadres* are necessary to support and implement the program of a faction, giving to a small body of men the semblance of a "mass" movement with widespread electoral support. In Maurice Duverger's terms, factions are *cadre* parties without rank and file members and with only a limited number of devotees.[10] The habitual supporters of a tendency are usually so loosely associated as not to constitute *cadres,* but they can provide the *cadres* for a new faction. The communications networks of groups are informal and intermittent, relying upon face-to-face contacts around the Palace of Westminster. The press can be manipulated in order to stimulate private conversations and combinations, but printed publicity is not a necessity. Editors themselves often appear more interested in supporting one or more tendencies than in supporting a single faction or giving blanket endorsement to an electoral party. Factional leaders or M.P.s representative of a tendency may enjoy the reward of office, being given ministerial appointment in order to decapitate potential opponents within the

[9] The excellent discussion of this problem in another context by MYRON WEINER, *Political Parties in India.* Princeton: University Press, 1957, pp. 241 ff., contains insights which can be applied to Britain.
[10] *Op. cit.,* pp. 62-70.

electoral party. The careers of many leading ministers indicate that a period of association with a minority faction or tendency is no barrier to reaching the highest offices. M.P.s whose limited talents or whose psychological characteristics disqualify them from high office may find that eminence within a faction or tendency is the highest position they may realistically hope for. The satisfactions which M.P.s seek are sufficiently varied so that official or shadow patronage will never bring into line all the nominal supporters of the electoral party leader.

The Conservative electoral party is pre-eminently a party of tendencies. The chief tendencies toward which politicians may gravitate can be approximately labeled reaction, defense of the *status quo,* amelioration and reform. The existence of these several tendencies without the firmness of factional groupings means that alignments within the Conservative Party are usually temporary and in flux. The authors of the Keele study of Early Day Motions conclude of Conservative M.P.s:

> Such disagreements as arise are struggles between *ad hoc* groups of members who may be left or right on specific questions; but as new controversies break out, the coherence of the former groups dissolves, and new alignments appear, uniting former enemies and separating old allies.[11]

Since this fluidity is usually combined with a high respect for electoral party leaders, the Conservative Prime Minister has wide scope for manipulating his followers—though he cannot rely upon the same hard core of support available to a factional leader such as Hugh Gaitskell. But the Conservative Party is also notable for the fact that its dissidents have normally confined public complaints against the leadership to a single issue or, like Peter Thorneycroft in 1958, have refrained from efforts to rally a faction and found themselves later readmitted to the Cabinet. Conservatives in favor of amelioration and reform would appear to constitute the nucleus of a political faction. Yet this collection of individuals has not coalesced into a cohesive and self-conscious group, and the leading extra-parliamentary spokesmen, the Bow Group, have gone to some lengths to repudiate the idea that they are a "party within a party" in the sense familiar within the Labour ranks.[12]

Reformism may be described as a tendency supporting change for its own sake, or "left" views on issues which are, in Anthony Crosland's terms, "left-right issues which are not socialist-capitalist issues."[13]

[11] S. E. FINER, *et al., op. cit.,* p. 106.

[12] See RICHARD ROSE, The Bow Group's Role in British Politics. *Western Political Quarterly,* 14, No. 4 (1961), 869 ff.

[13] ANTHONY CROSLAND, *The Future of Socialism.* London: Cape, 1956, pp. 520-21.

Reformism is a tendency which cuts across electoral party boundaries. Many individuals will support a particular reform through a special-purpose pressure group with "non-party" sponsorship. Some reformers—the Webbs up to 1914 being a notable example—have preferred to work through more than one electoral party, rather than narrow their influence by concentrating upon factional activity within a single electoral party. Conflicts between the policies and symbols of reform and those which provide the traditional basis of the unity of the Conservative and Labour parties inhibit conscious organization of reform factions. The Liberal electoral party has embraced the symbols of reform—but, as the debate on a possible Liberal-Labour merger in the winter of 1962-3 illustrated—the Liberals were unable to convince more than a handful of politicians in the major parties that support for reform could better be given outside the major parties rather than inside it.

The Labour electoral party has been since its foundation a party of factions, although it is not exclusively composed of factions and the left-wing faction has been notoriously schismatic. Notwithstanding many differences, conflict between right and left has been stable—whether between Aneurin Bevan and the supporters of Clement Attlee in 1951, between Sir Stafford Cripps and Transport House in the 1930's, or, as in the 1920's between the ILP, formally a party within a party, and the official party leadership. Hugh Gaitskell's period as party leader began by his accession to office as the chief spokesman of a recognized faction; during most of his time in office he not only acted as leader of a faction divided from another faction in the electoral party, but also as the nominal symbol of electoral party unity. (The contrast with Clement Attlee, who did not allow himself to become a symbol of controversy and disunity, is marked.[14]) The fight within the Labour Party on nuclear disarmament from 1959-61 brought into relief the inconsistency in Gaitskell heading the electoral party and the Campaign for Democratic Socialism faction. The Labour left as a faction shares a desire to transform Britain into a completely socialist society, and the need to act together, notwithstanding schismatic influences, in attacking the leaders of the Labour moderates. The persistence of left factions from generation to generation shows the deep roots of the left in the Labour Party. In the days of the Bevanites, the left held regular caucuses in the Palace of Westminster, with an agenda and minutes. It conducted a propaganda campaign through *Tribune* and held meetings in the constituencies. At

[14] A point that Harold Wilson appears to have noticed. See his remarks in an interview with Kenneth Harris, *The Observer* (London), June 16, 1963.

present, the *New Left Review* and the Campaign for Nuclear Disarmament perform the important functions of recruiting new adherents and providing an institutional focus for activity. The use of extra-parliamentary groups indicates the relative weakness of a faction now leaderless in Parliament. Parliamentary weakness can hardly deter many members of the left, however, since they have spent their whole political lives far from the centers of power.

The strength of factionalism in the Labour Party has placed a high premium upon non-aligned partisans. Their importance was dramatically demonstrated after the 1959 general election. First, this categoric group appeared to have been decisive in defeating Hugh Gaitskell's proposal to repeal Clause IV in the party constitution, a clause which embodied an important symbol of the electoral party. Secondly, the victory of Hugh Gaitskell in his fight against the nuclear disarmers appeared to have come from the mobilization by the moderate faction of non-aligned partisans in support of loyalty to the leadership and collective security. It remains to be seen whether or not the election to the leadership of Harold Wilson represents a re-emergence of Attlee's conception of the leader as a non-aligned politician, or whether the policies of Wilson and the problems the party faces will lead to the re-emergence of old factional differences, the emergence of new factions, or the conduct of intra-party disputes by *ad hoc* collections of men rallying to different tendencies.[15]

IV. CONSEQUENCES FOR THE POLITICAL PROCESS

The existence of varied, unstable policy parties within the formally united governing party maintains and strengthens a number of restraints upon the exercise of power by the Cabinet, which today is secure against defeat in the House of Commons because of the acceptance of the discipline of the two-party system by M.P.s and electors.

Policy parties act as a counterweight against pressure groups. The cooperation of pressure groups is important for the success of a government. But because pressure group allegiances have not been demonstrated to be strong enough to affect voting behavior significantly, organized group leaders can rarely succeed in punishing a recalcitrant government at the polls. But members of policy parties opposed to particular pressure groups may create trouble in Cabinet, in speeches leaked from

[15] Conflict cutting across factional lines had begun to show itself in the debate on the European Common Market at the 1962 Labour Party Conference, a few months before Hugh Gaitskell's death.

private party meetings and on the floor of the Commons itself. For instance, the Attlee government's nationalization of the steel industry was persevered in against the wishes of affected pressure groups and of important Cabinet members because of the strength of the left-wing tendency on this issue, including several ministers who had jumped outside their usual factional positions.[16]

A united Cabinet can fend off criticism from the opposition party indefinitely. (Concessions are more likely to be made to disaffected potential voters than to partisan opponents: witness the announcement of the repeal of the Schedule A tax on home-ownership following the Liberal victory at Orpington in 1962.) But the protest of a policy party within the governing party is immediately felt, especially if it involves sharp divisions during the private deliberations of the Cabinet. In at least four cases in this century,—1905, 1923, 1931 and 1951—policy divisions have been notable as major causes in a government in office defaulting, and going down to electoral defeat shortly thereafter. The possibility is always present, as the lobbying within the Conservative Party, including the Cabinet, showed in the week before the division in the Profumo debate of June 17, 1963. The threat to expel a group of several dozen M.P.s who vote against a party whip is meaningless, because such an expulsion would hurt the electoral party by making more clear-cut divisions within the ranks.

By voting together in Parliament, M.P.s in different policy parties reaffirm their common identification with a single electoral party. Voting together shows a degree of cohesion which political parties in many countries lack. But it does not provide continuously cohesive support for a party leader. Rather, the division lobbies represent only one phase in a lengthy process, a phase far distant in time from the one in which the most substantial decisions will be made about a problem. When problems arise salient to factions, ministers can anticipate to a considerable extent the nature of support and opposition to alternative policies under consideration. But lacking factional guidelines, ministers can only note the tendencies associated with policy alternatives, without being able to estimate so well the numbers of M.P.s who will associate themselves with the several tendencies. Only after the front bench takes a line can it find out whether the hints and threats of M.P.s lobbying them are in fact accurate predictions of opposition or part of the complicated game of bluff involved in situations of political uncertainty. Because public dispute within an electoral party can harm both sides in the dispute, a high premium is placed upon accurate information which

[16] See HUGH DALTON, *High Tide and After*. London: Muller, 1962, pp. 248 ff.

can be used to anticipate and forestall policy disputes. This accounts for the importance of party whips; they provide the two-way flow of information between the party leader and back bench M.P.s. Individual ministers have parliamentary private secretaries to warn them of impending difficulties. The object of this communication, from the point of view of a nominally impregnable leadership, is to keep the leadership informed about possible sources of discontent, and threats of factions forming around tendencies opposed to those prevailing among the dominant leadership group. In this way, the appearance of unity can be maintained by aborting public controversy. This was, for instance, the technique that Clement Attlee used when informal collections of M.P.s began discussing his replacement, by Sir Stafford Cripps or Ernest Bevin, during the 1947 economic crisis. Retention of Cripps in the Cabinet was essential at this point in order to forestall the conversion of a left-wing tendency into a strong left faction with a potential Prime Minister at its head.[17] More recently, Harold Macmillan has demonstrated in successive Cabinet changes since the 1959 general election an awareness of the importance of keeping his political associates divided and balanced against one another by the distribution of Cabinet posts.

The need to balance factions, tendencies and individuals against one another acts as a major restraint upon the power of the party leader, whether in opposition or as Prime Minister.[18] The recurring polemical discussion about the "constitutional" position of the leader of the Labour Party *vis-à-vis* extra-parliamentary followers, with emphasis given to affirming the pre-eminence of Parliament, has drawn attention from the question of what restraints might be needed upon the Prime Minister. One wonders whether British Prime Ministers are always so wise and dispassionate in their actions that they need no restraints. History suggests not, and provides recent examples. In practice, restraints are often imposed by divisions within the electoral party. Three Prime Ministers, Neville Chamberlain, Lloyd George and Asquith, were forced from office by defections of nominal supporters. Eden, Attlee, MacDonald and Balfour retired after intense strife within their parties. It is impossible to demonstrate the extent or the weight of Attlee's self-denying approach to the potential power of his office—but this does not deny the significance of the limitations upon his influence due to his self-effacing

[17] See H. DALTON, *op. cit.,* ch. 29; and LESLIE HUNTER, *The Road to Brighton Pier.* London: Barker, 1959, pp. 18 ff.
[18] The restraints upon the party leader are discussed in detail in RICHARD ROSE, Complexities of Party Leadership. *Parliamentary Affairs,* 16, No. 3 (1963).

approach and the dispersion of power during most of his period in that office.

Policy divisions help to maintain flexibility and diversity in a political system in which large nominal grants of power are made once every four or five years to one of two parties in duopolistic competition. Flexibility is desirable inasmuch as many major problems which face a government cannot be foreseen at a general election, by candidates or by electors, and during a crisis, an election is likely to be avoided by the party in office. But because a governing party contains a wide diversity of tendencies, a range of policies is likely to have some political support within a single electoral party. Since supporters are not united in their views, leaders have room for maneuver in choosing between alternatives. By manipulating the tendencies, and appealing for the loyalty of the non-aligned, a leader, especially a Conservative, may bring off a major public reversal of policy, as in Harold Macmillan's winds of change speech on colonialism in 1960, or his Common Market policy subsequently. If the Conservative Party had been monolithic, it would have proven less adaptable in both instances—and if divisions had been as long-lived and deep as those in the Labour Party's factions, shifts would have been far less easily and quietly accomplished.

In times of crisis, the British party system has shown flexibility by the making of new coalitions across electoral party lines, as in 1940, 1931, 1916 and 1886.[19] Electoral parties split in times of crisis not because they have suddenly lost a previously maintained unity, but rather in part because of pre-existing divisions which crises serve to heighten in intensity. The process is illustrated in slow motion by the gradual collapse of the Liberal Party and its replacement by the Labour Party, with Labour assimilating one section of the Liberals and the Conservatives another. Even without the formation of new parties from the amalgams of old factions and tendencies, Britain has often enjoyed coalition government. In the seventy-eight years since 1885, the country has been governed by a combination of parties for thirty-four years. Major policy problems, such as Ireland, the Depression of 1931 and total mobilization in 1940, have been handled by coalition governments, and the foundations for the present mixed economy welfare state were laid in the Coalition of 1940-5. The *ad hoc* building of coalitions within the limits of a single electoral party or between electoral parties has important consequences for consensus in the political culture

[19] See the insightful discussion of cross-party ties in R. BASSETT, *The Essentials of Parliamentary Democracy*. London: Macmillan, 1935, esp. ch. 3.

—that is, the acceptance by more than one party of important innovations in public policy.

Coalition governments do not endure in Britain, because once great hurdles have been taken, disagreements upon other policy issues become dominant, and the points of disagreement between electoral parties reassert themselves, or else new points of difference become permanent as old differences disappear. The party system is dynamic, involving periods of coalition across electoral party lines as well as periods of competition; both are necessary elements in what has aptly been described as a "moving consensus." [20] Movement is as important as consensus. The existence within the British party system of a large number of policy parties, whether tendencies or factions, facilitates movement. (E.g., the domestic and international policies of the 1940-45 coalition government were not those of the dominant policy groups within the Conservative and Labour Parties prior to 1940.) Non-aligned partisans are important in this process too, sometimes cushioning conflicts within electoral parties and sometimes resolving them. Since the government is not under the absolute control of any one policy party it is always able, potentially at least, to readjust its alliances. The surface cohesion of British parties reflects an equilibrium between forces pulling in different directions, not a unity obtained by a single, united thrust.

Divisions within electoral parties also serve to reduce the distance between electoral parties. Some Labour M.P.s have supported tendencies more in accord with those also claiming adherents within the Conservative Party than they have those in accord with their nominal colleagues of the left. The closeness evidenced can cause confusion to the voter and friction between electoral party colleagues. It also makes it easier for ideas to be assimilated across electoral party boundaries. For instance, domestic policies enacted by Labour from 1945-50 were first accepted by reformist Conservatives, and have then gradually been diffused through the electoral party from sources of influence inside Conservative ranks. In a complementary fashion, non-Socialist critiques of Socialist economic doctrines and principles of foreign policy have been diffused within the Labour Party.

Because of the areas of agreement which cut across electoral lines (though rarely reaching from the extremes of the Conservatives to those of Labour), the stakes at general elections in Britain are not such that either party actively fears the consequences of defeat. Election results and the accession of new governments involve shifts in the emphasis

[20] See ARTHUR W. MACMAHON, Conflict, Consensus, Confirmed Trends and Open Choices. *American Political Science Review*, 42, No. 1 (1948), 2 ff.

given to certain political tendencies as against others, by changing the label and the personnel of those engaged in holding together the governing party. The electorate is not defrauded or alienated in exercising its franchise by being asked to choose between two parties which are either interchangeable in programs or mutually exclusive. The mixture of policy parties within the electoral parties means that there is something for all sorts of people to attach themselves to, whichever party wins an election or is given their vote. It also means that those who find themselves at the apex of the structure of "winner-take-all" party government in Britain cannot govern without regard to a number of restraints built into the British party system.

❦ 5 ❦

Political Parties in Western Democratic Systems*

Leon D. Epstein

EDITORIAL NOTE: *This is perhaps the most comprehensive overview of the development and functioning of political parties in Western Europe, their distinctive traits and their most salient differences from American parties. It is symptomatic of the state of the literature that most of the author's observations are offered in the form of questions from which comparative studies may emerge. Comparative studies are few, but individual studies of Western political systems plentiful. For two perceptive comparative essays, the reader should consult Otto Kirchheimer's* The State of Parties in Western Europe, in Political Parties and Political Development, *Princeton, 1966, and* The Waning of the Opposition in Parliamentary Regimes, *Social Research (1957), 127-56.*

I

MY concern generally is with the problems of comparative study of Western democratic political systems. Parties provide the point of entry for an analysis which, I hope, will illustrate the general problems. The apparent universality of parties in Western democracies makes them a

* This paper was originally presented in the fall of 1964 as part of Indiana University's program commemorating the fiftieth anniversary of its Department of Government. It has since been published in a shorter and modified version in *Essays in Political Science* (Indiana University Press, 1966), ed. by Edward H. Buehrig. The ideas outlined here have been developed and altered for the author's forthcoming book on Western democratic political parties.

convenient as well as a significant subject. But I do not claim that parties are *the* significant subject or even any more significant than certain other possibilities. Interest groups or executive authority, to cite two rather different topics, might be at least as important and useful. Also much is to be said for an analysis not of agencies or institutions but of a particular political function like representation, socialization, or rule-making, taking into account any or all agencies performing the function in various systems.[1] There are many routes for comparative study. Which one each of us chooses depends on what questions are being asked. In my own case, having been impressed with the observable differences in organization and function between American parties and European parties, I seek the explanation for such differences (and for any similarities) in the historical, social, and institutional settings in which the various national parties have developed. By an explanation of this kind, I hope to be able to say something about the political systems as well as about the parties operating within these systems.

It would not be completely candid, however, to say that my comparative study of parties was motivated merely by observable cross-national differences. Many similar differences are insufficient to motivate study. What is special about this one is that it relates to a pragmatic policy question of long and great concern to American political scientists. To reform parties as a crucial step in changing the operation of government in the United States has been an article of faith for an important school of thought in the twentieth century.[2] Its most recent well-known spokesmen have been E. E. Schattschneider[3] and James MacGregor Burns.[4] Much of the time, although not often overtly, European and especially British parties have represented models for the American advocates of more responsible parties. Therefore, it seems to me that the comparative study of parties in Western nations can help us to estimate the validity of the suggested reform of parties in the United States. A political scientist should not have to apologize for this pragmatic concern. Our discipline, after all, is a policy science whose work should contribute ultimately to the making of judgments about our political institutions. The contribution may be indirect, as it would

---

[1] The best-known use of this method is by GABRIEL A. ALMOND and JAMES S. COLEMAN, *The Politics of Developing Areas*. Princeton: Princeton University Press, 1960, whose Introduction presents a functional scheme derived from Western models.

[2] AUSTIN RANNEY, *The Doctrine of Responsible Party Government*. Urbana: University of Illinois Press, 1954.

[3] *Party Government*. New York: Rinehart, 1922.

[4] *The Deadlock of Democracy*. Englewood Cliffs: Prentice Hall, 1963.

have to be in the present work as opposed to a work of applied research on a highly specialized problem, but the concern with relevancy is similar. The criteria of policy relevance do not and should not preclude a vast tolerance for what originally seems only the curiosity of individual scholars fascinated by problems of their own choosing. No more than in other sciences can we be sure how relevant our findings will turn out to be.

Uncertainty as to relevancy is likely to be greatest with respect to a broad subject like political parties in Western democratic systems. The primary purpose is not to present new data, but to arrange in meaningful relationships what has already been learned about particular parties. How meaningful these relationships can be is affected, in the first place, by the meaningfulness of the universe taken for analysis. This is not to question the usefulness of the comparative method, which is of the essence of our science and which is regularly used in purely national studies as well as in cross-national studies like the present one. But it is to question the conception of "Western democratic systems" as the universe for the study of political parties or other political phenomena. For many scholars, the conception is too broad because it includes nations too diverse to permit the limited but useful comparisons possible within, say, the universe of English-speaking Commonwealth nations or the universe of parliamentary systems. For other scholars, the conception is too narrow because it does not take advantage of the possibilities of generalizing on a really universal level from the experiences of the over one hundred nations now in existence. And, whether too broad or too narrow, "Western democratic" is hard to define without seeming arbitrary.

Arbitrary or not, I have defined Western democratic to include at least twenty nations. But since my method is mainly illustrative rather than systematic and is heavily dependent for illustrations on certain nations (principally Britain and the United States), I would not hesitate to cite the experience of nations marginal to the definition. The twenty clearly Western democratic nations are the United States, Great Britain, Ireland, Canada, Australia, New Zealand, Norway, Sweden, Denmark, Finland, France, West Germany, Italy, the Netherlands, Belgium, Luxembourg, Switzerland, Austria, Iceland, and Israel. A few of these provide almost no data. Marginal and so unlisted, mainly because of doubts about their Western rather than democratic status, are Japan, Greece, Turkey, and certain Latin American nations. Among the Latin American nations, Uruguay and one or two others would probably qualify on every count. Their exclusion can be justified only by the convention of treating all of Latin America with developing rather than Western nations. Conversely, Israel is included as Western because, despite its location, it is regarded, like Australia and New Zealand, as an extension or geographic transplantation of Western society. "Democratic," as is evident from the listing above, is also used in its conventional sense—that is, in its conventional Western sense—of free and open electoral competition for governmental offices. All of our listed Western nations now qualify according to this definition of democratic. As of thirty years ago, however, Germany and Italy would not have qualified, while Czechoslovakia would have. Nothing but the conventional criterion of contemporary relevance justifies the citation of post-1945 German and Italian experience instead of interwar Czech experience.

As suggested, I would be more troubled by the arbitrariness of the Western democratic definition if I were primarily concerned with generalizations to be established by counting the number of nations whose parties had similar characteristics. Then if there were one or two marginally Western nations, it could be consequential whether or not they had been included. But where for the most part we do not seek a primarily numerical basis for generalizing, it matters much less how we have defined our universe. Admittedly, it can matter to some extent even with our selectively illustrative method. We have to be careful to state that our illustrations do not exhaust the possibilities among either the twenty listed nations or the marginal nations.

So far I have indicated a very general problem of any comparative study of Western democratic nations. I should now like to mention some others, only slightly less general, before discussing the ways in which scholarly work on parties illustrates the limitations imposed. The *first* is the national approach which has characterized political science as it has history, out of which so much of our scholarly tradition comes. We have studied the politics of national units, our own or foreign, and we have tended to emphasize the distinctive features of each political system in terms of its own national background. That background, originally political history, has come to include a nation's economic and social structure, and so the impact on political science of sociological learning has often confirmed a national approach. The basic reasons for that approach were good and virtually uncontestable. Obvious advantages lie in comprehending a political system in national terms. Government itself is primarily national, and so are its related political phenomena. But there are disadvantages as well. Our political data and findings are so national in character as to render cross-national generalizing most difficult. The questions that have been asked about political parties in one nation are not often the same questions asked about parties in another nation. In this as in other areas of political science, usually only rather broad and gross comparisons are possible across national lines. It is not surprising, therefore, that the most justly famous "comparative" studies, like Tocqueville's *Democracy in America* or Bryce's *American Commonwealth,* are works written about a single nation other than the author's own. Then at least it is possible to ask questions about one nation that have meaning in terms of another.

The *second* limitation is closely related to the national approach. It is the divorce, notable in American political science, between American and European (or all foreign) subjects. The latter, as we know, we hopefully labelled "comparative," perhaps expecting thus to inspire American students to become Tocquevilles or Bryces in reverse. Our hope may not have been entirely wasted. The comparative label itself has occasionally inspired an American student of a foreign government to ask some questions derived from his own nation's system rather than only from the one he was studying. But admittedly most of our Western European studies have been as national—that is, European national—as American studies by Americans have been national in their way. Thus we have had intra-European and intra-Commonwealth comparative studies, but hardly any Euro-American comparative studies. American specialists have usually remained in their area, and European specialists in theirs. The result is a remarkable absence of any generalizing about the politics of Western democracies which is broad enough to include the United States along with Europe.[5] We already have more such generalizing about the new developing nations.

The *third* limitation is more basic and it may help account for the first two. Each of us has been limited in his access, linguistically, culturally and otherwise, to the range of knowledge apparently necessary for broad comparative study. It is rare for a scholar to master the political system of more than one country other than his own. And most of us do not comfortably rely on the research of others, especially when they have not asked the same questions about their nations as we have asked about the nations we have studied. For some Western nations there is little available research on which to rely.

Fourth, the highly promising cross-national survey research, represented by a few recent works of high quality, has tended, like national survey research, to be limited so far to only some of the questions of

[5] An important exception in the field of voting behavior is SEYMOUR MARTIN LIPSET, *Political Man.* Garden City: Doubleday, 1960. Another is ROBERT R. ALFORD, *Party and Society.* Chicago: Rand McNally, 1963.

concern to political scientists.[6] Relatively little, for example, is directly applicable to the study of party organization. That which is, however, is most useful.[7] There can be little doubt that the whole conception of cross-national survey research, systematically asking the same questions in several nations, provides the basis for eventually reducing the barriers to fruitful comparative study. Hopefully, such research will mean the collaboration of American and European specialists.

The limitations still existing may be observed in works on political parties. Almost everywhere parties have been accepted as well worth empirical study. The result has been a great deal of national and sub-national research. Excellent works of various kinds have been written on parties in each of the major Western nations and in some of the minor ones.[8] More detailed examinations exist for American parties, reflecting the preponderance of American work by Americans, themselves preponderant among political scientists of the world. The limitations of these national studies, in their uneven availability and in their divergence in questions asked, have already been noted. It is in the few but significant comparative works that special problems may be observed. The best-known major books are by M. Ostrogorski,[9] Robert Michels,[10] and Maurice Duverger.[11] The last commands attention because it is the most recent, in fact the only one to be at all recent, and because it seeks a broader coverage of countries than Ostrogorski and a wider range of topics than Michels.

Duverger, by the very prodigiousness of his effort, best illustrates most of the difficulties. Seeking to transcend the national approach by citing data from other Western countries besides his native France, the work is nevertheless distinctively French. It is so not just because Duverger uses more illustrations from France than from any other country, or because he is more sure-footed in discussing the French material. It is

[6] GABRIEL A. ALMOND and SIDNEY VERBA, The Civic Culture. Princeton: Princeton University Press, 1963, and PHILIP E. CONVERSE and GEORGES DUPEUX, Politicization of the Electorate in France and the United States. Public Opinion Quarterly, 26 (Spring 1962), 1-23.

[7] Notably STEIN ROKKAN and ANGUS CAMPBELL, Factors in the Recruitment of Active Participants in Politics: A Comparative Analysis of Survey Data for Norway and the United States. International Social Science Journal, 12, No. 2 (1960).

[8] Apart from American texts, there are outstanding books like ROBERT MCKENZIE, British Political Parties. London: Heinemann, 1963 ed.; and PHILIP WILLIAMS, Crisis and Compromise: Politics in the Fouth Republic. London: Longmans, 1964 ed.

[9] Democracy and the Organization of Political Parties. London: Macmillan, 1902.

[10] Political Parties. Glencoe, Ill.: The Free Press, 1949; first published in 1915.

[11] Political Parties: Their Organization and Activity in the Modern State. Trans. by Barbara and Robert North. New York: Wiley, 1954; first published in French in 1950.

also because the questions which he asks about parties in other countries
are essentially French questions. Thus one can understand his great concern with the election system and with the number of parties. Further
displaying the general limitations affecting comparative study is Duverger's Europeanism. Despite some use of American data, he suffers
almost as much from the divorce of American and European studies as
do American political scientists. For Duverger this meant asking
European, if not just French, questions about American parties. He was
not alone among political scientists, European and American, who
thus imposed criteria derived from European circumstances to judge
parties which had developed in response to different demands. But none
of these criticisms should make one fail to appreciate the scope of
Duverger's ambitious work. That even Duverger's learning and energy
should suffer from limitations is discouraging.

II

I have not been discouraged enough to preclude a start on my own
comparative study. Nor have I been kept, by what I have thought was
Duverger's national approach, from having a national approach of my
own. Rather I concluded that such an approach was unavoidable given
the state of our training and knowledge, certainly of my own, and that
the right thing was to be aware of the limitation and to make allowances
for it. My questions are American-inspired questions. If my study is
thus tilted, so that European parties are often observed in American
terms, I hope that by being explicit in this respect I make it easier for
European scholars to achieve their own balanced perspective. At least
I have anticipated their criticism. And I think that I contribute more
directly to balance because so much previous work, not just Duverger's,
is tilted heavily the other way.[12]

The same might be said for a more obvious limitation of my work:
the concentration on the parties of English-speaking nations, particularly
Britain and the United States. Not only are studies about these nations
most accessible, because of their quantity and language, but my own
first-hand research has been so largely confined to English-speaking nations that I am more confident about the relevance of illustrations from
the United States and Britain (and, to a lesser extent, from Canada).
This limitation may be so severe as to cause one to wonder why I have

[12] An example is provided by the useful anthology edited by SIGMUND NEUMANN,
Modern Political Parties. Chicago: University of Chicago Press, 1956.

not confined my entire study to English-speaking democratic nations. The thought has occurred to me, but I have rejected it on several grounds. First, the English-speaking nations are a large enough part of the whole Western democratic universe to permit tentative generalizations primarily from the fuller and more familiar illustrations that these nations provide. Secondly, there are available, if unevenly, useful works in English as well as in other languages on parties in continental European nations. Where their findings are relevant they can be used to support or refute tentative generalizations drawn from the narrower base. Thirdly, even if generalizations in my work have to rest almost entirely on illustrations from English-speaking nations, they could still be tested by other scholars more familiar with other Western nations. Happily neither I nor anyone else will regard my work as definitive. Fourthly, my concentration on explaining certain major differences between American and European parties makes it possible to use British parties, in many respects, as European prototypes without doing violence to the variations existing within Western Europe.

From what has already been said, it will be evident that my method is mainly that of non-quantitative multivariate analysis.[13] Finding parties with certain characteristics in certain nations, the problem is to find what other common characteristics these nations have to account for their parties in contrast to those elsewhere. While the method is more impressive when a large number of nations (or other units) are included within the analysis, it is useful with as few as two nations and certainly with three. When thus limited, our generalizations must be most carefully stated as tentative or suggestive.

One other aspect of the method should be made explicit. I usually treat parties as dependent variables. The main independent variables are general matters like constitutional structure, degree of federalism, timing of mass suffrage, stage of industrialization, pre-industrial social structure, and culturally-based political values. As in most political analysis, there is unlikely to be universal agreement about the classification of independent and dependent variables. Although everyone, even if starting from my perspective, grants that parties themselves affect the circumstances which are believed to be more basic, many political scientists have treated parties as independent variables, influencing the political environment more than they are influenced by it. This has been especially likely among parties specialists, who have tended to glorify their subject-matter by regarding it as causal.[14] Clearly party reformers do this

---

[13] I owe the term to my colleague, Herbert Jacob.
[14] This seemed especially true a decade or two ago of writers like Neumann,

because they intend to change the political system through changing the parties. By turning this around, as I have done in regarding parties mainly as responses to circumstances including the political system, it has to be admitted that I have tried to set the stage for a refutation of the party reformers. But no refutation is made unless I show how the circumstances, which I call independent variables, fashion parties in resistant forms. This is what I hope will emerge from my comparative analysis.

Before proceeding, "political party" must be defined. It means here, as it does in ordinary understanding, any group, however loosely organized, seeking to elect government officials under a given label. The recognizable label (which may or may not be on the ballot) is the crucial defining element. This allows us to use the word party for office-holders or aspiring office-holders who are without organized followings but who seek votes under a collective name. It is usual for such groups to have organized followings. So is it usual to have, or seem to have, principles and policies, even though it is possible to meet our broad definition of party without principles and policies as well as without organized followings. All that is required is the collective, labelled appearance before the electorate. This is enough to distinguish a party from a purely parliamentary faction. Only if the office-holding members of such a faction stand together in appealing for votes do they constitute a party, in our sense of the term. That sense is purely electoral. Nevertheless it also enables us to distinguish parties from interest groups because the latter, while often endorsing candidates, do not ordinarily provide the labels under which candidates stand for election. When interest groups provide such labels, then they are parties as well as interest groups.

Our definition can thus take into account all the various phenomena that are called parties in the several Western democratic nations: major and minor parties, broad coalition and interest-group parties, long-established and ephemeral parties, highly organized and solely electoral parties, social movement and non-movement parties, principled and opportunistic parties, democratic and totalitarian parties (as long as they compete in a democratic system). Within this large range, every Western nation has political parties. No one type is "normal," but it is evidently normal to have parties of some kind. No Western nation functions entirely without parties. Although it is conceivable that both electoral

---

Schattschneider, and Duverger (all cited above). It is not true of the very recent work by FRANK SORAUF, *Political Parties in the American System*. Boston: Little, Brown, 1964.

competition and governmental affairs could be managed in their absence, the fact that parties do everywhere function at least to structure electoral competition is enough to make us think that they are nearly essential agencies in modern democratic societies. Whenever a nation extended the right to vote to relatively large numbers, parties developed in evident response if they did not already exist. They had in several nations antedated the mass franchise. In others they had not existed except in the embryonic form of parliamentary factions not yet clearly labelling candidates in electoral competition. But with the mass franchise' there were sure to be parties. The presumption is strong that the regularized labelling, which parties perform, became necessary when large numbers of voters had to choose among candidates whose personal qualifications they could not know, and when candidates had to reach the large numbers of voters whom they could not know. (Only after parties existed was there a reaction in the form of the non-partisan elections adopted by many American cities.) It cannot, however, be assumed that the mass franchise or any other feature of modern democratic societies requires parties to do much more than the minimal labelling function. Indeed, to anticipate our analysis, the presumption is negative since only in some nations, not in all, have parties developed membership organizations or clear-cut doctrinal positions. Different kinds of parties function in different political and social systems.

Similarly there is nothing universal about the number of parties, even of major parties, which exist in the various Western democratic nations. This matter of number is worth passing attention although it does not figure so prominently in my analysis as it usually does in works that conceive the number of parties to be almost synonymous with "party system." Whether two or several parties seriously compete to elect candidates does not appear to be as fundamental and as important a classificatory device as much of the literature implies. One reason is that two-party competition is not here regarded as a democratic norm or as a universally more workable pattern.

Despite the Anglo-American bias of my research, I am impressed by the extent of continental European experience with multiparty competition. The experience is so extensive that we have, in our universe of twenty Western democratic nations, no more than six nations with long-term two-party competition—that is, with two parties each demonstrating its capacity to elect a majority of candidates sufficient to control the national government.[15] We may be stretching matters to reach the total

---

[15] Six is also the number of western two-party nations listed by ARTHUR S. BANKS and ROBERT B. TEXTOR, *A Cross-Polity Survey*. Cambridge: MIT Press, 1963, par. 141, where there are altogether only 11 two-party polities out of all 115 polities analyzed.

of six. The United States and Britain, despite the latter's persistent third party, are the most clear-cut, Australia, New Zealand, and Canada are conventionally counted. However, Australia has had a durable third party whose support is necessary for a majority led by one of the two major parties,[16] New Zealand now has a substantial third party,[17] and Canada has had several third parties which substantially affect the achievement of a majority by a major party.[18] The sixth nation is Austria and it is even more doubtful. True enough, Austria has two parties each at least close to majority status, despite other competing parties, but the two major parties, while competing against each other electorally, long maintained a grand coalition government after World War II. Thus they were not alternative governing parties in the usual two-party competitive fashion, but instead, in the words of a perceptive student of Austrian politics, their coalition was "a cartel formed to mitigate competition." [19] This means of mitigating competition was a much more important feature of Austrian politics than the existence of two major parties enabling us technically to classify Austria with two-party nations.

We have so classified Austria in order to be as generous as possible about the two-party category. Austria, it will be noted, is the only non-English speaking nation to be included. Hardly any other except West Germany is even close. Surely this suggests that two-party competition cannot stand as a norm. If it is supposed to be the result of a "natural political dualism" [20] of opinion, the dualism is evidently natural only to English-speaking nations. If it is supposed to be the kind of competition necessary for strong government because of its majoritarian election results, the necessity is accepted in relatively few nations. On the other side, these nations do bulk large in population, because of the United States, and in prestige as successful democracies. But at least one fairly large country, France, has had multiparty competition for nearly a century, and while its experience has been marred by the collapse of regimes, that has not been true for the smaller multiparty na-

[16] ULRICH ELLISM, *The Country Party*. Melbourne: Cheshire, 1958, and J. D. B. MILLER, *Australian Government and Politics*. London: Duckworth, 1954, pp. 67-68.
[17] R. M. CHAPMAN, W. K. JACKSON, and A. V. MITCHELL, *New Zealand Politics in Action*. London: Oxford University Press, 1962, pp. 272-75.
[18] HUGH G. THORBURN, Party Politics in Canada. Toronto: Prentice-Hall of Canada, 1963; and JOHN MEISEL, *The Canadian General Election of 1957*. Toronto: University of Toronto Press, 1962.
[19] H. PIERRE SECHER, Coalition Government: The Case of the Second Austrian Republic. *American Political Science Review*, 52 (September 1958), 791-808.
[20] DUVERGER, *op. cit.*, p. 215.

tions of the Netherlands,[21] Belgium,[22] and Scandinavia.[23] Nor it it true for the brief experience of Israel.[24]

The universality and so the normalcy of two-party competition may be questioned from another angle. Within our evidently two-party nations, even those so readily classified as the United States and Britain, most impressive exceptions are embedded. Apart from regional and local third parties, which as in Canada may really be first or second parties locally when they are only third parties nationally,[25] there are many areas in which one major party so dominates over time that the national two-party competitive classification is inapplicable. These one-party areas may be whole sections or states, or more limited urban, suburban, or rural areas forming constituencies where a given party's voters are clustered. The latter situation prevails in Britain where about two-thirds of the parliamentary constituencies have been regarded as safely Labour or Conservative over at least two decades. There is even one British region of one-party dominance: the Unionist (Conservative) enclave of Northern Ireland.

The American one-party pattern is more widely recognized. Its character in the South, when the Democratic dominance still retained its old staunchness, has been carefully described in one of the great books of American political science.[26] And we are familiar with long-time Republican dominance of certain Northern states. So frequently, in fact, has national two-party competition failed to find roots in large areas of the United States, apparently because the socio-economic basis for one of the national parties was locally or regionally insufficient, that intra-party electoral competition has been institutionalized through the direct primary. When this intra-party competition consists of clear-cut factionalism, especially of bi-factionalism like that between progressive and conservative Republicans in early twentieth-century Wisconsin, it is

[21] H. DAALDER, Parties and Politics in the Netherlands. *Political Studies,* 3 (February 1955), pp. 1-16.
[22] FELIX E. OPPENHEIM, Belgium: Party Cleavage and Compromise, in NEUMANN, *op. cit.*
[23] DANKWART A. RUSTOW, Scandinavia: Working Multiparty Systems, in Neumann, *op. cit.,* and *The Politics of Compromise.* Princeton: Princeton University Press, 1955.
[24] AMITAI ETZIONE, Alternative Ways to Democracy. *Political Science Quarterly,* 74 (June 1959), 196-214.
[25] C. B. MACPHERSON, *Democracy in Alberta.* Toronto: University of Toronto Press, 1953; and SEYMOUR MARTIN LIPSET, *Agrarian Socialism.* Berkeley and Los Angeles: University of California Press, 1950.
[26] V. O. KEY, JR., *Southrn Politics in State and Nation.* New York: Knopf, 1950.

virtually two-party competition.[27] The factional labels, even though they are not printed on the ballot, have all the significance of party labels. More often, however, intra-party factionalism has meant the personal and shifting politics that V. O. Key found in most Southern Democratic primaries.[28] Then intra-party competition is by no means the equivalent of inter-party competition. Voters, in choosing among candidates, are not guided by the established labels which parties would provide.

What can still be true of such primaries is a provision of fairly wide electoral competition even though voters may not have their choices structured any more than in the municipal non-partisan elections so widespread in the United States. In fact, primaries in one-party areas are essentially non-partisan elections unless there is intervention by an organization of the single party or by its factional equivalents. In any event, it is possible to have one-party electoral competition, however contradictory the phrase seems, as long as numerous voters, not just a relatively narrow organized membership, gets to choose the candidates to be elected under the dominant party label. Primaries may be inferior in other respects to the more closed methods of candidate selection, but at least they allow for electoral competition where otherwise there would be none that was meaningful. They are one kind of adjustment to the fact that under national two-party competition there are many one-party areas. These are numerous enough, as has been noted, to limit the general applicability of the two-party classification.

Once accepting the view that two-party competition is well short of being the usual Western democratic standard, both because it is less frequent than multiparty competition at the national level and because it contains large one-party pockets, there seems less point in concentrating on the number of parties in cross-national analysis. No longer can two-party competition be treated as a norm toward which systems tend in varying degrees. There is still some point, of course, since the number of parties at the national level in a given country may be importantly related to the nature of parties in that system. But I put this subject aside and turn directly to the kinds of parties.

III

There seem to me at least six significant ways to classify parties. In each case, I do so dichotomously for the sake of simplification. I appreciate

[27] LEON D. EPSTEIN, *Politics in Wisconsin*. Madison: University of Wisconsin Press, 1958, ch. 3.
[28] V. O. KEY, JR., *op. cit.*

that within each classification a range of possibilities exists rather than just the polar opposites I indicate.

First, in the manner of electoral organization, there is the *skeletal versus the mass-membership party.* The former consists only of a handful of leaders, including candidates for public office, plus a few retainers, and the latter consists of large numbers of dues-paying followers in addition to the leadership group. A really large-scale patronage party, like the old American city machines, fits somewhere between these two extremes. *Second,* judged by the way in which the important task of candidate selection is performed, parties may be *open to voters at large or closed to all except organized members* (however many or few). American primaries are the clearest examples of the open method, but even American conventions have often been relatively open affairs, especially when ordinary party voters elect the convention delegates. The closed method, on the other hand, permits no one outside the essentially private party association to help select candidates. The association may consist of a few leaders, as would have to be the case in a skeletal organization or as could happen by delegation from a large dues-paying membership. The control might be national, regional, or local although it is worth mentioning that it tends to be exercised by local associations in Britain despite impressions to the contrary.[29] *Third,* parties may be organized *nationally or federatively.* The inevitable local branches may be linked directly to the national party, or only indirectly through state or regional units. *Fourth,* parties may be *explicitly class conscious or explicitly non-class.* Chiefly, in recent times, this refers to the contrast between the socialist working-class party, along with avowedly capitalist or agrarian parties that are often co-existent, and the party which, while middle-class in its leadership, seeks support of all kinds across class lines. *Fifth,* there are *strongly programmatic and not so strongly programmatic* parties. Here no polar opposites can even be stated since all parties claim some program, policy, principle, doctrine, ideology, or whatever similar term we use. Even the old American patronage machines had policies, usually in favor of the status quo, which members implicitly accepted. Yet certain parties are much more programmatic or doctrinal than others. Program is simply more important in some cases. The range is from rigidly doctrinaire to highly opportunistic. *Sixth,* in their governmental representation, parties are *individualistic or cohesive.* Their candidates, when elected and perhaps even when they stand for office, may regard themselves as free agents in policy matters owing

[29] The power of local associations is stressed by AUSTIN RANNEY in his general study of British candidate selection (*Pathways to Parliament.* Madison, University of Wisconsin Press, 1965).

no more than acknowledgment of the party label which they carry. Or, at the other extreme, they may always accept the policy line of their party as that line is determined either by recognized leaders or by a caucus collectivity of which they are part.

In thus suggesting six typologies, I have no doubt that there are others useful for various analytical purposes. For my purposes these six happen to suit because they provide the basis for distinguishing between two party models: the American, and the generally European but particularly British. Neither in fact is the farthest conceivable extreme on a scale derived from any or all of the six typologies, but each is close enough to an "ideal type." Thus American parties are usually skeletal, their selection of candidates relatively open, their structure federative, their general character explicitly non-class conscious, their emphasis generally non-programmatic, and their governmental representation fairly individualistic. On the other hand, British parties (to let them serve as our European models) are mass-membership organizations, their candidate selection is closed and private, their structure is national, they include at least one major party that is explicitly class-conscious (though much more moderately so than many continental parties have been), they are proudly programmatic, and their governmental representation is highly cohesive.

Given this perspective, there is plainly a sense in which the American model seems the less highly developed. Organizationally, in particular, it is not surprising that both American and European political scientists have made this judgment. A skeletal organization, with or without patronage workers to man the precincts, is smaller, less elaborate, and less regularized than a mass-membership party. Therefore, it is bound to appear as a less highly developed form. A similar view of the American model tends to be confirmed by its other characteristics. Relatively open candidate selection seems to follow from a skeletal organization; without a mass membership base, the only "popular" means available is for voters to take a hand in the selection process. Even their federative organization, although it is connected to the federal system of government, looks less modern than national parties in a period of increasing centralization of governmental authority. Something like this appears to hold for the more individualistic governmental representation of American parties since it precludes the effective action as an organized entity which is possible for a party whose elected legislators act cohesively. Less apparently undeveloped are the explicit non-class consciousness and the relatively unprogrammatic character of American parties, but even on these counts forceful arguments have been made on the

ground that a large working-class party committed to a socialist program represents an advanced stage of development. Indeed this is the
core of Duverger's view of American parties as underdeveloped. Their
organizational limitations are emphasized, but he sees these in relation
to the absence of a large socialist working-class party.[30] It is such a
party which initiates mass-membership, for instance, and in this as
in other respects it represents organizational "contagion from the
Left."[31]

Possibly, however, the American model might be regarded as less
highly developed if the socialist working-class party itself were left
largely out of account. In either case, support appears to be given to the
proposal that parties in the United States can and should become more
like those in Europe. The assumption is that there is a progression
toward the more highly developed form.

One does not have to be an American chauvinist in order to question
this argument. There is a superficiality about the application of the developmental terminology. In what ways, aside from the most obvious
one, are the less fully organized parties also the less developed? Surely
the American parties are not less highly developed in the sense of belonging to, or responding to, a less highly developed social and economic order. And surely they are not less highly developed in the sense
of being newer political entities. The fact is that American parties are
the oldest democratic parties in the world.[32] The United States, because
it was the first nation to have a mass electorate, also had the first
political parties in the modern sense in which we use the term. It may
be recalled that white manhood suffrage was established in the United
States at least half a century before it was in Britain (by the acts of
1867 and 1885), and that many other Western European nations, including the Scandinavian, did not go this far until the two decades
preceding World War I.[33] Thus Europe, not the United States, has less
experience with democratic political competition and so with the political parties responding to such competition. The later European parties
could still be more modern than the American, just as the factories of
a more recently industrialized nation are often more modern than those
of an older industrial country. But that possibility would not clearly

---

[30] DUVERGER, *op. cit.*, pp. 4-5 ff.

[31] *Ibid.*, pp. XXVII and 25.

[32] WILLIAM N. CHAMBERS, *Political Parties in a New Nation.* New York: Oxford
University Press, 1963.

[33] A useful comparative chronology of suffrage extensions has been constructed by
STEIN ROKKAN, Political Participation, Paris: IPSA, 1961. The lateness of manhood
suffrage in Scandinavian nations is striking.

support the view that there are higher (more advanced) stages of development toward which parties inevitably tend. It might support this view if American parties, after an early, less highly organized period, began to resemble the European model. Unless this can be demonstrated, however, it seems more likely that American parties are simply different from European parties in ways that cannot be expressed in terms of stages of development.

The likelihood is strengthened by the realization that American parties were more highly organized in the middle and late years of the nineteenth century than they have been in the recent years of the twentieth century. The big city political machine, in its heyday, was the largest, most elaborate, and most effective party organization we have known in the United States. It is only because it is no longer typical that we now regard loose organization as a major aspect of the "American" party model. The terminology would have been unthinkable in the late nineteenth century. Then, when European parties were beginning to develop, American parties impressed observers as most highly organized—even as over-organized. Thus James Bryce described "the tremendous power" of American party organization in the 1890's: "It enslaves local officials, it increases the tendency to regard members of Congress as mere delegates, it keeps men of independent character out of local and national politics, it puts bad men into place, perverts the wishes of the people, it has in some places set up a tyranny under the forms of democracy." [34] Equipped with relatively few principles, American parties, Bryce thought, had strong enough organizations to substitute for principles. He wrote of "the remarkable cohesion of parties in America," and of victories at the ballot box which were won by "the cohesion and docility of the troops. . . ." [35] No American, Bryce said, would dream of offering himself for a post unless chosen by his party. Candidacies were controlled by the parties.[36]

Disregarding Bryce's now unfashionable moral disapprobation of machines, which may have led him as well as Ostrogorski to exaggerate their power, it remains undeniable that American parties of the 1890's were characterized by much more highly organized units than have lately been usual in the United States. One can understand why a few present-day American students of parties, evidently in despair about any newer ways of making American parties more "responsible," have be-

[34] *The American Commonwealth.* Chicago: Charles Sergel & Co., 1891, vol. 2, pp. 491-92.
[35] *Ibid.,* pp. 48, 72.
[36] *Ibid.,* pp. 74, 77.

gun to look back on the old big city machines as belonging to an organizational golden age.[37] This age, it should be emphasized, was relatively early in the history of the mass franchise in the United States. In fact, our city machines developed in almost immediate response to the rapid extension of the suffrage to masses of new immigrants. It is not far-fetched to suggest that this response was the American counterpart, mainly prior in time, to the European socialist working-class party which organized newly enfranchised industrial workers. Nor is it outlandish, therefore, to suggest that a relatively high degree of party organization belongs primarily to the early stages of mass enfranchisement. In this perspective, however, the earlier American and the later European organizational responses do not have to be regarded as identical or even similar in all respects. It is only that the older American machines were closer than are contemporary American parties to the European model on these typological counts: the machines put more flesh, by way of organized supporters, on the party skeleton; they exerted more organizational control over candidate selection; and their elected representatives were likely to act more cohesively in legislative bodies. On the other hand, they were no more national or programmatic, and they were no more explicitly class conscious (although their ethnic group consciousness may have been an American equivalent).

Both because of the early rise of the now declined city machine and because of more general aspects of socio-economic and political development which have been noted, it is necessary to search for a less simple explanation of the contemporary differences between the American and the European party models than that which regards the latter as the more advanced. In trying to gather material for a book on the subject, I am impressed by the magnitude and complexity of the task. I will indicate here only as much of the substance of my comparisons as are useful to illustrate my method as well as my difficulties. Basically my approach is to study the types of political parties as responses to different national circumstances, social and institutional, and to stress the importance of the circumstances existing at the time of initial party development in a given nation. The assumption is that parties, once started in a certain mold, are likely to persist in that mold even after the original conditioning circumstances have changed considerably. The parties too, it is appreciated, can and do change, but slowly and not in all respects.

[37] Not the most extreme but still a substantial admiration is expressed by FRED I. GREENSTEIN, *The American Party System and the American People.* Englewood Cliffs: Prentice-Hall, 1963, ch. 4.

IV

In successive sections of this paper, I propose to summarize first the
American and then the European circumstances that have provided the
social and institutional molds for political parties and which therefore
help to account for their characteristics. In the United States, for reasons already stated, the circumstances are especially those of the nineteenth century although the circumstances, like the responding parties,
have changed only gradually rather than by a revolutionary process.
This is evident when we discuss the *social and structural federalism* in
which American parties developed. We know that even with a vaster
area and many more people the United States of the twentieth century
is a more highly national entity, socially and governmentally, than it was
in the early days of the Republic. Yet we also know that both substantial regional differences and substantial state governmental units
remain vital enough forces in American life to continue to nourish the
essentially state organizational basis for political parties. While we cannot be certain that the remaining vitality would now be sufficient to
make parties state rather than national, if our parties were starting from
scratch in the middle of the twentieth century, there can be little doubt
about the original impact. Not only have our parties at the national
level been federative in organization, but in association with their federative character, they have tolerated individualistic political styles which,
in part, are sustained by divergent regional and state bases. Not too
much should be made of this latter point, however, because there is
evidence from Canada and Australia, the former of which surely has
both social and structural federalism, that cohesion rather than individualism can characterize legislative parties at the national level even
though external party organization is decidedly federative.[38]

This observation points to the strikingly important and durable American circumstance of the *separation of executive and legislative powers*.
No plainer difference exists between the United States and all other
Western democracies than that which flows from the constitutional fact
that the effective American executive is not dependent on a legislative
majority for its continuation in office. A political scientist seeking to
understand parties could neglect it only if most excessively zealous in
wanting fundamental social and economic explanations. Far from
neglecting it, I propose the separation of powers as the crucial circum-

---

[38] LEON D. EPSTEIN, A Comparative Study of Canadian Parties. *American Political
Science Review*, 58 (March 1964), 46-59.

stance in explaining the relative non-cohesiveness of legislative representatives elected under a given party label. This non-cohesiveness, or individualism in legislative voting behavior, we know to be a mark of American congressional parties in comparison with behavior in Britain and in other nations with working parliamentary systems. The fact that a similar non-cohesiveness is not uniformly characteristic of American state legislative parties should lead us to pause before concluding that the separation of powers is a sufficient cause for individualistic legislative voting behavior. But I do not go that far in making my case. I argue only that the separation of powers permits non-cohesive legislative parties in a way that the parliamentary system does not. The American government can and does work without continuous support by a legislative majority. The executive authority remains stable, with its own popular mandate, even if less effective in certain respects. The parliamentary system, however, really cannot work unless a legislative party, or a coalition of legislative parties, provides a consistent majority. "Cannot work" might better read "cannot work at all well given the modern need for stable executive authority." This allows for the experience of France and some other Western nations, where the absence of a cohesive majority in a parliamentary system contributed to the collapse of that system. In the American system, however, there is no such drastic result from the absence of majority legislative support. The separation of powers is permissive in a way that the parliamentary system is not.

Another way to put the point is to say that in a large and diverse nation like the United States it would seem likely that each of two major parties would contain significantly diverse elements whose cohesion, in legislative bodies or elsewhere, would have to be contrived. Yet it is contrived for certain limited purposes imposed even by the American governmental system. Each congressional party is cohesive when it comes to organizing the legislative body. And, more importantly, each national party achieves a temporary cohesiveness every four years in order to try to elect the President. Here the constitutional rules make it virtually necessary for a party to unite in order to achieve the collective benefits of power. No comparably strong institutional pressure exists —although some pressure assuredly exists—for congressional parties to be thus unified, certainly not continuously unified, as parliamentary parties tend to be.

A third American circumstance is the *largely pre-industrial and pre-urban environment* in which parties first developed. Some of their style was set by the Jeffersonian and Jacksonian eras, when white manhood suffrage brought forth political parties in what was still a rural nation, and still more of their style derived from the middle and late nineteenth century when the America of farms and small towns remained dominant despite the growth of industries and cities. In these respects, the United States was not unique. France, for example, remained relatively non-urban when modern parties developed in the Third Republic. But the United States was a good deal more rural at the earlier date of its modern party development. The point is worth emphasis because we know that more highly organized parties have been essentially urban phenomena in the United States and elsewhere. Thus in a still largely rural America we would not expect the national parties to reflect the high degree of organization that characterized even the American city machines. Farm and small-town America might have set the national style and then helped maintain it through various representational advantages which persisted after numerical superiority had disappeared.

A more specific if negative result of the development of American parties in a largely pre-industrial and pre-urban environment is that they occupied the democratic political arena before there was an economic basis for a large socialist working-class party. Not only was there white manhood suffrage before there were many industrial workers to organize, the significance of which in contrast to Europe has often been noted,[39] but there were also political parties already well-entrenched with the voting masses. American parties secured the votes of large numbers of ordinary electors long before the electors were primarily industrial and urban workers. Republicans and Democrats had popular bases capable of expansion to include members of the new working class. That class, it is true, grew rapidly both from rural migration and European immigration, but American parties were accustomed to appealing to both groups regardless of class. The rural migrants to cities had always been enfranchised, and the European immigrants were given the vote as soon as they established citizenship (if not sooner). They did not have to wait for the franchise because they were propertyless industrial workers. No such enfranchisement of a class had to take place in industrial America. Thus a frustrated desire for political participation, which along with economic demands provided a basis for the European working-class party, had no reality in the United States.

The free and prior gift of the ballot to the American working class does not stand alone as a factor in explaining the absence of a socialist

[39] Especially by SELIG PERLMAN, *A Theory of the Labor Movement*. New York: Augustus Kelley, 1949 ed., pp. 167-68.

working-class party. Another well known American circumstance, the nation's *material wealth,* is surely relevant. Compared to Europe, the United States was a rich and bountiful country before industrialization, and it was so afterward as well. There was so much wealth that there was even enough to raise the standard of living of the manual working class well above European levels. We do not have to ignore the disparities of wealth and income in American society, especially in the earlier stages of industrialization, in order to appreciate that the economic grievances of American workers were usually less sharp than those of European workers.

How much the widely accepted *openness of American society* has to do with the nature of American parties, and especially the absence of a large socialist working-class party, is less clear. We used to believe that the frontier provided a safety valve for discontented workers, but this has been seriously questioned. So has the belief in a greater occupational mobility in the United States than in Europe. We now think that about the same degree of occupational mobility characterizes every Western industrializing society.[40] This leaves the high American *valuation* of openness as a possible factor. However intangible, it might well have constituted an impediment to the growth of class consciousness and so to the growth of a large socialist working-class party. It is not just a matter of believing that one could move up occupationally. Also involved is the belief that this kind of mobility does not run against any really high social barriers. That, in turn, requires that the working class not be sharply separated or alienated from the rest of society. It seemed easier to avoid this separation in the United States because there was no pre-industrial tradition of a class society.[41] American parties exemplify American social values, or perhaps respond to them, by their broad electoral appeals and notably by their leaderships. These leaderships have always been heavily middle-class, including some who entered the middle class after upward mobility, educationally and occupationally, from working-class families. At no time have American party leaders been recruited in significant numbers directly from working-class ranks in the manner of European socialist parties.[42] Meeting the interests of

---

[40] SEYMOUR MARTIN LIPSET and REINHARD BENDIX, *Social Mobility in Industrial Society.* Berkeley and Los Angeles: University of California Press, 1959, and DAVID V. GLASS, *Social Mobility in Britain.* London: Routledge and Kegan Paul, 1954.

[41] LOUIS HARTZ, *The Liberal Tradition in America.* New York: Harcourt, Brace, 1955, p. 234.

[42] DONALD R. MATTHEWS, *The Social Background of Political Decision-Makers.* Garden City: Doubleday, 1954, and C. WRIGHT MILLS, The Power Elite. New York: Oxford University Press, 1956. The American data, showing a small minority of political leaders from the working class in both the 19th and 20th centuries, can be

the working class, as at least one major American party has done, did not require the class consciousness involved in adopting working-class leaders.

Much has been made of an *American ideological consensus* in connection with the relatively non-programmatic character of American parties. Insofar as this consensus has meant, as just suggested, less class consciousness, it can be connected to the absence of one kind of programmatic party—that which opposes a socialist economic order to a capitalist one. Often this is what students of ideology are talking about. For them ideology means socialist ideology and consequentially a meaningful party program. Consensus with respect to the capitalist economic order, therefore, means non-programmatic parties in the United States. Although this definition of ideology is rather constricted, it probably has to be so if the term is to be used to distinguish the basis of American parties. In looser senses, such as how much governmental intervention is ideologically acceptable, American parties do not seem committed to a given consensus. Of course, when it comes to views of the fundamental governmental order, there appears the same degree of broad American consensus as on the general economic order. No basis for programmatic parties can be found in disagreements about the legitimacy of the constitutional system. But this is hardly the basis for programmatic parties in any healthy democratic nation.

While in the area of intangible values, it is well to mention one other American circumstance related to the nature of parties. It is the *populist democratic tradition.* Perhaps direct democracy would be as good a name. What I am referring to is the American preference, unusual in degree among Western democracies, for reducing the barriers between voters and their elected officials. This has been expressed by the direct election of a host of state, county, and other local executive officers as well as legislators. It has also been expressed by the direct primary method of selecting party candidates. And generally it has meant a bias

---

contrasted with the sharp change in Britain from a complete absence of such leaders in the 19th century to their presence in large numbers with the Labour Party in the 20th century. I have made this contrast in British Class Consciousness and the Labour Party. *The Journal of British Studies*, 1 (May 1962), 136-50. Full British data are now available in w. l. GUTTSMAN, *The British Political Elite*. London: MacGibbon & Kee, 1963. While exactly comparable data have not been found for other European nations, what is known about the social backgrounds of leadership in several continental nations tends to confirm in those nations the British pattern of association of working-class leaders almost exclusively with the rise of working-class parties. From some research of my own, I have learned that Canadian leadership resembles the American pattern—just as Canada resembles the United States in not having a major socialist working-class party.

against party organization, surprising in a nation which has accepted high degrees of organization in so many other aspects of its life. To an extent, this populist tradition can be attributed to the rural circumstances which, as I have mentioned, set the tone for American politics. But the persistence, even the growth, of anti-organizational feeling with respect to parties creates a presumption that the populist tradition represents fundamental American values.

v

To a large degree the European circumstances for party development can be considered, as implied in the previous section, to be the reverse of the American. Thus in Europe, especially as exemplified by Britain, the circumstances have been non-federal, parliamentary, urban industrial, materially unwealthy, socially stratified, and ideologically divided. (We could add nonpopulist, or deferential to leadership however chosen, in order to complete the symmetry.) We may thus seem to be looking at Europe through American sights, but it would be equally true to say that we established the American circumstances in the first place by using European sights. The fact is that we try to see both in the comparative perspective of advanced Western nations. Certainly it should be apparent below that European circumstances are not crudely regarded as non-American.

This emerges, to start with, in talking about the non-federal conditions. Far from regarding these as peculiar, it must be stressed that they are usual among Western nations. To make the point, the circumstances should be labelled less negatively as the characteristics of geographically homogeneous nations. Their homogeneity, relative to the United States, is related to their smaller area. Regions within European nations may have considerable historical significance, but unless they coincide with linguistic differences, as in Switzerland, they have not provided the basis for a durable social or structural federalism. Originally they may have been more diverse than American regions, and yet ceased to be so by the time democratic government was established. For example, regions as distinct from England as Wales and Scotland had been subject to centralized national authority long before Britain adopted the mass franchise. What was democratized was the election of national not regional representatives. Thus it was natural, from the start, for there to be national parties. Significantly Switzerland, exceptional among European nations in its consistent federalism, is also exceptional in the federal organization of its parties (on the basis of cantons).[43] And Germany, with partially federal features at times during modern history, has partially but not primarily federal parties.[44] Otherwise it is fair to say that European nations generally provide the circumstances for national party organization. For it to be otherwise apparently requires structural federalism—that is, a federal system of government—along with the social federalism to sustain it.

Such conditions are met in the Western world, apart from Switzerland, only in the vast continental land areas of North American and Australia. Canada, Australia, and the United States do have size in common, and thus are less homogeneous in the purely geographical sense. But they have something else in common vis-à-vis most of Western Europe: all three achieved considerable measures of political democracy either before or nearly simultaneously with their establishment as nations. They had no prior national histories of centralizing authority except that of the outside imperial power. Meaningful regional units, becoming states or provinces, already had more or less popularly based governments before a national government was established, also on a popular basis. Interestingly, Canada, Australia, and the United States resemble Switzerland in this respect. At least certain Swiss cantons had long had popularly elected governments, still virtually unique in Europe of the early nineteenth century, and these governments antedated the establishment of Swiss national authority.

With or without the Swiss case, it is evident that what we conceive to be European about non-federal or geographically homogeneous circumstances is in fact more narrowly European than the sense in which I have sometimes used the term. Here it does not extend to all Western nations except the United States. Among those nations outside Europe itself, Canada and Australia must clearly be counted with the United States.[45] But this is not at all the case in discussing the next and probably more important circumstance: the *parliamentary system*. In varying ways, all Western democracies except the United States make their working executive dependent on legislative authority both for election and for continuation in office. It is true that Switzerland operates a

[43] GEORGE A. CODDING, *The Federal Government of Switzerland*. Boston: Houghton Mifflin, 1961, p. 127.
[44] DOUGLAS A. CHALMERS, *The Social Democratic Party of Germany*. New Haven & London: Yale University Press, 1964, pp. 155-56.
[45] On the provinces as crucial Canadian party elements, see R. MACGREGOR DAWSON, *The Government of Canada*. Toronto: University of Toronto Press, 1957, p. 529. On Australian federal party structure, see AARON WILDAVSKY, Party Discipline under Federalism: Implications of Australian Experience. *Social Research* (Winter 1961), 437-58.

rather special variant, and that France of the Fifth Republic has at least temporarily substituted a separately elected executive as the principal source of authority—yet without abolishing the traditional dependence of the working executive on the legislative body. Canada and Australia are as clearly parliamentary as Britain itself.

In comparative perspective, the relevance of the parliamentary system in Canada is especially significant. I have argued this at length elsewhere,[46] and I want only to summarize here. The principal point is that the parliamentary system is associated with the existence in Canada. of political parties which, in the vital respect of their parliamentary cohesion, resemble British rather than American parties. The association of the parliamentary system with cohesion is arrived at partly by a process of elimination. Nothing else but the demands of the parliamentary system would seem to account for the British and Canadian similarity in legislative party behavior. Other Canadian circumstances are much more like those of the United States than they are like Britain's or Europe's. Note Canada's intense social and structural federalism, its pre-industrial and pre-urban environment in which parties originally developed, its material wealth, and its American-type ideological consensus. Admittedly Canada's society seems less open and less populist than the American, but considerably more so than the European. Anyway these circumstances would be difficult to connect with the party loyalty of elected legislative representatives. In Canada as in Britain, Australia, and every European nation with a working parliamentary government, parliamentary party cohesion seems the response essential to make the system work. A parliamentary party, if it is a majority on its own or part of a successful majority coalition, functions on a continuing basis as a majority party's representation functions more briefly in the American electoral college. A single parliamentary majority party, in particular, registers the voters' choice of executive leadership, and then, unlike the American electoral college, re-registers this choice from time to time by votes of confidence. At least this is the fully developed British model. Even the Canadians may deviate occasionally from its perfected cohesion. And some Europeans do so more often.

Returning to more specifically European circumstances, it will save time to consider together those circumstances which seem related to the emergence of the socialist working-class party. These are the already considerable *industrial and urban environment* in which democratic parties developed, the *material hardships* accompanying the early industrialization, and the *stratified society* carried over from pre-industrial times. All

[46] LEON D. EPSTEIN, *op. cit.*

three circumstances, as previously observed, distinguish Europe from the United States, and in ways that seem meaningful in understanding why every European nation has had a large socialist working-class party while the United States and Canada have not. (Whether the labor parties of Australia and New Zealand can be considered European-style socialist working-class parties is debatable; the Australian qualifies in terms of class-consciousness if not in terms of socialist ideology. It is possible but not entirely satisfying to account for it as a consequence of the transplantation of late nineteenth-century British workers and their attitudes to an as yet unsettled political party system.)

That European parties, in contrast to American, developed in a more heavily industrial and urban environment does not itself explain the socialist working-class party. But it helps to supply an explanation when it is appreciated that not just parties but the suffrage on which parties are based came when large numbers of urban industrial workers were already present. In some nations, like Germany, the socialist party was the first major democratic party in the sense of appealing for the support as well as representing the interest of the propertyless masses.[47] Moreover in both Germany and Scandinavia,[48] for example, the socialist party existed even before the enfranchisement of urban workers and so took part in the effort to enfranchise what became its following. In other nations, of which Britain is the best example, the socialist party did not quite precede mass suffrage, but it came along soon enough afterward to represent what was a still newly enfranchised working-class aware, as was the rest of the community, of its special status. That status, in Britain as elsewhere in Europe, derived from other facets of experience in adition to late enfranchisement as a working class. The other facets were the economic squalor more widely characteristic of European than of American industrialization—labelled as the greater material hardship for the working class—and the residual feudal sense of class identification which both manual workers and their betters carried into the nineteenth and early twentieth century societies from the pre-industrial age—labelled as the marks of a more stratified society.

These circumstances together, it is not surprising, coincide with a kind of *ideological cleavage* that is another circumstance making European parties different from American. In varying degrees, the working class in European nations was sufficiently distinct as to support a different view of the nature of the economic order, and even sometimes

[47] CHALMERS, op. cit., pp. 5-6.
[48] RUSTOW, The Politics of Compromise, op. cit., pp. 10-85; and CARL ERIC KNOEL-LINGER, Labor in Finland. Cambridge: Harvard University Press, 1960, pp. 47-48.

of the political order, from that held by the upper and middle classes.

The European circumstances which have been noted in the last three paragraphs are plainly intended to account for more than the existence of the large socialist working-class party. They are also meant to help explain the mass-membership organization which characterizes some non-socialist as well as all socialist parties in Europe. The parliamentary system, let it be noted, cannot be used here. Logically there is no basis for connecting it to mass-membership parties, and the coexistence in Canada of the parliamentary system (and cohesive legislative parties) with skeletal external organization supports the logic. But all of the circumstances associated with the development of a socialist party seem relevant to mass-membership organizations generally. This is partly a matter of the socialist party itself being the prime exemplar of the mass-membership organization, and of non-socialist parties finding it useful to imitate socialist organization in order to compete with it—the contagion from the left, of which Duverger writes. But the circumstances making for a highly organized, class-conscious, and ideological party on the left may also directly make for the same kind of party on the right. The upper and middle classes in Europe, when forming highly organized parties, may not have responded only to the challenge of the socialist left. They may have directly responded to the same circumstances which produced working-class parties. Admittedly the necessity for organized dues-payers and for other forms of collective action would not have been so great as it was for the working class, whose strength lay entirely in numbers, but organization would still have been useful. More to the point, it would have been possible on the basis of class consciousness. The impressively large dues-paying membership of the British Conservatives, a class organization if there ever was one, provides an excellent illustration. Whether any such organization could be built and regularly maintained without class consciousness, at least comparable to the Conservatives' defence of capitalism, is open to doubt.

VI

Much of what we have described as accounting for the differences between American and European parties is historical. The parties are now —perhaps still—different, but the differences in conditioning circumstances may no longer exist in the same degree. Obviously this holds for the pre-industrial American environment versus the industrial European environment in which parties first developed. And it probably holds for the difference in class consciousness between the United States and

Europe since a diminution in the latter is widely believed to have taken place. But it is not true for the key institutional determinant flowing from the difference between the separation of powers and the parliamentary system. The results of this continuing difference in circumstances, plus the continuing habitual results of certain admittedly changing circumstances, seem likely to maintain American and European parties as distinctive political phenomena. They have come to perform different functions in their respective political systems, and the systems themselves have developed in accord with these differences. For example, a British party assumes responsibility for governmental policy in a way that an American party does not. But much the same degree of responsibility is assumed in the United States by the President as a public figure seeking support beyond his own party.[49] On the other hand, an American party may be even more important than a British party in structuring the vote at election time since the long ballot imposes this function in a special way.

Nevertheless, in light of those circumstances which changed or are changing, it is possible that American and European parties are becoming more alike in some respects. I prefer to put the point in this way rather than to adopt the more usual idea that American parties are coming to resemble the European, or the unconventional idea that European parties are coming to resemble American. I should be honest, however, and confess that I lean more to the latter. The major exception is in the tendency of American parties to become more national. While they are a long way from overriding the governmental federalism which, with social federalism, made and keeps the parties organizationally federative, there is a good deal of evidence of the nationalization of issues, elections, and political personalities.[50] This nationalization has so far had surprisingly few counterparts in organizational growth at the national party level, but the probability remains.[51]

In other respects, there are almost no signs of the Europeanization of American parties. None should be expected by way of greater legislative party cohesion as long as the European party cohesion is viewed

---

[49] Bipartisan support for a presidential program like that of the Civil Rights law of 1964 is well-known, but it is not so exceptional. Calculations in the *Congressional Quarterly Almanac* show that about one-third of the President's victories in the House and in the Senate during 1961 and 1962 required votes from the minority Republicans as well as from the majority Democrats.

[50] E. E. SCHATTSCHNEIDER, United States: The Functional Approach to Party Government, in NEUMANN, *Modern Political Parties, op. cit.*

[51] American national party committees are hopefully described by CORNELIUS P. COTTER and BERNARD C. HENNESSY, *Politics Without Power.* New York: Atherton Press, 1964.

primarily, as it has been here, as the product of a parliamentary system which we are not in process of adopting. Nor should any Europeanization be expected by way of mass membership, class consciousness, and more deeply ideological programs, as long as these characteristics are thought to flow from older and now diminishingly different European circumstances. The same can be said for any change from open to closed methods of candidate selection since the democratic credentials for the closed method involve a mass-membership party. Much, in fact, depends on whether the United States is developing mass-membership parties. Some observers might argue that such organizations are growing in the United States despite the absence of European circumstances of the late nineteenth and early twentieth centuries. The argument would have to rest on the slender evidence of the party clubs which have developed in certain American cities and suburbs during the last two decades. So far, however, these clubs have not usually been as large as their European counterparts, they have been limited mainly to middle-class citizens in both major parties, they have been sporadic even in most of the areas where they have existed at all, and they have been less highly organized than the old city machines which they seek in some instances to replace.[52]

While the decline in the old machines based on a vanishing mass patronage might seem conducive to the growth of policy-oriented membership organizations, there are many countervailing forces in modern society which make the last half of the twentieth century an unlikely time to build parties along those lines. Among the forces, deserving much fuller treatment than is possible here, are the new mass media of communication and the accompanying public relations and opinion survey techniques. All are enormously expensive. They require large sums to buy communication time and expert personnel. No significant portion of the necessary money can be raised through membership dues, which have to be modest if there is to be a large membership, and no significant portion of the work can be done by amateur volunteers. In other words, membership organizations seem largely irrelevant to what has become the major campaign method for candidates and parties. And this method, principally television, is likely to become more important. It is the efficient way for a party, through its leaders, to reach masses of

[52] The broadest study of the new clubs is by JAMES Q. WILSON, *The Amateur Democrat.* Chicago: University of Chicago Press, 1962. Reports may also be found in *Politics in Wisconsin, op. cit.,* ch. 5; CURRIN SHIELDS, A Note on Party Organization: the Democrats in California. *Western Political Quarterly,* 7 (December 1954), 673-84; and HUGH BONE, New Party Associations in the West. *American Political Science Review,* 45 (December 1951), 1115-25.

voters. Furthermore it suits the increasingly educated mid-twentieth century citizen who, especially in the United States, is already organized in interest groups designed to influence governmental policy and who can enjoy making a choice between candidates and parties on the basis of personal appeals over his television set. Neither the old patronage organization nor the mass-membership organization is needed as it might have been in earlier democratic times.

If there are technological trends now working against the development of mass-membership party organizations in the United States, they ought by now also to be operative in Europe so as to reduce the importance of such organizations as have existed. Television, public relations, and opinion surveys have in fact become prominent in European politics during the last decade or so. Their rise has coincided with an unusually sharp change in many of the circumstances which we have believed responsible for mass-membership parties in the first place. Thus it is hard to say what would have caused a decline in organized membership, but there is considerable evidence of such a decline espcially in Britain, Germany, and France.[53] Not only are there fewer members now than in former years, but the parties which have depended on such memberships rather than on newer campaign techniques have not competed successfully.[54] The less highly organized conservative parties have tended to pioneer the new style politics and to be followed, often slowly and reluctantly, by socialist working-class parties. The contagion is now from the right. And, in some respects, it is from the United States.

---

[53] British Conservatives dropped from a peak of 2,805,032 members in 1953 to about 2,250,000 in 1961 (MCKENZIE, *British Political Parties, op. cit.*, p. 187), and British Labour declined from a high of 1,014,524 individual direct dues-paying members in 1952 to 767,459 in 1962 (*Report of the 62nd Annual Conference of the Labour Party*, p. 47). The German Social Democrats declined from their postwar high of 875,479 in 1947 to below 600,000 in the mid-fifties before rising to 623,816 in 1958; the French Socialist membership decline has been even sharper (data for both countries in *Yearbook of the International Socialist Labour Movement*, vol. 2, 1960-61. London: Lincolns Prager, 1960, pp. 121-22 and 130-31). Socialist party membership in most of the smaller European nations has been fairly stable in the last decade.
[54] This was the lament of the German Social Democrats in the 1950's, and later of (or at least for) the British Labour Party. DAVID BUTLER and RICHARD ROSE, *The British General Election of 1959*. London: Macmillan, 1960, p. 25.

⁓ 6 ⁓

Direct Democracy in France

Henry W. Ehrmann

EDITORIAL NOTE: *The state of the political parties in France, their fragmentation, their multiplicity and in general their apparent ineffectiveness accounts for the development of direct democracy in France that Henry Erhmann examines here. His remarks clearly indicate, however, that the viability of democracy in France depends upon the future of the political parties. The best account of the state of political parties in France, especially under the Fourth Republic, is given in Maurice Duverger, ed.,* Partios Politiques et Classes Sociales, *Paris, 1956, which unfortunately has not been translated. On some recent trends Georges Vedel,* Depolitisation, *Paris, 1964, should be consulted. On the Gaullist system and its relations with the political parties, P. M. Williams and M. Harrison,* De Gaulle's Republic, *London, 1960, and R. C. Macridis and B. E. Brown,* The De Gaulle Republic—Quest for Unity, *Homewood, Illinois, 1960.*

> "Le suffrage périt par l'acclamation."
> —*Alain*

WHEN during the debate on a motion of censure in October 1962 Paul Reynaud challenged the government from the rostrum of the National Assembly with a scornful: "Here and nowhere else is France!" [1] the issue was well joined. To Reynaud, perennial deputy during three

---

[1] "Pour nous, républicains, la France est ici et non ailleurs." *Journal Officiel. Débats Parlementaires, Assemblée Nationale.* October 5, 1962, p. 3209.

republican regimes, General de Gaulle's projected referendum appeared as a two-fold attack upon French republican traditions. If adopted, the proposal to elect the President of the Republic by popular suffrage would divest the Assembly of its role as the sole bearer of national sovereignty. Moreover, to seek approval for such a change of the Constitution of 1958 without a prior vote of parliament deprived both houses of any participation in the amending process.

In 1958, as President of the Consultative Constitutional Committee, Reynaud had insisted that the possibilities of any direct appeal to the electorate be carefully circumscribed and hedged by parliamentary controls. He had obtained official assurances that the referendum would never be used by the executive as a means of arousing popular opinion against the elected assemblies. The final text of the Constitution had incorporated proposals by the Consultative Committee which strengthened the position of parliament whenever either a referendum or presidential emergency powers might create a plebiscitarian situation.[2]

Four years later, Reynaud's dramatic plea to defend "all our popular traditions and a long parliamentary tradition" still rallied a majority of deputies to its support. But the country which he had sought to identify with the National Assembly decided otherwise. The referendum on the constitutional amendment was approved by 62.25 per cent of the votes cast. In the subsequent elections, Paul Reynaud, a deputy since 1919, lost his seat to a proven supporter of De Gaulle who in the first ballot obtained 61 per cent of the votes.

I

The traditions which Reynaud had invoked do not know of the nation except through representation. In France, the identification of the republic with representative traditions had become so complete that any suggestion to give the electorate direct influence on legislation or on the designation of the executive was suspect as authoritarian. But an exclusively representative regime, lacking that link between voters and government which democratic mass parties provide, ended up by alienating the citizens from politics and turned them into passive and frequently disgusted onlookers.[3] The corrected democracy which emerged from the crisis of 1958 was, for all the changes it brought, committed

[2] See Travaux Préparatoires de la Constitution. *Avis et Débats du Comité Consultatif Constitutionnel.* Paris, 1960, pp. 203 ff.
[3] See OTTO KIRCHHEIMER, France from the Fourth to the Fifth Republic. *Social Research,* 26, No. 4 (Winter 1958), 382.

to classical parliamentary traditions. In 1962 General de Gaulle decided to break with them when, after the end of the Algerian war, a return to the political life of earlier republican regimes appeared likely.

Tension between a commitment to Rousseau's notion of popular sovereignty and the need for political representation had led to incongruities in the early days of the French revolution. The Constitution of 1791 had formulated (Ch. III; art. 2): "The nation which is the source of all powers can exercise them only by delegation. The French Constitution is representative. . . ." But it also incorporated specifically (as would the constitution of 1958) the Declaration of Rights which had paid homage to Rousseau: "The Law is the expression of the General Will. All citizens have the right to take part in its formation *either directly* or by their representatives." [4]

The talented exchanges in the First National Assembly of 1789 revealed precise insights into the democratic potentialities of Rousseauan thought. But such insights clashed soon with the conviction, ably expounded by Sieyès and shared by a majority of delegates, that the people, "lacking instruction as well as leisure," needed qualified representatives to ascertain their own will through effective legislation.[5] The spokesmen for the *tiers état* knew that the experiences of antiquity with which Rousseau was saturated had little meaning for them. Most of them scorned direct democracy in which "everybody wants to be a master." [6] The farther the debates progressed, the clearer became the sometimes oligarchic, sometimes corporatist, tendencies latent in the idea of representation. In the end Rousseau's notions appeared in many speeches as extraneous metaphysical justifications of an exclusively representative system. It was consistent with such beliefs that the National Assembly rejected all mandatory instructions to the representa-

---

[4] This article of the Declaration and especially the words italicized in the text were used in the referendum campaign of 1962 to justify the direct appeal to the electorate on a question of constitutional revision.

[5] As early as September 1789, Sieyès had argued that citizens "without alienating their rights can commit their exercise" to those best qualified to represent them. The ablest analysis of the debates on the problems of representation is still ROBERT REDSLOB, *Die Staatstheorien der französischen Nationalversammlung*. Leipzig, 1912. See also KARL LOEWENSTEIN, *Volk und Parlament nach der Staatstheorie der französischen Nationalversammlung von 1789. Studien zur Dogmengeschichte der unmittelbaren Volksgesetzgebung*. München, 1922.

[6] In such words Kant condemned what he called "democracy" as an *Unform* in contrast to the representative republic which he praised. See *Zum Ewigen Frieden*. Königsberg, 1795, pp. 26 f., and esp. Metaphysische Anfangsgründe der Rechtslehre, in *Sämtliche Werke*, vol. VII, Leipzig, 1868, p. 159. Kant's implied criticism of Rousseau's notion of direct popular rule is identical with that voiced by the majority in the National Assembly, even though Kant's often quoted *Antwortschreiben . . . an den Abt Sieyès in Paris* is now recognized as a forgery.

tives as an undue interference with the ideal of a just and rational legislation. To interpret the intentions of the sovereign people that had elected them was a mission exclusively incumbent upon the deputies.

The fight for popular participation in legislation which Robespierre and other undismayed disciples of Rousseau had lost in the National Assembly, was won by the Montagne in the Convention. The Constitution of 1793 distrusted "representative despotism" [7] and regarded elected assemblies as expressing only a partial rather than the general will. It organized annual elections, the right of the electorate to veto legislation and to take the initiative in amending the Constitution. "For otherwise it is not true that men are equal before the law," as Robespierre stated in the spirit of radical egalitarianism which is characteristic of all manifestations of direct democracy.[8] In accordance with a decree issued when the monarchy was abolished, the Constitution was submitted to popular approval. But this first referendum was already little more than a plebiscite by which the authors of the recent insurrection called in July 1793 for a vote of confidence. It was granted by an overwhelming majority—of the 25 per cent of the qualified voters who cared to cast a ballot.

The only republican Constitution which had sought to lend immediate rather than represented expression to popular sovereignty was superseded by revolutionary rule before it came into existence. The referendums organized by the two Napoleons discredited the direct consultation of the electorate to such an extent that shortly after the fall of the Second Empire any direct appeal to the people was stigmatized as a manifestation of "supreme decadence." [9] Bonapartist ideology had been frankly antirepresentative. The power of the chief of state rested upon the direct will of the nation to the exclusion of any intermediaries. Any infringe-

[7] This is Robespierre's term; see, also for the following, J. L. TALMON, The Rise of Totalitarian Democracy. Boston, 1952, p. 98 and passim. For the Constitution of 1793, J. M. THOMPSON, The French Revolution. New York, 1945, pp. 393-97, gives a more balanced account than Talmon.
[8] ALBERT SARRAUT, Le Gouvernement Direct. Paris, 1899—an interesting doctoral thesis by the radical-socialist leader—makes the point (pp. 175 ff., 214) that Robespierre's passion for direct democracy was not unconditional. More circumspect than the constitution-makers of 1848, he rejected the idea of a popularly elected executive. Dreading the emotions of an uneducated populace, he also warned against using a referendum to decide the fate of Louis XVI.
[9] So the Minister of Justice Ernoul during the constitutional debates of 1873, see ibid. p. 342. The brilliant analysis of the plebiscitarian ideology of Bonapartism in ROBERT MICHELS, Political Parties. New York, 1962, pp. 212-19, remains extremely valuable. New insights into the phenomenon of democratic cesarism are provided by H. GOLLWITZER, Der Cäsarismus Napoleons III. im Widerhall der Oeffentlichen Meinung Deutschlands. Historische Zeitschrift, 173, No. 1 (February 1952), 23 ff.

ment of constitutional and other laws by the ruler could be given legitimacy by popular approval. The Napoleonic plebiscites combined the threat of social chaos which would follow the demise of the providential leader with the flattery of the masses who were given a voice in choosing their master.

In the *senatus-consultus* of 1870, the liberal Empire made a belated attempt to consort features of a representative regime with the referendum on constitutional texts and amendments.[10] But the Third Republic returned to an undiluted representative system, becoming the classical "Republic of the Deputies"; the Fourth Republic soon fell into a similar pattern.[11] The defense of constituency interests and the close control of an ever-suspected executive were the foremost functions of the deputy, "entrenched, fortified and undefeatable in his constituency like the feudal lord of old in his castle." [12] Atomistic rather than global representation reproduced the cleavages of society. It did not take explicit instructions from the constituents to make of Chamber and Senate that "congress of ambassadors from different and hostile interests" against which Burke had warned. The absence of a modern party system in France made it impossible to correct, as other European democracies have done, the anachronism inherent in a mode of representation conceived for another age.

The modern mass party introduces elements of direct, i.e., plebiscitarian, democracy into a purely representative regime. The modification of classical atomistic representation by the emergence of structured and disciplined parties may be able to meet the dangers threatening both types of democracy: the oligarchic deformations of representative and the caesaristic temptations of plebiscitarian systems.[13] Where modern mass parties exist, politically active citizens have more than a theoretical

---

[10] The Constitution of May 21, 1870 was largely inspired by the monarchist and former enemy of the Empire, Prévost-Paradol, who throughout the Third Republic was considered by many as the foremost theoretician of representative government. By its division of the amending power between the head of state and the people, the text of 1870 resembled the constitutional situation which General de Gaulle created in 1962.

[11] ROGER PRIOURET, *La République des Députés*. Paris, 1959, gives a fascinating historical account of the representative tradition in France.

[12] ALAIN, *Eléments de la Doctrine Radicale*. Paris, 1925, p. 42. The classical picture of the relationship between the citizen and his deputy, was painted by ANDRÉ SIEGFRIED, *Tableau des Partis en France*. Paris, 1930, shortly before the decline of the representative system began. But even during the censure debate of 1962, a conservative deputy, M. Motte, still assessed his own role in similar terms. He too was not reelected.

[13] On this point see ERNST FRAENKEL, *Die Repräsentative und die Plebiszitäre Komponente im Demokratischen Verfassungsstaat*. Tübingen, 1958, esp. pp. 6-11.

possibility of influencing the choice of policies and leaders through the party organization or through its parliamentary group. Binding instructions leave to the member of parliament little room for independent decisions based on constituency considerations, but determine instead the course of action for government or opposition. "Parliament is transformed from the representative corporation which it was into a plebiscitary expedient." [14]

Only during the "abnormal" years of *tripartisme* (1945-47) has the French republic been governed under the aegis of organized mass parties. Aside from the Communists, the majority of voters never cast their ballots for candidates who were compelled to follow party directives.[15] Not only the number of parties but also their structure and, partly, an over-ideological commitment which proved meaningless for concrete political decisions, deprived elections in France of the characteristics of a popular referendum which they have become in other Western democracies.[16] American parties have been called antiparties because, instead of gathering together segments of power and wielding them as one, they serve to disperse power.[17] This has been true also of French parties, in a unitary rather than a federal republic. But in the United States the increasingly plebiscitarian nature of presidential elections gives to the electorate a voice in determining who should govern and who should be replaced at the helm of the government. This has in fact

[14] GERHARD LEIBHOLZ, The Nature and Various Forms of Democracy. *Social Research,* 5, No. 1 (February 1938), 99. With more details on the role of the modern party as a manifestation of direct democracy, see the same author's Der Strukturwandel der Modernen Demokratie, in *Strukturprobleme der Modernen Demokratie.* Karlsruhe, 1958, pp. 78-129.

[15] Foreign, and occasionally even the best French, observers have been overimpressed by the apparent increase in party discipline in the Fourth Republic. It is significant that the organizational structure of both the SFIO and the MRP, especially in regard to the relationship between party and parliamentary group, differed rather markedly from that of other socialist and christian-democratic parties in Europe.

[16] The last elections in the Fourth Republic (1956) offer an excellent example of total confusion, giving the deputies free rein how to interpret the "popular verdict"; for details see the remarkable essay by MAURICE DUVERGER, Esquisse d'une Théorie de la Représentation Politique, in *Evolution du Droit Public. Etudes en l'honneur d'Achille Mestre.* Paris, 1956, esp. pp. 217 ff. In an opinion poll held before the elections of 1956, 14% believed that their vote would have a "great" influence on future political developments, 26% hoped for some influence, 33% were convinced it would have none. Only 2% designated the future Premier M. Mollet as their choice for that post; see *Sondages,* 17, No. 4 (1955), pp. 11, 18. But two years later, a majority of voters still showed little inclination for a modern political party system; only 18% (hence far less than the number of Communist and Socialist voters) believed that a deputy should vote with his party; 50% wished to see him reach his own individual decision; for 21% the answer would vary according to the question to be voted upon. See *ibid.,* 22, No. 4 (1960), 49.

[17] MORTON GRODZINS, American Political Parties and the American System. *The Western Political Quarterly,* 12, No. 4 (December 1960), 997.

narrowed the gap between the American and the British, the presidential
and the parliamentary systems.[18]

In France, neither disciplined parties nor popular elections of the
executive have allowed that involvement of the electorate which gives
strength and legitimacy to representative institutions. An executive in-
sulated from the electorate could neither control nor check parliament.
It was left to deputies and senators to translate as they saw fit the viewpoints and preferences of the voters into political decisions. The widely
assumed and frequently proven insensitivity of the regime to the wishes
of the citizenry substantiated the belief that a professional oligarchy,
enjoying the "games, poisons and delights" of the parliamentary system,
preempted for itself the expressions of the general will. Mosca's stereo-
type of a "political class" wilfully ignoring the impulses of the *pays réel*
was of anti-democratic coinage. But in contemporary France the term
has acquired the democratic respectability which Rousseau gave to his
indictment of the parliamentary oligarchy of eighteenth century England.
Michel Debré was not alone in speaking of the rupture between public
opinion and the "princes" who dominate political life.[19] It is true that
such criticism often reeked of neo-romantic notions which see in all
parties a threat to an assumed national unity. Many of the critics
failed to perceive that in France the absence of valid parties rather
than their omnipotence has hampered the formation of a political will.[20]

The virtues of an exclusively representative system were not seriously
questioned as long as the style of political life under the Third Republic
was in harmony with the style of authority common to large strata of

[18] See OTTO KIRCHHEIMER, Parteistruktur und Massendemokratie in Europa. *Archiv
des Öffentlichen Rechts,* 79 (1954), 314. Using a somewhat different terminology
(contrasting direct democracy and *démocratie médiatisée*), Maurice Duverger has
reached similar conclusions. See especially his *La VI° République et le Régime Présidentiel.* Paris, 1961. For a recent analysis of the relationship between parties, elections and the executive in various Western democrats, see RICHARD LÖWENTHAL, ed.,
Die Demokratie im Wandel der Gesellschaft. Berlin, 1963.
[19] FRANÇOIS GOGUEL in his essay Six Authors in Search of a National Character, in
In Search of France. Cambridge, 1963, p. 395, speaks about "the political class" as
a narrow group of "not more than fifteen or twenty thousand persons at most."
The term is widely used in the columns of *Le Monde* or a liberal magazine such
as *Esprit,* but was denounced as anti-republican by a socialist deputy in the censure
debate of October 1962.
[20] In present-day Europe, confused anti-party propaganda in which various strands
of mostly conservative thought are merged, is not confined to France; see LEIBHOLZ,
Strukturprobleme, op. cit., pp. 122-23. After the demise of the Fourth Republic,
an opinion poll found that most voters considered the frequent change of governments and the multiplicity of parties the main reasons for its failure. Far fewer
believed that its weakness resulted from parliament having too much or the executive too little power. On the last points there was, however, a definite division of
opinion according to party preferences, MRP voters siding with the right, radical
voters with the left. See *Sondages,* 20, No. 4 (1956), p. 6.

French society.[21] Proposals to submit a controversial bill to a referendum came usually from a small conservative minority and were considered contrary to the Constitution by both parliament and the experts on public law. During the decade preceding World War I, sometimes the extreme right or the extreme left put forward the idea of a consultative referendum on major political issues, such as Church-state relationships, the military service or the electoral system.[22] Other proposals, equally unsuccessful, suggested the direct consultation of the electorate on the local level, to counter the effects of overcentralization.

After the crisis of the 1930's, which had undermined the unquestioning faith in representative institutions, spokesmen for the authoritarian right had a somewhat wider audience when they called for the use of the referendum to limit the prerogatives of parliament.[23] R. Carré de Malberg, whose teachings and writings strongly influenced De Gaulle's foremost constitutional advisers, considered the possibility of balancing an extravagant parliamentary sovereignty by a legislative and constitutional referendum. Quite characteristically, he hoped that the referendum might facilitate the expression of the general will "destroyed by the party regime," and that it might have the effect which, in his opinion, "frequent dissolutions" of Parliament produced in Great Britain.[24]

Since the referendum had become a weapon in the anti-republican and Bonapartist arsenal, it came as a surprise when General de Gaulle proposed to consult the electorate on the constitutional problem in the spring of 1945, in a climate of democratic frenzy. It seems that at the time the President of the Provisional Government was impelled to organize the referendum by two seemingly contradictory suggestions. Respected mainstays of the Third Republic, such as Herriot, argued that the legitimacy of the regime of 1875 was unbroken, so that De Gaulle, sensitive as he was to all questions of legitimacy, wondered whether he had not overstepped the bounds of legality when he had discarded the earlier Constitution during the war.[25] On the other hand, a critic of the

[21] Cf. the excellent remarks by STANLEY HOFFMANN, Paradoxes of the French Political Community, in In Search . . . op. cit., p. 16.
[22] LÉON DUGUIT, Traité de Droit Constitutionnel. Paris, 1923, vol. 2, pp. 481 ff.
[23] See, e.g., ANDRÉ TARDIEU, L'Heure de la Décision. Paris, 1934.
[24] Considérations théoriques (sic!) sur la question de la combinaison du référendum avec le parlementarisme. Revue du Droit Public et de la Science Politique, 48 (1931), 225-44. Interestingly enough, the author refused at the end of his article to take a stand on the question as to whether or not the referendum should be adopted. Rigorous analyst of the representative system that he had been in the writings of a lifetime, Carré de Malberg was obviously aware of the incongruity of the referendum within a strictly representative system.
[25] For the events in 1945, see GORDON WRIGHT, The Reshaping of French Democ-

past such as René Capitant, steeped far more deeply in a Rousseauan
than in the representative tradition, insisted that the moment had come
to return to the people their constituent power and to utilize the referendum as a check on the constituent assembly.

The three referendums held in 1945 and 1946 gave back a modicum
of republican respectability to the direct consultation of the electorate.
The parties, whatever their misgivings, could not openly contest the
legality of the chosen procedure. The political atmosphere in which
the referendums were held seemed to clear them of plebiscitarian sus-
picions, although the rejection of the first constitutional draft had some
of the characteristics of an anti-Communist plebiscite. General de Gaulle
himself later interpreted the vote of October 1945 as a mark of confidence in his person and as a condemnation of "party omnipotence." [26]

The door to a modification of an exclusively representative regime
which the consultations of 1945 and 1946 had opened, was kept merely
ajar in the new Constitution. Its Art. 90 provided for a referendum on a
constitutional revision only if the proposed amendment had not obtained
certain qualified majorities in parliament.[27] When De Gaulle, in his
Bayeux speech, developed alternative proposals to the second constitutional draft, his suggestions remained entirely within the framework
of a representative regime and made no allusion to the institution of a
referendum.

But once the Gaullist RPF had entered the political arena as an opposition party, it called for the extensive use of the referendum on constitutional amendments, major legislation and international treaties. At
party conventions, M. Capitant linked his attacks upon the "illegitimacy"
of parties and upon the claims of a "sovereignty of elected representa-

---

racy. New York, 1948, pp. 78 ff, and for a fascinating, broad historical view of
De Gaulle's position, LÉON BLUM *in L'Oeuvre de Léon Blum.* Paris, 1958, vol. 6, esp.
pp. 31-34.
[26] See CHARLES DE GAULLE, *Mémoires de Guerre.* Paris, 1959, vol. III, *Le Salut,*
p. 270. RENÉ CAPITANT, *Cours de Principe du Droit Public.* Paris, 1952-53, pp. 235 ff.,
argues quite convincingly that the majority which voted "yes" in answer to both
questions asked in the referendum of October 1945 expressed twice its preference
for "popular sovereignty" over the representative regime: they rejected the ultra-
representative Constitution of 1875 and accepted the proposal to submit the text
of the Constituent Assembly to a referendum.
[27] The sole revision of the Constitution, in 1954, avoided the referendum procedure.
The discussions of the Constituent Assembly in 1946 reveal that art. 90 was the
outcome of intense political bargaining; see Assemblée Nationale Constituante,
élue le 2 juin 1946, *Scéances de la Commission de la Constitution.* Paris, 1946,
esp. pp. 750-51. Substantial parts of the provision were transferred unchanged to
the Constitution of the Fifth Republic, only to become the focus of the constitutional crisis of 1962.

tives" with demands that popular sovereignty be restored by institutions of direct democracy.[28]

Such, however, was not the temper of the Constitution of 1958.

II

After the May crisis, historical circumstances, General de Gaulle's estimate of his own role, and M. Debré's commitment to the constitutional thought of nineteenth century liberalism, combined to establish what was described as a "true" parliamentary system.[29] It is as yet impossible to ascertain what parts conviction, ideological rationalization, opportunism or improvisation have played in the writing of the Constitution. If the experiment inaugurated in 1958 has failed, this was due far less to a lack of internal coherence of the system than to faulty assumptions as to the causes of political instability and, consequently, as to effective remedies.

Once the separation of powers and the presidential system were rejected as "dangerous" and contrary to the "traditional republican image", the National Assembly remained the only legitimate representative of the sovereign people; the republican dogma of an undivided sovereignty was kept intact.[30] Yet, since it was still necessary to protect the nation from "the effects of its perpetual political offervescence" (De Gaulle at Bayeux), parliament would either have to be transformed or its role diminished. A regime which considered parties as agents of political disruption had little inclination to assist in the emergence of modern mass parties. It adopted the electoral system seemingly least

[28] See, e.g., RENÉ CAPITANT, *Le Changement de Régime* (Rassemblement du Peuple Français. Assises Nationales de Paris, 9-11 Novembre 1952), 11. While in opposition, the Gaullist movement was unable to reconcile various strands of constitutional thinking. This explains in part the astonishing fact that there existed no definite project of constitutional reform at the moment of De Gaulle's return to power.

[29] Historical antecedents and the circumstances of constitution-making in 1958 are excellently analyzed by STANLEY H. HOFFMANN, The French Constitution of 1958: I. The Final Draft and its Prospects. *The American Political Science Review*, 53, No. 2 (June 1959), 332-57; and by NICHOLAS WAHL, II. The Initial Draft and its Origins. *Ibid.*, pp. 358-82. Professor Capitant, whose constitutional thinking had been ignored temporarily, described the text as keeping within the liberal traditions of the last century. See his "Préface" to LÉON HAMON, *De Gaulle dans là République.* Paris, 1958, p. xviii.

[30] Debré's address before the Council of State is indispensable for an understanding of the concepts underlying the text of 1958; it was reprinted in *Revue Française de Science Politique*, 9, No. 1 (March 1959), 7-29. For an analysis of the neo-liberalism which M. Debré's thinking reflects, see CARL J. FRIEDRICH, The Political Thought of Neo-liberalism. *The American Political Science Review*, 49, No. 2 (June 1955), 509-25.

conducive to the formation of disciplined parties.[31] An exclusively atomistic representation was still unlikely to produce stable majorities. But it was expected that a strict limitation of parliamentary prerogatives, together with elaborate techniques enabling the executive to check every move of parliament, would produce the efficiency which the previous *régime d'assemblée* had lacked. Once the "political class" was shorn of its powers to harm, a dormant general will could easily be mobilized, and what Debré was wont to call the "depolitization of the national essential" became a possibility.[32] The parallel belief that a President freed from executive responsibilities and removed from politics would be able to define the general interest and to insure its triumph by "arbitration," placed the system clearly within those traditions of constitutionalism which regarded a monarch, crowned or republican, the ordained representative of all.[33] What M. Debré's intellectual ancestors had called the "royal dissolution" was regarded in 1958 also as the foremost guaranty of governmental stability. Although the threat of an appeal to the electorate was to discipline parliament, dissolution was still not considered a political decision but merely as a means by which the President sought the decision of the electorate. Nor did dissolution violate the representative principle, since the President entered only into a momentary dialogue with his people and presumably therefore could not turn the expression of universal suffrage into a plebiscite.

The widely criticized election of the President by a college of 80,000, drawn mostly from provincial notables, was hardly more anachronistic than the constitutional framework within which it was placed. Those who came to its defense praised the electoral college because it avoided both the designation of the President by parliament alone and the

---

[31] In his pre-1958 writings, M. Debré had criticized the single-member district system with run-offs as disastrous. The fact that General de Gaulle decided to adopt it might have been indicative of an early divergence of views between him and Debré on the role of parliament in the new republic. Also in regard to the electoral system Gaullist doctrine had wavered.

[32] See, e.g., his first speech before the National Assembly, *L'Année Politique* (quoted hereafter as *A.P.*) *1959*. Paris, 1960, pp. 603-11.

[33] See among others BENJAMIN CONSTANT, *Principes de politique, applicables à tous les gouvernements représentatifs et particulièrement à la constitution actuelle de la France*. Paris, 1815; Lucien-Anatole Prévost-Paradol, *La France Nouvelle*. Paris, 1868; CHARLES BENOIT, *La Réforme Parlementaire*. Paris 1902; and the monumental work by Carré de Malberg, *Contribution à la Théorie Générale de l'Etat*. Paris, 1920, 1922. In all of these writings, one discovers elements of what the Constitution of 1958 tried to enact. Particularly interesting is ROBERT REDSLOB, *Die Parlamentarische Regierung in ihrer wahren und in ihrer unechten Form*. Tübingen, 1918, because it has a marked influence on the Weimar Constitution. There are notable parallels between the Weimar Constitution and that of the Fifth Republic, especially after its structure was modified in 1962.

political contest into which popular elections could degenerate. The
college would function as the "filtered plebiscite" of which the conservative critics of the Third Republic had written. Here the intermediaries
would not be the distrusted parties but local representatives who owed
their functions to status, prestige or personal merit rather than to a
political label.[34] Since the President was to bestow unity on a society
rent by supposedly artifical discord, was it not fitting to see him elected
by a college which denied equal representation to modern and urbanized
France?

While the Algerian war lasted, the republican monarchy which the
constitution had striven to install, was transformed into a Roman
dictatorship. The notion of the President as an impartial arbitrator was
abandoned early. Gradually the sphere reserved for presidential action
was enlarged, that of governmental responsibility and parliamentary
control correspondingly reduced. Where in the Fourth Republic parliament had frequently invaded the sphere of governmental decision, now
the presidency reduced the cabinet in all important matters to an agent
of technical execution. None of the members of the government enjoyed
a prestige comparable to that of the President.[35] In major crises, Premier
Debré had to admit that legitimacy in the new state had not accrued
to institutions but only to one man. He insisted that, although the
government remained responsible to parliament, the President had assumed overwhelming responsibility for the country's destiny—on the
basis of the Constitution, sanctioned by the referendum of 1958.[36] This
was an admission that the Fifth Republic had failed to perform the task
which Debré had assigned to it: to recreate *un pouvoir* and to do so

---

[34] In 1958, M. Debré /exalted the "earthy" composition of the electoral college.
MARCEL PRÉLOT, *Institutions Politiques et Droit Constitutionnel*. Paris, 1961, p. 630,
pointed out that the critics of the electoral college failed to understand how much
it was in harmony with the spirit of a "senatorial" constitution. During the referendum campaign of 1962, De Gaulle destroyed such justifications rather cruelly
when he declared that he had known "from the beginning" that the President
would have to be elected by universal suffrage. See *A.P. 1962*. Paris, 1963, p. 678.
[35] In the spring of 1961, when 71% of the voters were "highly" or "rather" satisfied
with the President of the Republic, only 39% expressed similar feelings towards
the Debré government. At the same time, 84% were confident that De Gaulle
would be able to solve the Algerian problem. Among the voters of the MRP and
of the SFIO parties that were to oppose De Gaulle in 1962, such confidence was
expressed by 91% and 74% respectively. See *Sondages*, 23, No. 1 (1961), 13-15, 29.
[36] As examples see Premier Debré's declarations before the National Assembly,
Journal Officiel, Débats Parlementaries, Assemblée Nationale, October 14, 1959,
1734 ff. and February 3, 1960, 115 ff. President de Gaulle himself from the very
beginning had interpreted his role without much concern for the wording of the
Constitution: "*Guide* of France and chief of the Republican state, I shall exercise
the supreme power in all the breadth it now carries and according to the new spirit
to which I owe it." See *A.P. 1958*. Paris, 1959, p. 567.

on the foundations of a traditional if renovated parliamentary regime.

In the relation between parliament and the executive, the anticipated "dialogue, cooperation and equilibrium" never materialized.[37] The new rules which the Prime Minister enforced with didactic punctiliousness proved disconcerting to the players in the parliamentary game. The government, convinced that parties and interest groups were the main obstacle to administrative and political efficiency, provoked frequently the very attitudes which it criticized. Deputies and senators considered a situation in which the fountainhead of decision-making was outside their reach as a *provisorium* imposed by the war. But a *provisorium* offered little incentive for political realignments or for a reform of structures and ideologies. Cut off from channels of influence which in the past had insured the effective defense of constituency interests, the "political class" moved in an atmosphere of even greater general indifference than before.

In 1959, 47 per cent of the voters believed that parliament would be of little significance in the life of the nation and only 31 per cent disapproved of such a development. After the elections of 1962, 35 per cent expressed little or no confidence in their deputies or senators for the defense of their interests, while 60 per cent were willing to put their trust in their trade unions or other interest groups. At least subjectively, such diffidence towards parliamentary institutions was not regarded as an expression of political indifference: in December 1962, 32 per cent declared themselves as "highly" or "rather" interested in politics as against 9 per cent in October 1958; in 1962 only 30 per cent (as against 42 per cent in 1958) confessed to a total lack of political interest.[38] A careful if inconclusive study of the phenomenon of *dépolitisation* found that although important changes in political style and a notable decrease of ideological commitment had occurred, there was no general decline of political concern or of participation in public life.[39]

---

[37] Constitutional and political developments during the first years of the Fifth Republic have been described among others by NICHOLAS WAHL, The French Political System, in SAMUEL H. BEER et al., *Patterns of Government.* 2nd ed., New York, 1962, esp. pp. 397-466; by HENRY W. EHRMANN, Die Verfassungsentwicklung im Frankreich der Fünften Republik. *Jahrbuch des Öffentlichen Rechts der Gegenwart,* 10 (1961), 353-96; and with emphasis on the executive-parliament relationship, by JEAN-LUC PARODI, *Les Rapports entre le Législatif et l'Exécutif sous la Ve République.* Paris, 1962.

[38] See *Sondages,* 21, No. 2 (1959), 45; 22, No. 3 (1960), 67; No. 4 (1960), 49. Figures from more recent polls have been communicated to me by the *Institut Français d'Opinion Publique* to which I express my gratitude. Some of the data are now published in *Revue Française de Science Politique,* 13, No. 2, (June 1963), 428-32.

[39] See Association Française de Science Politique, *La Dépolitisation—Mythe ou Réalité?* Paris, 1962, esp. pp. 99-145.

The frequently incoherent behavior of the popularly elected deputies and their subservience to various lobbies merely confirmed longstanding convictions of De Gaulle and his advisers. But the unexpected and strenuous opposition which the government met in the Senate was taken as proof that all intermediaries, not just the traditional political parties, were impeding the defense of the common good. The *corps constitués*, the local notables who designated the Senators as well as the President of the Republic, had been held in esteem by both De Gaulle and Debré as an expression of the "true," *viz.* unorganized, nation. Hence they explicitly assigned the task of checking a possibly unruly National Assembly to the upper house, not to the electorate. When it turned out that the Senate had become a haven for the personnel of the Fourth Republic and that it had revived the political mores of the Third, this "revolt of the notables" added further to the estrangement between executive and parliament.

As soon as the end of the Algerian war was in sight, it became obvious that the attempt to reform political life by constitutional rules and parliamentary standing orders had been futile. For lack of cohesive majorities, the most disturbing features of the previous regime reappeared even in the parliament elected at the height of the Gaullist tide in 1958. Many deputies were convinced that the situation in which a charismatic leader was needed had come to an end. They were undisturbed by their own isolation from public opinion, since they believed that the return to normalcy would restore dignity and usefulness to the representative function. If they expressed such hopes during the censure debate of 1962 by asking for a "return to the Constitution of 1958," it was because many of them wished to make sure that the Fifth Republic without De Gaulle would not depart from representative traditions. Once the college of notables had elected a suitable personality to the Presidency of the Republic, the executive weapon of parliamentary dissolution could easily be blunted. As after 1877, an authentic republican regime could replace the republican monarchy.[40]

For the author of the Constitution of 1958, the lesson was unmistakable. M. Debré now declared that it was no longer acceptable to consider parliament as an expression of national sovereignty. "To have a government depend on parliament which is a mosaic of parties and factions, of social and regional claims, means not to want a govern-

---

[40] Shortly before the referendum of October 1962, 47% of the voters believed that, if given a chance, the traditional political parties would return to a regime "of the type of the Fourth Republic." A few months earlier, only 25% thought that the existing constitution could survive De Gaulle.

ment." [41] Such a change in the basic philosophy underlying the constitutional framework called for readjustments. In order to legitimize political decision-making by a President who was independent of parliament, the unity of the *volonté générale* had to be recreated, since it could no longer find its sole expression in parliamentary elections and an occasional referendum.[42]

III

Incessant discussions of institutional changes marked most of the first years of the Fifth Republic. The debate in which critics of the regime as well as its spokesmen participated, pertained primarily to the presidency whose character and functions had been so totally transformed by political realities.[43] The carefully spaced and frequently oracular statements of General de Gaulle were marked by an acknowledged pragmatism, obviously designed to keep all institutional arrangements flexible until they had been tested by experience. There was, however, little doubt that in De Gaulle's eyes those aspects of the constitutional experience had proven most viable which had long suited his own temper. Upon his return to liberated France he had been careful, or so he said later, to "accept for my power no other investiture than that which the voice of the masses would give me directly." [44] Since 1958, the presidential trips to the provinces have been turned into manifestations of undifferentiated popular acclaim for the leader who found in them psychological encouragement when the political climate in the capital had proven oppressive.[45]

[41] See his statement before the Central Committee of the UNR, *Le Monde*, October 14-15, 1962. A comparison with an earlier speech in which M. Debré proposed a much more limited constitutional reform affords an interesting insight into the development of his thinking. See *ibid.*, March 11, 1961. As before, he rejected a presidential regime which, in his opinion, results in "the complete effacement of parliament" (sic!).

[42] Carré de Malberg, from whose writings M. Debré drew so much inspiration, had frequently criticized a rigorous separation of power as violating the unitary postulates of democratic government: "a duality [of power] without a crowning unity cannot exist for long," *La Loi, expression de la volonté générale. Etude sur le concept de la loi dans la Constitution de 1875.* Paris, 1931, p. 201. In the name of that principle, the author praised the Weimar Constitution for having combined the parliamentary system with a popularly elected president.

[43] For an excellent survey see JEAN-LUC PARODI, Quatre années de Controverses Constitutionnelles. *Revue Française de Science Politique*, 12, No. 4 (December 1962), 845-76.

[44] See *Mémoires de Guerre*. Vol. II, *L'Unité*, Paris, 1956, p. 368; and vol. III, *op. cit.*, p. 14.

[45] For the role of presidential voyages, see PIERRE VIANSSON-PONTÉ, Les Gaullistes. *Rituel et Annuaire.* Paris, 1963, pp. 35 ff. The extra-parliamentary methods by which

The unforeseen development of the referendum did much to give the regime its increasingly plebiscitarian texture. De Gaulle's memoirs had lauded the consultation of the electorate by referendum.[46] To the contrary, in his early comments on the constitution, M. Debré's defense of the referendum had been halfhearted: he apparently realized that the new institution was structurally alien to the parliamentary system which he wished to erect. The language of Art. 11 dealing with the referendum seemed to assign to it a less than secondary place; most French and foreign commentators doubted that it would open opportunities for practices of direct democracy.[47] Already, however, the constitutional referendum of 1958 had proved far more useful to the regime than the subsequent national and local elections which, to a varying degree, attested the resilience of traditional political structures.

The greater his impatience with the representative features of the new regime, the more General de Gaulle became convinced that his was indeed the role of the *"guide"* in the sense in which Rousseau had used the term. The *Contrat Social* had assigned to the leader the task of formulating correctly the few questions which were to be put before the people in such a way that the general will may "see things as they are [and] sometimes as they ought to appear to it." [48] Accordingly, the two referendums held on January 8, 1961 and April 8, 1962, asked the sovereign to manifest the general will by approving De Gaulle's Algerian policies.

Both consultations bore the earmarks of plebiscites. Each time the voters were invited not to arbitrate between equally available solutions but to endorse an already established policy from which no return to

---

the leader in a plebiscitarian democracy wins confidence and commands faith have been classically described by MAX WEBER, in *Gesammelte Politische Schriften.* München, 1921, p. 212.

[46] *Op. cit.,* vol. III, p. 240. The same passage speaks somewhat cryptically of the "popular designation of the Presidency" without any reference to an electoral college. While this volume of De Gaulle's memoirs was written, presumably, before his return to power, it appeared in print after the new Constitution had already shown its weak points.

[47] See HOFFMANN, The French Constitution . . . , *op. cit.,* p. 343; CAPITANT, *Préface, op. cit.,* regretted (p. xix) the insignificant role of the referendum: "we are very far from popular sovereignty." Only C. J. FRIEDRICH, The New French Constitution in Political and Historical Perspective. *Harvard Law Review,* 72, No. 5 (March 1959), recognized, 811 ff., the potentialities for a plebiscitarian development. For an uncertain evaluation of the referendum see KARL LOEWENSTEIN, The Constitution of the Fifth Republic. A Preliminary Report. *Journal of Politics,* 21, No. 2 (May 1959), 216-17.

[48] See J. J. ROUSSEAU, *Du Contrat Social.* Amsterdam, 1762, bk. II, ch. VI; also the comments by TALMON, *op. cit.,* pp. 46-49 and, with reference to a similar statement by Saint-Just, p. 117.

the status quo ante was possible. An act of faith was demanded from the electorate in order to isolate the opposition and to discourage rebellion. At the same time, the providential leader declared that he could not continue in office without a massive vote of confidence, thus raising the spectre of unending war in Algeria and of political chaos at home. As in the case of other plebiscites, the bills that were submitted to the electorate wrapped several propositions into one. This not only maximized the chances for approval but tied the sanction of the past to an acceptance of the future, as when the referendum of April 1962 asked for a new grant of almost unlimited presidential powers.[49] In both campaigns De Gaulle stressed that he was appealing to each citizen as an individual, "above all intermediaries," that the referendum was a "personal affair" between himself and the nation. With such assertions as to the nature of what he called "the clearest, the frankest, and the most democratic of procedures," came the announcement that in the future direct appeals to the people would multiply and "mark profoundly the character and functioning of republican institutions." [50]

Party and group leaders realized fully that the deliberate shift to a plebiscitarian form of government violated the rules of the game as they had understood them when they approved the Constitution. Moreover, the referendum on the Evian accords also violated Art. 53 of the Constitution, and it was widely known that the Council of State had reported adversely on the legality of the new presidential powers.[51] Nonetheless, it was left to the discredited protagonists of the *"Algérie Française"* and to some tortured expressions of individual doubt, to voice protests against the unconstitutionality of the referendum. Outright violations of the constitutional text had occurred before and had been challenged only weakly so long as the war lasted. The absence of an effective constitutional jurisdiction and the rapid transformation

---

[49] See the characterization of plebiscites by KIRCHHEIMER, *op. cit.,* p. 403. For the text of the bills submitted to popular vote see *A.P. 1960.* Paris, 1961, pp. 663-64; and *ibid., 1962,* Paris 1963, p. 650.

[50] The authoritative and complete account of the referendums, reproducing all of De Gaulle's campaign speeches, is to be found in the volumes published by the French Association of Political Science, *Le Référendum de Septembre et les Elections de Novembre 1958.* Paris, 1961; *Le Référendum du 8 janvier 1961.* Paris, 1962; *Le Référendum du 8 avril 1962.* Paris, 1963. The referendum and the elections of October-November 1962 will be treated in similar fashion in a forthcoming volume. For the time being see the summary analysis by FRANÇOIS GOGUEL, Le Référendum du 28 octobre et les Elections des 18-25 Novembre 1962. *Revue Française de Science Politique,* 13, No. 2 (June 1963), 289-314.

[51] On the question of constitutionality, see PHILIP WILLIAMS and MARTIN HARRISON, The French Referendum of April 1962. *Parliamentary Affairs,* 15 (1962), 294-306. Very critical also, JACQUES FAUVET, Un Régime Nouveau. *Le Monde,* April 8/9, 1962.

of power relations between governmental organs, gave to the President, as if by default, the position of guardian of the Constitution. His discretionary interpretation of an often obscure text had met with little resistance in the past.[52] When the Evian agreement promised the end of the seven-years war, constitutional scruples carried little weight.[53]

The large majorities of "yes" votes in the first three referendums of the Fifth Republic (see Table I) were not the only indication that the electorate looked favorably on the referendum as an institution. In opinion polls held in 1961 and 1962, 57 per cent and 65 per cent, respectively, of the voters approved of being consulted directly on the Algerian policy. If in October 1962 the popularity of the "repeated use" of the referendum had decreased, more voters endorsed the idea of a direct consultation than there were to be "yes" votes (51 per cent as against 46 per cent of votes cast).[54]

A historical situation in which representative institutions were discredited and in which there seemed to be available no reasonable alternative, was undoubtedly the principal reason for the popular acceptance of a fairly novel and hitherto widely distrusted device. Normally, the regime held public opinion at arm's length and provided a "counter-pedagogy" rather than the political education for which Debré had called before 1958.[55] But the referendum, not unlike the provincial visitations of the President, provided a temporary mobilization of the citizenry. If the direct appeal is flattering, the commitment exacted is fleeting and maintains the distance between the leader and his followers which appears particularly desirable in a society characterized by a dislike of face-to-face relationships.[56]

In the 1961 referendum, only 18 per cent of the registered voters had

---

[52] For an (incomplete) list of constitutional violations, see MAURICE DUVERGER, *Institutions Politiques et Droit Constitutionnel*. Paris, 1962, pp. 491, 516 f, 591. FRANÇOIS GOGUEL, *Les Institutions Politiques Françaises*. Cours professé à l'Institut d'Etudes Politiques de l'Université de Paris 1961-1962, Fsc. I, pp. 174-76, concludes that the President is entitled to an authoritative interpretation of the Constitution, at least outside the rather narrow competences of the Constitutional Council. See also GEORGES BERLIA, Les Pouvoirs du Président de la République comme Guardien de la Constitution. *Revue du Droit Public et de la Science Politique,* 75 (1959), 565 ff.

[53] An (unpublished) *Mémoire* by the Institut d'Etudes Politiques in Paris concluded that the general press, and presumably its public, paid scant attention to questions of constitutionality.

[54] For the 1961 figures see *Sondages,* 23, No. 1 (1961), 15.

[55] Excellently on this point, GEORGES LAVAU, Réflexions sur le Régime politique de la France. *Revue Française de Science Politique,* 12, No. 4 (December 1962), 820; and Hoffmann, Paradoxes . . . , *op. cit.,* p. 101.

[56] For a penetrating analysis of French concepts of authority, see MICHEL CROZIER, La France, terre de commandement. *Esprit,* 25, No. 256 (December 1957), 193-211.

cast a "no" vote, although the parties and deputies that urged a negative vote had mustered a combined strength of almost 40 per cent on the first ballot of the preceding elections.[57] This goes far to explain why after Evian none of the traditional political formations recommended the outright rejection of the referendum. The acceptance of the peace settlement in 1962 by 90 per cent of the votes cast was easily interpreted by the government as a popular verdict rejecting "legalistic" wrangles. It was, nevertheless, short of satisfactory to De Gaulle. This time, the approval of peace in Algeria had submerged the vote of personal confidence for which the President had called once more. The deliberately authoritarian style of his addresses had failed to drive even the Communists off the bandwagon.

If elections were held before the regime was able to differentiate itself in some dramatice fashion from the traditional parties, there was danger that the parties might reestablish their identity and their habitual clientele. Therefore, De Gaulle refused to dissolve parliament and to call for the new elections which had been generally expected to mark the start of a new phase for a parliamentary regime at peace.

IV

The nearly successful attempt on the President's life, in August 1962, precipitated his decision to seek the long debated and often postponed constitutional revision by the shortcut of an unconstitutional referendum. Art. 89 of the Constitution had regulated the amending procedure by combining features of the two preceding republics. One of two alternative ways of revision provided for a referendum on an amendment which had been adopted in identical form by both houses of parliament. Hence the electorate had at best a veto, not the initiative in matters of constitutional revision.[58] Since Art. 89 gave Senate and National Assembly an equal voice, the upper house had more weight in the amending process than in ordinary legislation. In line with the general outlook of a "senatorial" constitution, the chamber of notables was to afford

---

[57] Since the right was divided, it is difficult to give an exact figure. There is little doubt that in 1961 an even larger number of Communist voters than in 1958 ignored party orders to vote "no." See Le Référendum du 8 janvier . . . , op. cit., p. 203, and passim.
[58] In 1958, Professor Capitant commented on the fact that the amending power was still reserved to parliament with the remark: "Napoleon would never have permitted such a provision" ("Préface," op. cit., p. xxiv). Should one conclude that when this power was divested from parliament, President de Gaulle had found his way to Bonapartism?

protection against an Assembly which might try to upset the reforms of 1958.

When four years later not parliament but the executive felt the need for constitutional revision, its project which proposed presidential elections by popular suffrage, was certain to meet parliamentary opposition. At least the upper house would not readily endorse the liquidation of an electoral college which, in composition and character, was very similar to its own. Nonetheless, it would not have been impossible to obtain from parliament the desired constitutional reform which was known to be popular.[59] The government could have made fullest use of the means at its disposal to discipline parliament, including dissolution and the threat of altering election procedures for the Senate by ordinary legislation.[60] However, to seek the reform in the constitutionally prescribed manner would have required considerable time and seemed therefore unsuitable at a moment when the President had to reckon with the imminent possibility of violent death. Since after his demise a return to the traditional forms of republican government appeared likely, General de Gaulle might well have feared that his inability to leave a lasting imprint on the country's political institutions would mar his historical image.

Nearly all experts on public law agreed that the government was violating the Constitution when instead of observing the amendment procedures it decided to submit a change in the method of presidential election (Arts. 6, 7) to a popular referendum, provided for in Art. 11.[61] The spokesman for the government retorted with a variety of arguments which, for all their nuances and internal contradictions, asserted that

[59] In November 1961, 52% of the voters favored the election of the President by popular suffrage, 17% were opposed, 31% were undecided or refused to answer; i.e., 3 out of every 4 voters who expressed an opinion approved of the reform when it was as yet unknown how it would be carried out.

[60] On such a possibility see GOGUEL, Les institutions . . . , op. cit., pp. 700-12. Writing in the spring of 1962, the same author declared that the plans to revise the constitution by way of Art. 11 existed only in the "creative imagination of certain journalists."

[61] For many others, see GEORGES BERLIA, Le Problème de la Constitutionalité du Référendum du 28 October 1962. Revue du Droit Public et de la Science Politique, 78 (1962), 936-46; GEORGES VEDEL (Dean of the Paris Law School), De Gaulle peut-il modifier la Constitution? France Observateur, May 31, 1962, and MAURICE DUVERGER, various articles in Le Monde, September 4, October 14 and 21/22, 1962. See also the remarkable (anonymous) article, Le Respect de la Constitution. Ibid., September 19, 1962; and GASTON MONNERVILLE (President of the Senate), La Constitution ne peut pas être modifié sans l'accord du Sénat. Ibid., March 2, 1962. For a full and well balanced account of all sides to the controversy, see J.-L. QUERMONNE, La révision constitutionnelle et la crise du régime. La Croix, October 11, 12, 13, 14, 15, 1962. The text of the proposed bill on the popular election of the President is to be found in A.P. 1962. Paris, 1963, pp. 676-77.

the *vox populi* was capable of vindicating any innovation. The popular verdict would have to resolve an alleged contradiction between Art. 11 and Art. 89.[62] A constitution which had reasserted (in its Art. 3) the historical claim that "national sovereignty belongs to the people" could be changed by the people at any time.

The referendum debate thus echoed memories of 1789, when a *pouvoir constituant originaire* (constituent power) had been recognized as overriding whatever formalities might have been prescribed for the exercise of the *pouvoir constituant institué* (amending power). When Sieyès had declared that the constituent power knew no constraints, he seemed for a moment to revert to the principles of the *Contrat Social*.[63] However, the constitution of 1791 stipulated that it was "in accordance with national interest" to exercise the "imprescriptible" right of constitutional revision only in ways prescribed by the constitution itself. Afterward, Napoleon was the first among many to manipulate with great ease the *pouvoir constituant originaire* incarnating the national will.[64] But modern French constitutional theory has always denounced the argument that the soverign people possessed an unalterable constituent power as "sophistry" and as an attempt to "legitimize" almost permanent revolutionary action.[65]

In 1962, the government's appeal was anything but a call for revolu-

[62] Such arguments turned partly around the wording of Art. 11 speaking about "any government bill dealing with the organization of public authorities." But even in what has been called "the worst written text" of French constitutional history, it is clear that constitutional revision is only dealt with in Art. 89. The sole constitutional expert to defend the government's stand was Professor Capitant; as examples of his numerous writings during the referendum campaign, see Réfutation du "Non." *Notre République,* October 4, 1962; Oui quant au fond. Oui quant à la forme. *Ibid.,* October 18, 1962; and "Oui" pour confirmer la souveraineté populaire. *La Croix,* October 24, 1962. Premier Pompidou offered the most complete juridical defense of the government's position during the censure debate, *op. cit.,* pp. 3220-24. During the same debate, the speakers for the opposition, among them many lawyers, demonstrated the unconstitutionality of the procedure.
[63] Of particular interest is Sieyès' "Reconnoissance et Exposition raisonnée . . ." of July 20, 1789, before the constitutional committee, published in *Procès-Verbal de l'Assemblée Nationale.* Paris, 1789, f. II, B3, pp. 20-21. Rousseau himself contradicted his statement that the people could never bind itself (*Du Contrat Social,* bk. I, ch. VII) by admitting in his *Considérations sur le Gouvernement de Pologne.* London, 1782, p. 94, that it may be useful to formalize the exercise of the amending power.
[64] Cf. HANNAH ARENDT, *On Revolution.* New York, 1963, p. 162.
[65] So ADHÉMAR ESMEIN, *Eléments du droit public.* 7th ed., Paris, 1921, vol. I, p. 570. Carré de Malberg's remarks in *Contribution . . . , op. cit.,* vol. 2, pp. 522 ff., read today like an explicit refutation of the main arguments used during the campaign by René Capitant (see above n. 62). For a detailed discussion of the development of the constituent and of the amending power in France see EGON ZWEIG, *Die Lehre vom Pouvoir Constituant.* Tübingen, 1909.

tionary action. Instead, the voters were admonished to insure the continuation of political stability and economic well-being by preventing the departure of De Gaulle, which would be inevitable if the referendum were to fail. In many ways, October 1962 reenacted the situation which had arisen when the enabling act of June 3, 1958 ignored the amending procedures of the preceding Constitution. Then as now, De Gaulle symbolized a merging of constituent and constituted power. The majority of voters who each time sanctioned the constitutional text proposed to them, did so not because of the inherent value of its provisions but because they wished to see De Gaulle in power. Hence they were prepared to grant him the instrumentalities of power for which he asked.[66]

Both the circumstances under which the first President of the Fifth Republic had been elected and the transformation of the Presidency which had taken place since then, reinforced the official argument that the electorate was asked merely to sanction a de facto development. In 1958, De Gaulle undoubtedly had been "the people's choice." To ensure governmental stability his successor would need the vastly broadened power which he would inherit. But then he too should be elected by the nation, not merely by 80,000 notables who might have a penchant to choose a man of minor stature. For such reasons, the question of the constitutionality of the plebiscite was still not a decisive factor for a majority of voters, even though at this time it had considerably more weight than during the preceding referendum. In an opinion poll taken in December 1962, 76 per cent declared that it would be "grave" if a government did not respect the Constitution "integrally." [67] Did the voters wish to ignore the fact that many of them had just endorsed the lastest of many instances in which a French Constitution had become the victim of French politics?

On the other hand, the fact that in the lastest referendum only 46 per cent of the registered voters cast an affirmative vote lent little

[66] In 1958, 40% of the voters declared that their vote was determined by the intrinsic value of the Constitution; for 41% the personality of General de Gaulle was decisive. See *Sondages,* 22, No. 4 (1960), 44. After the referendum of 1962, 62% of those who had voted "yes" said their decision was motivated by their desire to see De Gaulle remain in power, and 20% had wished to prevent a return to the Fourth Republic; only 20% were primarily interested in the election of the President by popular suffrage. It is interesting to compare these results with those of a year before, as reported above, n. 59.

[67] Ten per cent viewed a possible future violation without concern, 14% gave no answer. Of those who had voted "no" in the referendum, 47% gave as their foremost reason the unconstitutionality of the procedure; 23% had so voted because they wished De Gaulle to resign; 23% because they were opposed to popular presidential elections.

credibility to the claim that the plebiscite had been a manifestation of the sovereign's constituent powers.[68]

v

A comparison with the constitutional referendum of 1958 shows that four years later the "no" votes had almost doubled. They outweighed the "yes" votes in fourteen Departments, something that had not happened anywhere in the previous consultations. In sixty-four Departments less than 50 per cent of the registered voters sanctioned the proposed constitutional amendment; the number of abstentions remained high. There were some fairly significant variations, according to socio-economic status, sex, etc.[69] The real differences, however, were regional. East and North-West of the country supported the government strongly. While votes in the industrial North corresponded to the national average and Paris fell only slightly below it, opposition waxed strong South of the Loire River: here, since 1958 the "yes" votes had diminished by more than 30 per cent. In the Bas-Rhin, 88 per cent of the votes cast declared for De Gaulle, in the Aude only 41 per cent: Strasbourg and Carcassonne were seldom farther apart.

Contrary to 1958, the traditional divisions of the country reappeared in the geography of the 1962 referendum. With a few insignificant exceptions, all Departments with a majority of "no" votes had consistently voted "left" since the fall of the Second Empire (and sometimes before). All except five of the Departments (among them, it is true, the industrial regions of the North) with a higher than 60 per cent "yes" vote had been consistently in the conservative camp. Particularly suggestive of the permanence of electoral attitudes is a comparison with the results of the vote on the Constitution of the Fourth Republic in October

[68] M. Debré seemed to have justified the referendum merely by the "gravity of circumstances" (see the censure debate, *op. cit.*, p. 3217). For André Malraux, speaking as a member of the government between referendum and elections, things were yet simpler: the Constitution had to be in the service of France, not France in the service of the Constitution, *Pour la Ve République*, No. 2, November 1962. For a sincere and highly sensitive discussion of the political and constitutional reasons for voting either "yes" or "no," see GEORGES LAVAU and PAUL THIBAUD, Positions sur le Référendum. *Bulletin Intérieur* of the journal *Esprit*, October, 1962.

[69] Forty-four per cent of the workers, but 61% of the farmers, favored the "yes" (64% and 76% respectively of those expressing an opinion); only 17% of the women expected to vote "no" as against 33% of the men. In the larger cities the proportion of those voting "yes" was 1.5:1, in towns between 2,000 and 5,000 population almost 3:1. The opinion polls from which these data are drawn were held 5 days prior to the referendum and predicted the actual outcome with great accuracy.

TABLE I. FRENCH REFERENDUMS, 1946–1962

(Voting in Metropolitan France)

Date	Registered Voters (millions)	Abstentions		"Yes" Votes			"No" Votes		
		In Millions	% of Registered Voters	In Millions	% of Registered Voters	% of Actual Voters	In Millions	% of Registered Voters	% of Actual Voters
13 October 1946	25.07	7.89	31.2%	9.04	36.1%	53.6%	7.83	31.2%	46.4%
28 September 1958	26.61	4.01	15.06	17.67	66.41	79.25	4.62	17.38	20.74
8 January 1961	27.18	6.39	23.51	15.20	55.91	72.26	5.00	18.37	24.73
8 April 1962	26.99	6.59	24.41	17.51	64.86	90.70	1.79	6.65	9.29
28 October 1962	27.58	6.27	22.75	12.81	46.44	61.75	7.93	28.76	38.25

1946. (See Table I.) In both cases, constitutional texts were adopted by a minority of registered voters. In both situations, De Gaulle had appealed to the electorate to ignore the directives of M.R.P., Socialists and Communists: after 16 years, substantially the same proportion of the registered voters, about 46 per cent, followed him. With very few exceptions, the map of the "yes" votes in 1963 corresponds to that of the "no" in 1946, and in 1946, too, observers agreed that the division corresponded largely to that between the classical right and left.[70] After the liberation and again at the height of the Algerian crisis, it appeared for a time as if old political alignments were giving way, each time with De Gaulle as a pole of attraction. In both cases, a few years later—in 1947 as well as in 1962—the political landscape appeared to reemerge unscathed, with De Gaulle followed by a definite segment of public opinion.

If one considers the referendum of 1962, however, as a contest between the *"guide"* of the French people and the "old parties," the results take on a rather different significance. With hindsight, political leaders have expressed regret that by opposing the constitutional amendment and by censuring the government, parliament had accepted General de Gaulle's challenge.[71] Undoubtedly, the tactics of the opposition made it easier to ask the electorate for a direct expression of that confidence in De Gaulle which the deputies had just refused. The political parties had in fact vastly overrated the attractiveness of their own, if only covert, suggestion to return to the traditional forms of parliamentary government. Their patent inability to agree on a coherent constitutional alternative after the dissolution of the Assembly reinforced the public image that their coalition was held together only by opposition to a still popular leader.[72]

The parties that had voted the motion of censure and were campaigning for the "no" had represented on the first ballot of the 1958 elections

---

[70] The 46% "yes" votes in 1962 are compared here with the sum of the 31% "no" and of the 31% abstentions in 1946. About 15% of "structural" abstentionism must be subtracted in order to arrive at an estimate of those who heeded De Gaulle's warnings against the new Constitution. For a detailed analysis of earlier elections and of the October 1946 referendum, see FRANÇOIS GOGUEL, *Géographie des Elections Françaises de 1870 à 1951*. Paris, 1951, pp. 102-05, and Géographie du Référendum du 13 octobere et des Elections du 10 novembre 1946. *Esprit*, 15, No. 130 (February 1947), 237-64. For a comparison of the "no" votes in 1946 and the "yes" in 1962 see the maps, *ibid.*, p. 232, and *Le Monde*, October 30, 1962.

[71] See, e.g., the remarks by Edgar Faure (a radical-socialist senator) in his "Préface" to *A.P. 1962*. Paris, 1963, pp. vii-xvi. Prior to the crisis F. Goguel had demonstrated why a "trap" set by Arts. 11 and 49 of the Constitution made it most inadvisable to ever censure a government when the latter proposed a referendum; see *Les institutions . . . , op. cit.*, vol. II, p. 196.

[72] During the referendum campaign, the fluctuations in De Gaulle's popularity were no greater than in preceding years: at the lowest point 30% of the voters were dis-

not less than 82 per cent of the votes. Yet, in the referendum the actual "no" vote amounted to only 38 per cent, which demonstrated what the previous consultations could not show: when the political parties were pitted against the plebiscitarian appeal of the new regime, they were poorly followed by their habitual clientele. Opinion polls indicate that only Communist voters followed their party's directives fairly faithfully. One-third of the Socialist voters cast a "yes" vote and so did about one-half of the Radicals and Independents. About 85 per cent of the followers of the M.R.P. refused to sanction their party's opposition to De Gaulle and thus repeated their performance in the referendum of October 1946; they could not be induced to vote with the left.

The referendum drove a wedge between leadership and rank and file not only in all parties (with the exception of the Communists and the UNR), but also in numerous interest groups and traditional "spiritual families." During the censure debate, Paul Reynaud had claimed correctly that the regime had estranged the intellectual, political and working-class "elites" of the nation. But the results confirmed what had already become apparent during the campaign: these very elites as well as most of the local notables were losing much of their following. The prefectures had reported that about 73 per cent of all mayors were in favor of the "no"; an almost unanimous Senate reelected M. Monnerville as its President, just after he had accused the Prime Minister of "criminal abuse of authority." Yet, in general, the population of villages and small towns cast a more favorable vote than city dwellers. A number of political interest groups had to proclaim their neutrality in order not to be disavowed by their membership.[73]

Four presidential addresses and a carefully orchestrated official propaganda exploited governmental control of radio and television to the fullest, but did not abuse it.[74] The main theme was an ever increasing

---

contented and 60% satisfied with his conduct. At about the same time, 54% of the voters believed that the parties were opposing the constitutional amendment "to defend their own interests," only 25% believed that the parties were acting out of "a concern for the orderly functioning of the institutions."

[73] If the majority of "no" votes in the South can be attributed to anything else but stubborn republican traditions, it is assumed that the energetic campaign for the "no" which the major regional newspapers had conducted had a far greater impact than the views of notables and parties. For a general evaluation of the election results, see the analysis by PIERRE VIANSSON-PONTÉ and JACQUES FAUVET in Le Monde, October 30, 1962.

[74] While spokesmen for the opposition were given radio and television time, it is true that governmental influence was constantly felt in the presentation of news and features. The careful analysis by RENÉ RÉMOND and CLAUDE NEUSCHWANGER, Télévision et comportement politique. Revue Française de Science Politique, 13, No. 2 (June 1963), 325-47, concludes that television had far less influence on voting behavior than is sometimes assumed.

scorn for all "intermediaries" and for their attempt to prevent the leader and the nation from accomplishing great things *ensemble*. One of the rare outside supporters of the constitutional revision and of the main themes of the Gaullist campaign became the royal pretender. The Comte de Paris saw in an elective presidency the antidote to "caesarism and dictatorship." Fountainhead of all important decisions, the exalted office would happily blend the traditions of the Capetian kings and the expression of the general will.[75]

The constitutional referendum presented all those who had long advocated the transformation of the Fifth Republic into a presidential regime, with a painful dilemma. In their opinion, the failure of the 1958 constitution had provided additional evidence that history and sociology denied to France the prerequisites of a successful parliamentary system. Only a genuine presidential regime would put an end to the alternate confiscation of popular sovereignty by either an uncontrolled executive or by self-promotional deputies. Their proposals had won the sympathy not only of intellectuals and students, but also of the younger *militants* in a number of interest groups and civic organizations.[76] In 1962 they realized fully that the spirit in which de Gaulle presented the constitutional reform was alien to their own ideas and that a mere change in the mode of presidential elections might compromise rather than lead to a balanced presidential regime. Nevertheless, many of them hoped, as did numerous voters, that a victory of the referendum proposal would at least bar the return to the Fourth Republic.[77]

There was no doubt as to General de Gaulle's intentions: the referendum was to produce, by shock as it were and at the expense of parliament, that irreversible strengthening of executive power which

[75] See La Source du Pouvoir. *Bulletin Mensuel d'Information du Bureau Politique de Mgr. le Comte de Paris,* September 12, 1962. The role now attributed to the elected President had been described in earlier monarchist propaganda as that of the modern king; see HENRI, COMTE DE PARIS, *Faillite d'Un Régime. Essai sur le Gouvernement de Demain.* Paris, 1936, esp. pp. 99 ff, and 235-37. It is often considered significant that the present Constitution has omitted the customary republican reference declaring any member of families which have previously reigned over France ineligible for the presidency.
[76] The best statements of this position are to be found in Pour un vrai régime présidentiel. *Bulletin du Club Jean Moulin,* No. 31 (June-July 1962), and in MAURICE DUVERGER, *La VIᵉ République et le Régime Présidentiel.* Paris, 1961. For a critical comment see FRANÇOIS GOGUEL, Réflexions sur le Régime Présidentiel. *Revue Française de Science Politique,* 12, No. 2 (June 1962), 289 ff.
[77] As an example of this position see the "Lettre à l'Express," signed by a number of well-known liberal personalities in *L'Express,* October 18, 1962. In a similar vein and apparently typical of the numerous intellectuals who voted "yes" in spite of their criticism of form and content of the referendum, is MAURICE DUVERGER, Une pièce en deux actes. *Le Monde,* October 21/22, 1962.

the neo-liberal formula of 1958 had not secured. But the constitutional framework, which the amendment left essentially intact, had been built on the assumption of a balance between executive and parliament. If after the referendum the voters had elected a parliament out of harmony with the intentions of the "General-President," a sharpening of the political crisis might well have ensued.

VI

In his sole televised appearance between referendum and elections, De Gaulle castigated once more the "disastrous party regime" and admonished his listeners to vote in such a way at to "confirm" the choice they had made by voting "yes" in October. Prophecies that by thus descending into the arena of party politics the President was risking his popularity and, like MacMahon in 1877, inviting defeat, overlooked that the elections were transformed into another plebiscite. They gave to the French voter the satisfaction which, for lack of a valid party system, he has seldom enjoyed: that of designating his government directly (or expressing his opposition to it). In 1946, General de Gaulle's public image as a national hero served ill his attempt to play his own political game; in 1951, he had become too completely a party leader to command a large enough following. But to consider his identification with a party label in 1962 as perversion of the presidential office meant clinging to the unrealistic concept of a national arbiter.[78]

The pervasively plebiscitarian character of the elections makes it difficult to assess their significance for long-range political developments. Did they indicate an inclination of the voters to accept the logic of a presidential system and the simplification of the party system which it invites? Will it seem attractive to transfer permanently to the election of deputies some of the characteristics of a semi-direct democracy? Or were the results merely an aspect of the De Gaulle phenomenon, so that the modifications of the political mechanism will not outlast his departure from the scene? While an analysis of the election results shows that traditional attitudes are by no means uprooted, a restoration of the classical French forms of representative government has become less likely than it was before referendum and elections.

The two outstandingly novel phenomena of the elections, the high

[78] For this view on De Gaulle as a party and national leader, see RAYMOND ARON, La République Gaulliste continue. Prevues, No. 143 (January 1963), 3-11.

rate of abstentionism and the large share of votes captured by a single party, can both be understood as an outgrowth of a continuing charismatic situation. (See Table II.) The rate of abstention (31.3 per cent) was higher than in any national election since 1881, but there had been a proportionately greater decline of electoral participation between the referendum of 1958 and the subsequent elections. In both situations, many voters seem to have felt that the elections were a superfluous repeat performance of the preceding plebiscite. Yet it is true that the number of non-voters exceeded "structural" abstentionism by about 4.5 millions. Their future return to the ballot boxes could modify the party picture considerably.

The UNR rode to unprecedented success (31.9 per cent of the votes in the first and 40.5 per cent in the second ballot) unaided by an electoral system that was, rather, expressly designed to act as a breakwater against the tides of public opinion. Neither its lack of local implantation nor the virtual absence of any political program prevented the triumph of its candidates, among them many *homines novi,* and the defeat of experienced politicians. Its propaganda was national in character, even though decentralized to fit the anachronistic forms imposed by the electoral system. It capitalized on the popularity of De Gaulle as much as on the need to ensure the smooth working of the institutions by sending faithful Gaullists to parliament.[79] If a desire for continuing political stability motivated many voters, the influence of economic well-being should not be overrated: in the North and East prosperity and success for the UNR coincided; but the party also showed great strength in regions of little productivity, while the Communists increased their vote in some of the richest and most modernized regions of the country. At least subjectively, the voters saw little connection between their economic status and their attitudes towards the regime.[80]

The geographic distribution of the votes suggests again that tradition

[79] The UNR conducted its campaign with (nationally used) posters, such as: "You have said 'yes' to De Gaulle. Vote for *this* candidate." "Defend your 'Yes': UNR." "So that De Gaulle may continue, insure the victory of those who support him." etc. After the elections, 56% of all voters believed that the main reason for the victory of the UNR had been a desire to vote for De Gaulle; 28% thought that the most important motive had been the wish to defeat the parties of the Fourth Republic.

[80] In December 1962, at a time when 64% expressed satisfaction with General de Gaulle's policies, only 20% thought that they were better off than before 1958; 28% considered that their situation had worsened. These statements are all the more subjective since they reflect the traditional unwillingness, especially of farmers, to admit an improvement in one's economic situation.

TABLE II. FIRST BALLOT OF FRENCH ELECTIONS, 1956–1962

(Voting in Metropolitan France)

	1956		1958		1962	
Registered Votes, in millions	26.77		27.24		27.53	
Abstentions, in millions	4.63		6.24		8.60	
in %	17.3%		22.9%		31.3%	
Parties	Votes (millions)	% of Votes cast	Votes (millions)	% of Votes cast	Votes (millions)	% of Votes cast
Communists	5.53	25.74%	3.88	18.90%	3.99	21.78%
Socialists	3.18	14.80	3.17	15.50	2.31	12.65
Misc. Left Wing	0.45	2.09	0.35	1.04	0.45	2.45
Radicals and Allied	2.88	13.38	1.71	8.30	1.38	7.56
Gaullists (UNR)	0.95	4.42	3.60	17.60	5.85	31.90
MRP	2.37	11.05	2.41	11.15	1.63	8.92
Conservatives	3.09	14.36	4.74	22.92	2.54	13.87
Extreme Right	2.86	13.33	0.67	3.03	0.16	0.87

and temperament rather than contentment or dissatisfaction were decisive factors. The strong correlation between "yes" votes in the referendum and success for the UNR indicates that the party has fallen heir to traditionally conservative strongholds.[81] The UNR's gain of 14.4 per cent in the first ballot over its vote in 1958 corresponds exactly to the combined percentage losses of the right and of the MRP—exceeding them, it is true, in absolute figures by about 300,000. In many constituencies, and those of Paris among them, the UNR unseated the right and the MRP from long-held bastions. The disintegration, which had started when the voters of the now defeated parties refused to cast the "no" vote urged upon them, had, therefore, proceeded in two stages.[82]

Although the UNR in the elections captured an amalgamate of conservative votes, its style and vocabulary as well as the perspective of its leadership place it far closer to Bonapartism than to other historical strands of the French right.[83] Today's Gaullism shares with Bonapartism (and Boulangism) a professed preference for the support of the masses rather than the elites, and for an expression of national sovereignty by plebiscites rather than elections. There is a similar pragmatism accompanied by contempt for "abstract ideas" and systembuilders, an equal distrust of "intermediaries," but also little inclination to establish itself as a totalitarian party.[84]

If one compares the share of the votes which Communists, Socialists and Radicals obtained in the last two elections (see Table II), the combined strength of the left appears equally unchanged and altogether un-

[81] Exceptions were mainly due to the fact that for a variety of reasons about 20 electoral districts had no Gaullist candidate. For an overall evaluation of the election results see JACQUES FAUVET, Le Gaullisme et l'Opposition. Le Monde, December 11, 1962.

[82] The otherwise convincing article by ANDRÉ PHILIP, The Crisis of Democracy in France. Social Research, 30, No. 1 (Spring 1963), 34-35, lumps the MRP votes with those cast for Socialists and Radicals, in order to prove that on the first ballot the non-Communist left outnumbered the UNR votes. His conclusion that this opens hopeful perspectives for a non-Gaullist candidate at the next elections is all the more dubious since the referendums of 1946 and of 1962, and to an extent also the last elections, have shown that the MRP meets disaster whenever it tries to oppose a position identified with De Gaulle or too closely allied with the left.

[83] In January 1963, 46% of the voting population considered the UNR as a party of the right, 28% as one of the center. For a brilliant comparison between Bonapartism and Gaullism, see RENÉ RÉMOND, L'Enigme de l'UNR. Esprit, 31, No. 314 (February 1963), 307-319 ff.

[84] Particularly suggestive of the similarities is a comparison of present-day Gaullist propaganda with the proclamation by the Prince-President Louis-Napoleon of January 14, 1854, reproduced in MAURICE DUVERGER, Constitutions et Documents Politiques. Paris, 1960, pp. 101-04. There is little evidence to substantiate the claim made by M. Chalandon (former Secretary General of the UNR) that the voters had found in "Gaullism . . . The attractiveness of an ideology." See Le Monde, January 23, 1963.

affected by the mutations of political life in the Fifth Republic. But these parties had suffered substantial losses in the 1958 elections, when their votes had declined from the 56 per cent of the vote which they had mustered in 1956 to 44.5 per cent, and from 11 million votes to 9.2 millions (shrinking further to 8.1 millions in 1962). Aside from such overall weakening since 1956, the Left showed its greatest strength in the latest elections wherever the "no" votes in the referendum had been the most massive, drawing therefore, exactly like the UNR, on old-established traditions. Electoral tactics, and especially the discipline of Communist voters in following party directives on the second ballot, insured a gain of 60 (and a total of 148) seats for the three parties. But momentary electoral alliances between heterogeneous formations gave little promise of a cohesive opposition in the new National Assembly where the UNR and its affiliates occupy 233 out of a total of 482 seats and can count on the support of an additional 32 Republican Independents.

VII

President de Gaulle has greeted the results of referendum and elections as the "solemn confirmation" of the institutions of the Fifth Republic.[85] Such confirmation as may have taken place has not put an end to extreme constitutional flexibility. It is therefore unlikely that the constitutional crisis which has now lasted for thirty years has come to an end. Instead a precedent has been set which allows the executive to seek plebiscitarian approval for any constitutional revision it wishes to enact. In a juridically dubious but politically almost unavoidable decision, the Constitutional Council has declared that the popular verdict will never be subject to any review or control.[86] Those who wish the transformation of De Gaulle's Republic into a presidential regime know that there are neither in nor out of parliament forces strong enough to alter the present constitutional arrangements, which are fundamentally autocratic even though they are being used to dispense liberal policies.

For the time being it remains dubious whether the very question of General de Gaulle's immediate succession can be settled by means other

---

[85] In his address to the newly elected Assembly; see *A.P. 1962.* Paris, 1963, p. 693.
[86] For the text of the terse decision by the Constitutional Council and the request to the Council by M. Monnerville to declare unconstitutional the law which had been adopted by referendum, see *ibid.,* pp. 687 f.

than a "political testament." The newly devised write-in primaries, which entrust the selection of the candidates for the Presidency to the suspected "intermediaries" and yet shroud them in anonymity, will hardly meet the test of practicability. They are probably little else than another *provisorium*.[87]

The loss of faith in the traditional representative institutions has led to an as yet tentative but fairly widespread acceptance of plebiscitarian practices, administered by a popular hero figure. The self-liquidation of a plebiscitarian democracy and its conversion into a caesaristic dictatorship is always a historical possibility.[88] In present-day France such a development would be a surprise, although it is well to remember De Tocqueville's dictum, that the political reactions of Frenchmen are sometimes as surprising to them as they are to foreigners.

The problem of bestowing legitimacy upon republican institutions remains. If one wishes to avoid the alienation of the citizenry by an ultra-representative regime no less than the authoritarian concentration of uncontrolled power, a transformation of the party system seems to be a necessity. Elections will not always remain what they became in 1962: a confession of faith and the confirmation of the leadership by acclamation. Yet, the electorate might no longer be satisfied with the limited role which was reserved to it in the previous republics. In a system in which executive leadership owes its position to popular approval, the mediation of parties and other groups is necessary to insure an adherence to the rule of law.

There is fairly wide agreement on the need for a renovation of the French party system.[89] Whether the outcome of the constitutional crisis of 1962 will further or hinder such a renovation cannot be determined as yet. After the elections, a greater number of voters than before expressed their belief in the importance of political parties; an equally large majority was favorable to a regrouping of existing parties into two or three

[87] For the text of the organic law which was adopted in the referendum, but does not form part of the Constitution, see *ibid.*, p. 677. Lists of candidates for the first ballot of presidential elections are to be established by the Constitutional Council on the basis of nominations by "at least a hundred citizens, members of parliament, of the Economic and Social Council, elected members of the departmental councils or mayors." However, the names of those making nominations are to be kept secret.
[88] Relevant to this point is Max Weber's discussion of the "transformation" of the charisma in *Wirtschaft und Gesellschaft*. Tübingen, 1922, pp. 758 ff.; see also FRAENKEL, *op. cit.*, esp. pp. 10-11.
[89] See for many others, CLUB JEAN MOULIN, *L'Etat et le Citoyen*. Paris, 1961, esp. pp. 164-81; GOGUEL, *In Search . . .* , *op. cit.*, pp. 401 f; LAVAU, *op. cit.*, pp. 837 ff. For the point of view of a leading member of the UNR, see *Albin Chalandon, Comment peut-on sauver la démocratie?* La Nef, No. 6 (April-June 1961), 74-80.

formations.[90] In characteristic fashion, President De Gaulle moderated his anti-parliamentarian stance as soon as the government was assured of majority support in parliament and rejected specifically the idea of a *parti unique*. Professor Capitant, who had lent to the referendum campaign its jacobin fervor, received no encouragement from the Elysée when, as the new chairman of the Assembly Committee on Legislation, he played the Robespierre and denounced the opposition as "enemies of the people." [91]

On the other hand, it is by no means certain that the UNR will be permitted to develop a national organization. Its continuing proximity to executive power could solidify its ranks and provide it with some meaningful idea for future action. At present it is not the discipline of its elected members that makes the UNR unsuitable for the role of a modern mass party, but the inability of its leadership (not to speak of a practically non-existent rank and file) to participate effectively in decision-making. This leaves doubts as to whether after De Gaulle's disappearance the new-styled pragmatism of the UNR will become the model for other parties, or whether it will evolve into the opportunism which led to the dissolution of the earlier RPF.

The future of the parties which are presently in opposition is similarly unfathomable. Their relationship to the Communists is not less problematic than their own realignment and reorientation. The discredit into which political parties have fallen has given rise to confused expectations that interest groups and other *"forces vives"* could be transformed quasi-automatically into political forces capable of organizing a representative democracy.[92]

In several important aspects the situation bears resemblance to that of Imperial Germany under Bismarck's rule. To preserve parties and parliament as strong and viable institutions had been all that seemed politically possible during the 1870's and 1880's. It was hoped that they could function effectively once the outstanding leader had been re-

---

[90] Seventy per cent and 64%, respectively, believed that parties had an important role to play in the representation of citizens and in controlling parliament; 17% and 21% considered the parties to be almost useless for such functions. Sixty-six per cent were highly, or rather, favorable to a two- or three-party system. Further questioning revealed great uncertainty about the forms and possibilities of any regrouping of existing parties.

[91] See *Le Monde,* February 15, 1963.

[92] For an analysis and criticism of such opinions see HENRY W. EHRMANN, Bureaucracy and Interest Groups in the Decision-Making Process of the Fifth Republic, in *Festschrift für Ernst Fraenkel.* Berlin, 1963, esp. pp. 74-77. In present-day terminology the opposite to the *"forces vives"* are the *"forces politiques."*

placed by politicians of more ordinary ability. Yet, as Max Weber concluded when he commented later on these developments, Bismarck's legacy was a level of political education for lower than it had been twenty years before, a powerless parliament and an emaciation of political will due to blind and prolonged confidence in an infallible *guide*.[93]

[93] See MAX WEBER, Parlament und Regierung im Neugeordneten Deutschland, in . . . *Schriften, op. cit.,* pp. 134-39.

～ 7 ～

The Immobility of the French Communist Party

Roy C. Macridis

EDITORIAL NOTE: *In all elections between 1945 to 1958, the French Communist Party has averaged about 25 per cent of the vote. After a slump in 1958 the party seems again to be gaining strength. An expression of protest, a symbol of an overriding ideological commitment that embodies many of the features of French left-wing ideology, the party's stability and strength continue to surprise all observers. Ideology, one is inclined to argue, may not be dead after all. Yet the French Communist Party has grown and become entrenched within the political system—both the Fourth and Fifth Republics—by qualifying its ideological stand in favor of electoral expediency. This article was written in 1958 but despite developments in the last decade its main thesis remains, I think, valid. For an overall study see Jacques Fauvet,* Histoire du Parti Communiste, *2 volumes, Paris, 1965-1966.*

THE growing Soviet military strength and the apparent successes of Soviet diplomacy have not led to a strengthening of the discipline and the ideological commitment of the Communist parties within or without the Soviet power orbit. The British Communist Party, the Italian Communist Party, the Communist parties in Poland and Hungary were confronted with many internal dissensions which raised issues that disturbed Communist orthodoxy and led to an ideological soul-searching that was bound to undermine the conformity of world Communism and endanger Soviet political control. For in a number of instances, the soul-searching among many Communists went even beyond the already explosive implications of national Communism. It questioned Communism itself as a philosophy of life and Communist party discipline, organization and action as a medium for its realization. Criticisms in which "old" ideas such as the rights of man, the freedom to criticize and the moral autonomy of the individual were resurrected brought about a crisis in the organization of many Communist parties, causing widespread defections, resignations and apathy and leading to the growth of "oppositional" factions.[1]

The only Communist party that may be considered to be an exception to this generalization is the French Communist Party. Neither the leadership nor the organization of the party appear to have been affected. In its attitude, the party continues to follow the same line of *sovietization à outrance*. There is no better illustration of this than the indignation of its leaders with the Khrushchev report and their consistent efforts to rehabilitate Stalin at the very moment when the adoration surrounding him had given place to sharp criticism. The theme, that the Soviet Union is always right, and the slogan, that the leadership of the party must be obeyed (for without such obedience the party would degenerate into many warring factions and lose its cohesiveness and strength), continue to characterize the attitude of the French Communist Party. In a country where individualism and intellectualism are, according to an astute observer,[2] two of the most significant characteristics of its political life, the discipline and the cohesion of the party and its ideological immobility constitute, against the background of fairly widespread dissatisfaction and criticism in the Communist world, an anomaly that calls for some explanation.

I. STRENGTH AND WEAKNESS OF THE FRENCH COMMUNIST PARTY: A BALANCE SHEET

The two events that caused widespread consternation among the Communist leaders of the world—the publication in June, 1956, of Khrushchev's report to the Twentieth Congress of the Communist Party of the Soviet Union held on February 25, and the Soviet military intervention in Hungary in October-November, 1956—found the leadership of the French Communist Party well entrenched. In the post-war years it

[1] For the writings of the Polish and the Hungarian Communists, see La Revolte de la Hongrie. *Les Temps Modernes* (January 1957), and *"Le Socialisme Polonais"* (February-March 1957); also PAUL ZINNER, ed., *National Communism and Popular Revolt in Eastern Europe, A Selection of Documents of Events in Poland and Hungary February 1-November 1956*. New York, 1956.
[2] See JACQUES FAUVET's recent study, *La France Dechirée*. Paris, 1957.

had met successfully the challenge of Titoism, the criticisms against Thorez and Duclos, and the veiled attacks against Madame Vermeersch, Thorez's wife. Whatever the significance and the strength of the criticism, it was dealt with in typical Stalinist fashion. Marty, Tillon Lecoeur, and Pierre Hervé were expelled from the party.[3] Tillon remained silent and was reinstated in the beginning of 1957. Marty died when the Soviet troops were again in control of Budapest, after giving his own interpretation of what had happened in the French Communist Party by blaming the "Thorez clique" for everything and by expressing his solidarity with the Hungarian people. Pierre Hervé and Lecoeur have continued their political activity[4] by organizing splinter left-wing parties. They criticize, in the name of Marxism and Leninism, Thorez's tight control of the party, its internal bureaucratization and its blind submission to the ever-changing Soviet directives. But there is no substantial evidence to indicate that their criticisms have undermined the strength of the leadership among the rank and file or the strength of the party among the voters;[5] nor is there proof enough to substantiate Lecoeur's allegations of widespread defection from the ranks of the party among the militants.[6]

However, since a number of weaknesses in the party have been pointed out, it might be appropriate to review their significance. The membership of the party has fallen from a peak of 906,727 (perhaps over a million) members in 1946 to 430,603.[7] There is no doubt that this is a serious indication of its weakness, and there is corroborative evidence to indicate that it is of concern to the Communist party leaders. On the other hand, it should be pointed out that there has been an even more widespread reduction in the membership of all political parties in France, and that the Socialist and the MRP lost relatively *more* members than the Communists, to say nothing of the chaos that prevails today among the Radicals.

[3] See JEAN TOUCHARD, De l'Affaire Lecoeur à l'affaire Hervé. *Revue Française de Science Politique,* VI (April-June 1956), 389-98, and the bibliography cited.
[4] For their respective attitudes, see LOUIS BODIN and JEAN TOUCHARD, L'Election Partielle de la 1ière circomscription de la Seine in *Revue Française de Science Politique,* VII (April-June 1957), 271-512. Hervé campaigned with the support of Lecoeur for "democracy and national communism." In the second ballot Hervé urged his supporters to vote for the Socialist candidate.
[5] Early in 1957 two clandestine papers circulated among the members of the party— the *Etincelle* and the *Tribune des Debats.* Within six months only one survived and at the time of this writing there is none.
[6] *L'Autocritique Attendue.* Paris, 1955.
[7] For the figures, compare ALAIN BRAYANCE, *L'Anatomie du Party Communist Français.* Paris, 1954, pp. 205-11, with JACQUES FAUVET, *op. cit.* For the circulation of the Communist press, see BRAYANCE, pp. 173-89 and J. FAUVET, p. 133.

Three more considerations should be mentioned: first, when the figure of 906,727 was released it was thought to be a propaganda figure; secondly, even if the figure was accurate, it reflected a peak in a drive for membership in the years immediately after the war. In the days of the post-war national euphoria when De Gaulle was proclaimed the *premier résistant,* when Thorez extended his hand to the Catholics, when *tripartisme* blurred the distinctions that came out into the open with their usual sharpness in 1947, and finally when the record of the resistance had confused patriotism and Communism, the door of the party was opened to practically everyone. But March, 1947 was the dividing point, not only in French foreign policy but also in French domestic policy.[8] The subsequent developments were something of a test, not only to the many people who had joined the party, but also to the party itself. Many dropped out and the overall figure was reduced to perhaps less than forty per cent of the peak. Third, the usual turnover of the party membership is 30,000 members. This indicates that since 1947, approximately 30,000 *new* members have entered the party every year, a record unexcelled by any other party except perhaps by the Radicals in the year of Mendès-France's leadership. Such a record also indicates that, despite the overall decline in total membership, the sources of recruitment remain remarkably stable.

It is also pointed out that the total circulation of the Communist press and periodicals has declined sharply. From a total of 2,700,000 in 1946 it has declined to about 800,000. Again, these figures must be interpreted with caution. The figure of 2,700,000 is excessive. But even if correct, it represents the same post-war trend of *tripartisme* in which the Communist Party was a government party. Furthermore, this reduction should be evaluated in the context of an overall decline in the circulation of the political press in France. The Socialist Party has no publications that even approach the character of mass media of communication. The MRP had to discontinue its official organ *L'Aube* and now must rely upon a number of Catholic newspapers which are not directly affiliated with the party. Excepting the Socialist Party, there are no parties that have their *own* daily newspapers. And even the great dailies like *Figaro* and *Le Monde,* which are not directly affiliated with a party, have a circulation that is smaller than that of *L'Humanité.*[9] Despite the decline of the circulation of the Communist publications, the Com-

---

[8] See the excellent article of J. B. DUROSELLE, The Turning Point of French Politics—1947. *The Review of Politics,* XIII (July 1951), 302-28.
[9] The daily newspaper with the highest circulation is the *Paris-Soir* which is apolitical and aims to entertain and to inform rather than to propagate a party point of view.

munist Party press continues to reach a relatively greater number of readers than any other political party organ and perhaps more than all the newspapers of the other political parties put together.

It is usually pointed out that the CP's control over organized labor has declined. The reformist *Force-Ouvrière* broke away from the Communist-controlled CGT, and the CFTC has been gaining in strength. Still the CGT comprises a larger section of organized labor (some four millions).[10] Despite the excessive use of the political strike (notably in 1947-48, 1950 and 1952) and the efforts made by the other parties to undermine the control of the Communist party over organized labor, Communist leadership continues to have a strong weapon in its hands. The roles and the relative strengths of Communists and Socialists with regard to organized labor in the post-war period appear to have been irrevocably reversed. The CP controls at least two thirds of organized labor today.

The Communist Party not only emerged from the post-war period as the party with the largest number of voters, but has consistently maintained this position. What is more, with the exception of 1951, it appears to improve in absolute terms its position in every election. In 1945, it polled 5,005,336 out of 19,189,799 votes cast; in 1946, the respective figures were 5,119,111 and 19,880,741; in the first election for the National Assembly in 1946, the figures were 5,489,288 and 19,203,070. In 1951, it polled 4,910,547 out of 19,129,064; and in the last election of 1956, it polled 5,514,403 out of 21,298,934.[11] A number of explanations have been given to account for the voting strength of the Communists, the most widely accepted being the one that considers the Communist vote as a protest vote which therefore absolves the voters of a direct attachment to the Communist revolutionary policy. This explanation obscures the real issue by considering the Communist Party of France a revolutionary party. It is far more important to note that the Communist Party has not only succeeded in becoming the symbol of protest, but has been able for a whole decade to maintain this symbolism among the voters.

With a strong organization, with a controlling position in organized labor, with a large press and, what is perhaps even more striking, with

[10] For an excellent account of the post-Liberation trade union movement, see CAL LORWIN, *The French Labor Movement*. Cambridge, Mass., 1954, esp. pp. 99-142. Commenting on the character of the political strike, the author rightly points out: ". . . The same apathy among workers which made even communists reluctant to strike prevented any real revolt or breakaway movement in the CGT or the Communist Party" (p. 142).
[11] MAURICE DUVERGER, *Constitutions et Documents Politiques*. Paris, 1957, pp. 238-39.

the largest and most loyal number of voters, the CP was well prepared to meet the crisis caused by the Khrushchev report and the military intervention in Hungary. What is the record?

II. KHRUSHCHEV'S SPEECH AND BUDAPEST

With the exception of one Communist Deputy, Aimé Cesaire, who was returned from Martinique and who is an intellectual, not a single member of the Communist parliamentary group has resigned in the past three years. Not a single member of the editorial board of *L'Humanité* has voiced criticism; not a single member of the Central Committee has expressed factional points of view; not a single member of the section and the departmental committees has defected; no overt opposition among the militants and the members has been reported. *L'Humanité* claimed in a number of instances in November and December, 1956, an increase in the membership of the Party.

In the elections of November 2, 1956, the Party's vote increased in absolute terms *though it fell* in relation to the total number of votes cast by less than one per cent. Through 1956, the Communist party improved its voting strength in all cantonal and municipal elections by two to four per cent with one exception where it showed a decline of 0.2 per cent.[12] In a number of local municipal elections held since June 30, 1956, the party's votes have shown a small increase. In six cantonal elections held between October 15 and October 30, 1956 (that is, after the Khrushchev Report and the events in Poland and during the Hungarian uprising), the Communists retained and even improved their positions. In Tours they received 38 per cent of the vote as compared to 31.6 per cent in the corresponding elections in 1955; in Etampes, they lost only 3 per cent; in Tarn and in Mantes the party gained.

What is more important, however, is the record of parliamentary by-elections held since the Hungarian uprising when the issue of Communism and Soviet intervention was fully exploited by the non-Communist candidates. In an important by-election held in January, 1957, in the first electoral district of Paris the Communist Party received 72,374 ballots as compared to 72,525 it received in a by-election held in the same district in 1952![13] In a second by-election held in Ain

[12] *L'Année Politique, 1956*. Paris, 1957, Statistiques Électorales, pp. 537-40.

[13] LOUIS BODIN and J. TOUCHARD, *op. cit.* The authors indicate, however, that there was a relative weakening of the Communist Party vote by comparison to the 1956 national elections. In the latter the party received 26.3% of the ballots cast while in the by-election of January 1957, it received 23.2%.

in March, 1957, the Communist Party which had polled 35,954 ballots in the general election of 1956 and 24.6 per cent of the ballots cast polled 29,501 votes *and 26.3 per cent of the ballots cast,* an increase of 1.7 per cent. Finally, a by-election held in Lyon to replace Edouard Herriot in May-June, 1957 indicated the same stability in the Communist vote. In two more by-elections in 1958, held in Nievre and in the third electoral district of the Department of Nord, in March 16 and March 23 respectively, the Communists made impressive gains. In Nievre they polled 38.6 per cent of votes as compared to 29.3 per cent in the general election of January 2, 1956, and in the Nord they polled 43.4 per cent as compared with 37.4 per cent. So in the face of massive opposition against the Communists because of the Hungarian events, and in a climate of nationalism provoked by the Suez adventure and intensified by the war in Algeria, the record indicates a remarkable stability of the Communist Party voting strength.

The balance sheet, however, might indicate one possible area of growing weakness: the inability of the Communist leaders to use the CGT as an instrument of political propaganda and the corresponding decline of the effectiveness of the political strike. In the last few years, non-economic protest strikes have generally failed. But more significantly, during the Hungarian uprising the Communist leadership was unable to get a resolution (in favor of Soviet intervention) passed in the Bureau of the Confederation. On the contrary, a communiqué issued on November 14, 1956 stated . . .

> The duty of each one of us is to make sure of the unity of the CGT in which there should be no interference with the expression of opinions. . . . Nothing in our Charter prevents a federated organization from having, on a particular point, its own opinions, while another organization has the same right to express a different opinion.[14]

In the national Congress of the CGT held in June, 1957, Benoit Frachon, the secretary general and a member of the Politbureau of the CP stressed the same theme of unity and spoke strongly against the "organization of tendencies" within the Federation, advocated by Pierre Le Brun.[15] The same Bureau in which the Communists have a controlling position was re-elected, and Le Brun subsequently retired from it. There is no doubt that the Communist leadership continues to control the key positions within the CGT; the only question which cannot be easily

[14] *Le Monde,* November 16, 1956.
[15] *Le Monde,* June 18, 1957.

answered is the one concerning the effectiveness of their control. The decline of the political strike is one indication of a lack of effectiveness; the success of economic strike, usually in cooperation with the CFTC and often the FO, is another. It remains to be seen whether the decline of the political strike reflects the weakness of the leadership rather than its ineptitude and bad choice of strategy.

III. THE IDEOLOGICAL COMMITMENT

The organizational and electoral stability of the party is coupled with an ideological commitment which has called for complete subservience to the Soviet Union. In 1934, 1939, 1941, 1947 and finally since 1954, the attitude of the party has reflected the changing patterns of Soviet diplomacy and has played, with no variations, the theme enunciated in Moscow. The only embarrassment was that which was caused by the de-Stalinization movement before, and particularly after, the Krushchev report and by the criticisms against the "cult of personality," so dominant within the French party. While the Italian Communist Party was quick to start the debate, and while the Polish and Hungarian Communist Parties began to draw their own conclusions, the French Communist Party refused to deviate from the logic of Stalinism.[16]

Writing in April, 1956, Thorez devoted only one page to the discussion of the errors of Stalin and to the cult of personality. Referring to the 20th Party Congress of the Soviet Union, the French Communist leader wrote:

> The Congress noted that there had been in the past serious infractions of the Leninist rules of Party life. It paid much attention to the reestablishment and the re-affirmation of the principle of collective leadership. . . . The mistake of Comrade Stalin was the fact that he failed to recognize, in the last period of his activity, certain rules on the life and the direction of the party which he had himself taught to the Communists of the world, particularly in his "Problems of Leninism."

Attacks against Stalin were exploited, he pointed out, by the bourgeois

---

[16] *The Anti-Stalin Campaign and International Communism, A Selection of Documents,* ed. by the Russian Institute, Columbia University. New York, 1956. It is unfortunate that the editors of this excellent compilation failed to include Thorez's lengthy and extremely revealing article, Quelques Questions Capitales posées au Congres du Parti Communiste de l'Union Sovietique. *Cahiers du Communisme* 32 année, April 1956. The publication of the Khrushchev speech had not as yet intervened, but there is little doubt that more than rumors of its contents must have reached by then Thorez and the leaders of the party.

and reactionary circles; and he attempted to show how insignificant the accusations against Stalin were:

> . . . As if the general direction of the Communist Party of the Soviet Union had not led the party and the country from one triumph to another on the road to wealth, cultural development and national grandeur!
>
> As if the necessary criticisms of certain errors could ever undermine the historic merits of Stalin! Stalin defended and developed the thought and practice of Lenin. He initiated and directed the realization of the Five Year Plans and the construction of Socialism in one-sixth of the world. He played a crucial role in defeating the enemy groups . . . who would have brought about the destruction of the revolution. . . .[17]

If one reads carefully the report of the Central Committee of the Communist Party of the Soviet Union issued on June 30, 1956, he cannot fail to note that the remarks made concerning Stalin's role and the explanation given of his deviations from the Leninist line are remarkably close to Thorez's conclusion.[18] For a long time the French Communist Party refused to accept the "so-called" Khrushchev Report. In a speech before the Plenum of the Central Committee of the Communist Party in November 22, 1956, Thorez went so far as to indicate that it was incorrect to refer to "Stalinism" since the phenomenon had never existed.[19]

In presenting the Report of the Central Committee before the Congress of the French Communist Party held on July 18-21, 1956, where the leadership of the party was re-elected unanimously,[20] Thorez failed to mention Khrushchev's name even once but admitted that certain errors had been committed by Stalin. He pointed out, however, in discussing the recommendations of the Soviet Party Congress, that he himself had argued in favor of the theory that there are different paths to socialism and that there was never a question in his mind but that France, "with a rich and glorious political tradition" of her own, would follow a different path to socialism from the one followed by the October Revolution. He quoted Marx and Engels to show that specific forms of revolution could indeed vary and reminded the Congress that Engels had admitted that " one could conceive" of a peaceful evolution towards socialism. Reemphasizing, in line with the resolutions of the

---

[17] Thorez, *Quelques Questions,* p. 392.

[18] *The Anti-Stalin Campaign and International Communism,* 275-306.

[19] *Le Monde,* pp. 23, 1956.

[20] *XIVᵉ Congrès du Parti Communiste Français,* Le Havre 18-21 July 1956; *Cahiers du Communisme, Numero Special,* July-August 1956.

Soviet Party Congress, the necessity of a *Front Unique* with the socialists, he pointed out

> the possibility of grouping around the working class, the farmers, the artisans and the intellectuals, that is, the majority of the French people and of transforming, thanks to an alliance between the proletariat and the middle classes, the Parliament itself from an instrument of bourgeois dictatorship to the legitimate instrument of the people's will. . . . Already [he added], socialists and Communists have together close to a majority in the National Assembly.[21]

Ample illustration was given the party's willingness to cooperate. They helped to elect Socialist Le Troquer to the presidency of the National Assembly in 1954, 1956 and 1957; they voted for the investiture of Mendès-France, and Guy Mollet; and on two occasions the "conscience" of the party was sacrificed to the strategic exigencies of the formation of a popular front. On two crucial issues in 1956, the Communist Party voted for the credits to continue the war in Algeria and to give to the government extraordinary powers to fight the rebellion.

Though overtures for cooperation have continued to be made, the Suez adventure and the Budapest rebellion have forced the Communist Party, even if temporarily, into a position of isolation. For Budapest provided another opportunity for the party to reassert its pro-Soviet stand, and to reconcile it with its earlier assertion that there were different paths leading to socialism. Thorez now wrote: ". . . the variety of forms has nothing to do with the content of the dictatorship of the proletariat. This content must always be the same." It was provided by "the country of the October Revolution which, for the first time in the history of humanity, has constructed victoriously a new socialist life." [22] Thus the conclusion is inescapable. Because the ultimate form of the proletarian revolution is international, the various Communist parties must subordinate their policies to the international logic of the Revolution. Since this logic, however, leads to the acceptance of the leadership of the first country which has realized this revolution, it follows that acceptance of the leadership of the Soviet Union and its corollary, obedience to the Soviet leadership, is the very essence of revolutionary probity.

---

[21] *Ibid.*, p. 43. "We condemn all discord, all unfriendly attitudes towards the workers who are members of socialist, christian or other organizations. We stretch our open hand to all the workers, no matter what their philosophic opinions and beliefs are. We want the unity of the entire working class." *Ibid.*, p. 47.

[22] *L'Humanité*, November 22, 1956.

The French Communist Party has never wavered from this position. The intellectuals, Thorez pointed out

> are still unable because of their petit-bourgeois past to reconcile, as every Communist must, the national cause with the international proletariat.
> In a question like that of Hungary there is not a single revolutionary worker who will hesitate for a second.[23]

The Hungarian national entity must, therefore, be recognized only if it is proletarian and revolutionary, i.e., in accord with the Soviet Union. Strictly speaking, the same interpretation applies not only to the Algerian "national problem" but also to the French national problem. They cannot be understood without reference to the proletarian revolution whose ultimate realization calls for a continuing but varying re-interpretation of the role of the party in the nation. There is no doubt that when Thorez stated in 1949 that the French workers would not fight against the Soviet Union under any circumstances and when he now takes a position in favor of Algerian autonomy, he is acting for the realization of the *real*, the revolutionary, the pro-Soviet interests of France at a dialectical level that few intellectuals and few non-Communists can grasp.

At a time when the Communist world was beginning to entertain possibilities for the development of more freedom for the individual Communist parties, when the development of a multi-centered Communist world appeared likely, Thorez was reiterating in most dogmatic terms to the traditional Stalinist position. He was binding the French Communist Party to the same doctrinaire position that had virtually caused a rupture with Tito and the Polish Communists, that condemned the militants and the intellectuals within the party to complete servility and that undermined seriously the role of the party at home. The fact that such an attitude was endorsed by the French Communist leaders is not so difficult to explain as is the fact that such an attitude did not affect the strength of the party and did not produce any serious demoralization or weakening among the ranks.

IV. A MASS PARTY

At the organizational, ideological and voting levels, the Communist Party represents a remarkable phenomenon of stability. Nothing seems

[23] *L'Humanité,* November 15, 1956.

to have stirred its ideology; nothing seems to have disturbed the loyalty of the militants or to have endangered the position of its top leadership, in office for almost a quarter of a century. Thorez, Madame Vermeersch and Duclos hold the decision-making powers, while a number of younger recruits of the caliber of Garaudy, Servin, Frachon and Casanova revolve around their orbit; nothing seems to have disturbed the monotonous loyalty to the party of some 20 per cent of the voters.

To understand this immobility, we ought to point to three party characteristics: the socio-economic character of its supporters, the class character of the party and its protest character.

The Socio-economic Factors

In contrast to the MRP, the Radicals and perhaps the Socialists, the CP is a mass party in terms of the distribution of its electoral strength. In only three Departments did the Communists obtain less than 4 to 7 per cent of the registered voters in the elections of 1956; in seven they obtained between 8 and 11 per cent; in eleven between 12 and 15.9 per cent; in fifteen they exceeded 24 to 27.9 per cent and in ten they had over 28 per cent. They are strong in almost all departments and particularly so in departments of diametrically opposed socio-economic configuration. Their strongholds are in the Northern France and the Paris regions, in the South and West of the Massif Central, some of the most industrialized and the most backward sections of the country. The party received 2,888,820 votes in the 26 advanced Departments of France and 2,625,583 in the 64 Departments that are below the national average of industrial production—23.1 per cent and 18.4 per cent in the "dynamic" and "static" France, respectively.[24] Its voters include winegrowers, small property-owners, industrial workers, artisans, civil servants, teachers, doctors and lawyers, intellectuals, and students. The Communist vote cuts across all regions, occupations and classes, excluding of course the industrialists, the large property owners, the shopkeepers and those areas where Catholic practices are still strong.

In the elections of 1951, for instance, only 38 per cent of the vote received by the CP was a working class vote, while 47.8 per cent of all workers in France voted for the Party. This would indicate that while the workers consider it their party, it is not a workers' party! This is corroborated by the opinion polls taken by the *Institut Français d'Opin-*

[24] *Les Elections du 2 janvier 1956,* Association Française de Science Politique, Paris, 1957, the excellent article of FRANÇOIS GOGUEL, Geographie des Elections du 2 janvier. 467-505.

ion Publique and reported in *Sondages*.[25] Many members of the middle
class vote Communist. According to the opinion surveys of 1952, 8 per
cent of the salaried (as contrasted to wage earners), 5 per cent of the
civil servants, 5 per cent of the merchants and shopkeepers, 3 per cent
of the liberal professions and 3 per cent of those living on retirement
pensions or rentiers vote Communist. The very organization of the
party indicates its changing social composition. For example, only 22
per cent of the total number of cells are factory or civil service and office
cells; 34 per cent are rural cells and 44 per cent are "local" cells.[26]

Class Character

At the same time, the Communist Party attempts to maintain its
"class" character. It continues to pay lip service to the theory of class
struggle; it rejects the capitalistic economy and continues to favor socialism. In 1955, it revived two theories that played a very important
role in its ideological propaganda among the workers, that of the class
struggle and that of the progressive pauperization of the workers. The
seriousness with which these two topics were discussed by the French
intellectuals, and the embarrassment of many of the French economists
when they were unable to show in any conclusive manner that the real
wages of the workers were above the 1938 level, indicated the success of
the Communists in using, whenever convenient, genuine Marxist slogans.

Only the symbolisms and slogans used by the Communists in spreading the ever-present wave of discontent and protest among the French
disguise the extent to which the class character and the mass character
of the party would seem to contradict each other. The anti-clerical forces
have realized that the Radicals have lost interest in what used to be
their strongest political weapon and that the Socialists can no longer
be relied upon to sustain actively the cause of laïcité; the artisans, agricultural laborers, the petit-bourgeoisie, and often the middle classes and
the farmers South of the Loire vote Communist only because they are
the heirs of the revolutionary tradition and of radicalism and for whom
an anti-state and anti-government philosophy has been, since the days of
Alain, the very definition of the Republic.[27]

[25] *Sondages.* Revue Française de l'Opinion Publique, 1952, No. 3, Numéro Special,
pp. 50-63.
[26] *Partis Politiques et Classes Sociales en France.* Paris, 1956, p. 182.
[27] For an excellent study of the Communist strength among the rural groups see
the excellent study of HENRY W. EHRMANN, The French Peasant and Communism.
The American Political Science Review (March 1952), 19-43. The decline of
Gaullism and the emergence of Poujadisme account, at least in part, for a relative
weakening of the CP vote in the rural areas and a corresponding strengthening in the
industrial areas.

A Party of Protest

The protest character of the Communist vote has certain peculiarities that should be noted. First, it is republican, inasmuch as it evokes the principles of 1789 and the cause of laïcité. Second, it combines in a subtle way the traditional elements of protest with the class mentality of the French workers; in this sense, the symbolism of protest assumes a national character in which workers and various other groups join forces. Third, the protest character of the party appeals directly to a number of pressure groups—the bouilleurs du crû, the artisans, the schoolteachers, the wine growers in the South, the veterans, the aged and incapacitated who live on pensions, and the students. The party becomes their spokesman—a self-appointed lobby for the protection of their interests—in the National Assembly.[28]

We may attempt, then, to give a tentative explanation of the immobility of the Communist Party. It evokes different images to different groups; it provides for different means of action among different groups; it is both a revolutionary and a reformist party in the eyes of the voters. It is in favor of economic modernization but also supports all the marginal groups that impede it; it is for socialization and for private property. It is the party of the "Revolution" in terms that satisfy both past (the Revolution of 1789) and the future (the Communist Revolution)! It is both national, emphasizing the greatness and the civilizing mission of France, and international. It is proletarian but at the same time the staunchest supporter of the small farmer of the South; it is against the curé but for the Catholics and ready to cooperate with them. With an uncanny perception of the most basic historical predispositions of the French voter, it has used every theme and slogan to reinforce those inclinations and to make the voter identify them with the party. This accounts for both the wide support it receives among so many socio-economic groups (a fact which continues to baffle all observers), and for the remarkable strength it has in regions that appear to be so different—the "static" and the "dynamic" France.

But by appealing to the many predispositions—even if contradictory —of the French and by trying to bring into the party many groups with

[28] This is easily demonstrated by the attitude of the Communist parliamentary group in the National Assembly, more at the committee level than in the formal pronouncements and votes and amendments proposed. In 1955, trying to forestall Poujade, the Communists introduced a bill "for the purpose of establishing an equitable tax policy by making the rich pay." Earlier Duclos declared himself in favor of fiscal amnesty for the "small and average taxpayers." On a number of instances, shopkeepers, artisans, wine-growers, including the bouilleurs de crû, were singled out for special favors.

many and very often contradictory interests, the party has also reached a common denominator. Its own image of its role has changed. If, according to the early post-war slogan, it is a "party to be counted in the millions," it is slowly becoming a captive of the many and diverse forces whose support it has cultivated. It has reached a dead center of compromise and synthesis beyond which there can be no movement in one direction or another without serious electoral, and perhaps organizational and ideological, dislocations. The party is becoming progressively embedded in the social and idelogical structure of France, and as a result is beginning to reflect within itself the very contradictions of the French society. The past is beginning to weigh more heavily than the future to which the party is in theory dedicated.[29]

It is this phenomenon, characteristically enough, that accounts for the immobility of its leadership and ideology. The leadership is entrenched, not only by virtue of its ability to manipulate the militants and the rank and file in the best Stalinist tradition, but because the balance of forces within the party provides for a mechanical stalemate in which no group can gain ascendancy. By playing the one against the other, the leadership can stay in power and avert any frontal challenge to its position. Second, the mass character of the party and its electoral successes have given to the leadership a great variety of patronage that can be judiciously dispensed: deputies, mayors, municipal councillors, departmental councillors, other elective posts in the Economic Council, the social security, the nationalized industries. It was not without reason that Duclos reminded the Communist Party Congress of 1956 that there were 1300 Communist mayors and 25,000 municipal councillors![30] In addition to financial advantages, such positions give status and prestige, participation and influence, something which, as the Radicals knew so well, is the most important reward a party can bestow in the provinces. By comprising with the various forces mentioned and by acting as a lobby for them, the party has carved for itself a permanent position in the French political and social system. But it has also impaired its position not only by neutralizing these forces but by neutralizing itself.

Superimposed upon the electoral mass of French Communist voters

---

[29] For a similar point of view see E. DREXEL GODFREY, JR., The Communist Presence in France. *American Political Science Review* (June 1956), 321-38. According to public opinion polls 40% of the Communist voters believe that the party should under certain circumstances take power by force while 40% favor reform. The rest "do not know."

[30] *XIVᵉ Congres du Parti Communist Français. Cahiers du Communisme,* June-July 1953, No. 6-7; DUCLOS, Les Municipalites aux Services des Masses, p. 105.

and upon the rank and file of the party is only a small group of permanent and semi-permanent party members—the hard core of the militants. Ever since the accession of Thorez to the leadership of the party, they have been so frequently appointed by him that there is hardly any opposition to be expected from them. Trained in the Stalinist school, they have learned that administration, propaganda and activation is their work, and that policy and directives will come from the top. They are bureaucrats, and Communism is for them the philosophy that best rationalizes their bureaucratic role. Secure in their position by virtue of their appointment, without the fear that the masses of members and the electorate will attempt to or be able to disturb the domestic balance of forces that reflects the party's policy, the *militants* can be counted upon, because of both their training and roles, not to bring forth new ideas that will become sources of controversy and disturb the leadership. We may conclude, therefore, that the vaunted strength of the party is based upon a negative compromise rather than upon a positive synthesis of various social, economic, regional and ideological forces. The party has reached a level of immobility, even if the immobility of the leadership gives the illusion of discipline and strength.

V. THE DANGER OF THE INTELLECTUALS

It is precisely this *modus vivendi* that the intellectuals are likely to criticize, and it is not surprising that criticisms against the party and the pro-Soviet stand during the Hungarian revolution came primarily from them, particularly from sympathizers. What has been more surprising, however, is that such criticisms were relatively few and that the intellectuals were unable to lead a sustained offensive against the leadership. Four Communist writers—Claude Roy, Roger Vailland, J. F. Rolland and Claude Morgan—voiced outright criticism of the Soviet intervention. Two of them, Rolland and Claude Roy, were subsequently expelled while the other two accepted with good grace a reprimand. Picasso and a number of other intellectuals demanded the convocation of an extraordinary Party Congress to discuss the Soviet intervention in Hungary, for without it "the revolutionary probity" of the party was at stake. Their request was peremptorily dismissed by the Central Committee and nothing has been heard from them since. Frederic Joliot-Curie, the President of the World Council for Peace, a Soviet Front organization, who stated in the Party Congress that he had never been so free (*"Jamais je ne me suis senti si libre"*),[31] issued a statement on behalf of the organization's French Bureau. The statement deplored the Suez attack, condemned the many mistakes of the Hungarian government, the manner in which they were exploited by foreign propaganda, and offered a resolution in favor of the withdrawal of the Soviet troops on the basis of an agreement betwen Hungary and the Soviet Union.[32]

The most bitter attack came from Sartre.[33] The man who only a year earlier had stated, in arguing with Pierre Hervé, that "the party has manifested an extraordinary objective intelligence so much so that it rarely errs," took a stand against the Soviet intervention and against the French Communist Party which supported it. "For me the crime is not only the attack on Budapest but that it was made possible and perhaps imperative, because of twelve years of terror and stupidity."

Though Sartre had never been a member of the Communist Party, he was intimately associated with the Communist cause for some four years; and his attacks hurt deeply. For ever since the Liberation, the party had made a consistent effort to woo the intellectuals[34] since they performed the important service of delivering the ideas of the Communist leadership to the public. With them the party was assured of the sympathy of the most important media of communications in France— the theater, the novel, the press and the conference. Without them, the party would find itself in isolation.

The French intellectuals themselves presented a special case which made their adherence to the party in the post-war period easier, but which also raised serious problems concerning their loyalty to the leadership. Torn by their deep sense of guilt for their failure to participate in the construction of a better society; tormented by their social isolation and more particularly by their failure to associate with the working class and understand its mentality and aspirations, many of them flocked into the Communist Party immediately after the Liberation. In a perceptive analysis,[35] Professor Aron has shown how many intellectuals accepted without any critical examination the myths of Revolution, class-struggle, the notion that progress and revolution were inextricably associated and, finally, Marx's attribution to the workers of a messianic role

[31] *XIVᵉ Congres*, etc., 265.
[32] *Le Monde,* November 27, 1956.
[33] Sartre's first attack appeared in *Express,* November 9, 1956, Après Budapest: Sartre Parle. A comprehensive critical essay appeared in *Les Temps Modernes* (January 1957), Le fantôme de Staline, 577-696.
[34] See Thorez's remarks in the Party Congress . . . *XIVᵉ Congres,* etc., pp. 64-67.
[35] RAYMOND ARON, *L'Opium des Intellectuels.* Paris, 1955.

according to which the working class alone was the hope of the future. The intellectuals showed in the post-liberation period a remarkable zeal to discover the working class. With the passion of the Russian Populists, they sought among the workers the virtues that the latter had sought among the Russian farmers—their integrity, intelligence, class probity, revolutionary spirit—and admired the privations and miseries they endured in the name of the historical necessity which was inevitably propelling them towards their mission of historical greatness. "Humanity [Sartre had written] is in the process of realizing a new youth through the working class. . . "; he maintained "that it is impossible to fight against the working class without becoming the enemy of mankind and one's own self. . . ;" [36] "The vocation of the working class cannot be found in history but rather in the transformation of history. . . " [37]

But the intellectuals are not workers. Despite their efforts to submit to party discipline and to identify their consciousness with that of the working class, they are still social deviants. They are men and women who belong to clubs and talking societies and who make a living by the use of their wits, mostly for the purpose of creative criticism. Membership and submission to the party produced a kind of social reintegration but led them to an alienation far more painful—the alienation of their minds from freedom. As early as 1953, Duclos, in presenting the Report of the Central Committee at the 13th Party Congress, issued a warning against the independence of the intellectuals. It was not a question, he pointed out, of a division of tasks within the party between intellectual work, propaganda, political action, reorganization and the like; the party was the one and only directing force on all issues and all phases of policy, be they artistic, scientific, intellectual or political. "We must watch carefully not to permit the notion to develop according to which the intellectuals are the only natural exponents of the national culture." [38] Indeed, "the intellectuals must be made to assimilate the policy of the party." On all questions the intellectuals are, like everybody else, "the soldiers" of the party. Questions of science, art, painting and philosophy are determined by the party; and it is the task of the intellectual to defend them and to show their superiority to "bourgeois" culture.

The enthusiasm with which the party originally welcomed the intellectuals has been slowly transformed into caution. The events in Hungary demonstrated that this caution was not only warranted but that it

---

[36] Les Communistes et la Paix. *Les Temps Modernes* (July 1952), 5.
[37] *Ibid.*
[38] *XIIIᵉ Congres du Parti Communist Français. Cahiers du Communisme*, June-July 1953, No. 6-7, pp. 640-95.

had produced results. For every Sartre there is an Aragon; for every
Picasso there is a Signac and a Leger; Joliot-Curie, as we have seen, protested the Soviet intervention by criticising the West. Answering
Roland's criticisms, Eric Servin, a young intellectual himself, put it up
to him and to all the intellectuals in clearcut terms: "Nobody asked
him to come to the party he now criticizes. Nobody is forcing
him to stay in the party. If he does not like it can go!" [39] For every
Roland, he claimed there were scores of workers and students that were
asking to become members of the party—a painful reminder that some
intellectuals were once more committing the *lèse ouvrière* which, by
their own admission, had been their original sin. Answering Sartre,
Garaudy pointed out that all the arguments advanced by him against
the Soviet intervention would be used by the "reaction" against the
Communist world and against the working class.

What are the most significant criticisms of the intellectuals, and how
effective have they been? Some seemed to direct their criticism against
Thorez's personal rule of the party and to favor a national Communism similar to that of Tito. But Hervé and a number of sympathizers, notably Sartre, seemed to favor an overall de-Stalinization of
the party (involving the abandonment of the cult of personality with
which Thorez's leadership has been associated for so long), democratization of the party (with freedom of expression for the various
tendencies) and, of course, a new formulation of the relation between
the party and the Soviet Union, stressing equality and allowing for
freedom. "Democratization," wrote Sartre, "is something that can take
place only after complete revision of the relations between the Soviet
Union and the satellite countries" [40] so that the individual countries
and the individual Communist parties may follow a policy compatible
with their own aspirations. The implication is clear. As long as the
Soviet Union attempts to maintain by force its position in the satellite
countries, it will also be prompted to consider its relations with the
other Communist parties in the world in terms of inferior-superior
relations and hence to deprive individual parties of freedom of action
and with it freedom of internal discussion and criticism.

These demands have been successfully resisted thus far by the
leadership. ". . . we cannot tolerate [said Thorez] the constitution of
fractions which will become real parties within the party." Paraphrasing
an old aphorism of Stalin, but without mentioning his source, he

[39] *Le Monde,* November 23, 1956.
[40] Le fantôme de Staline. *Les Temps Modernes.*

reminded his followers that the party was a party of action "which prepares for its revolutionary tasks." It was not a club or a school of controversy.[41]

There is no evidence to indicate, however, that the Communist Party members are moved by this controversy. Ever since the creation of the Popular Front, and more particularly since the Liberation, the workers, the artisans, the small farmers and many intellectuals have shown a remarkable confidence in the leaders of the Communist Party and have followed the directives of the party with admirable zeal. For them, Communism has been an expression of their hopes and interests. Many refuse to read any newspapers other than *L'Humanité* and to believe any news other than that which is propagated by their leaders and agitators. The insularity, the self-imposed censorship of the Communist masses in France, is a remarkable phenomenon. Perhaps some of them may be so discouraged as to abandon the party and fall back on an attitude of benevolent neutrality; perhaps a number of marginal groups —some of the voters, some of the Front organization including even some of the Federations of the General Confederation of Labor—may become disaffected and reassert their autonomy in the name of freedom and syndicalism. But there is no evidence that the bulk of the workers, the farmers and the intellectuals will abandon their allegiance to the party in favor of new solutions. On the contrary, for many of the workers and the voters the party is their best spokesman within a system they are unable to change and would rather reform in a manner that gives them a higher percentage of the national income. To abandon the party means to abandon their best lawyer in the course of the perennial lawsuit that goes under the name of class-struggle against the social and economic groups which have shown little concern with their post-war economic situation, indeed, which have remained traditionally indifferent to their well-being.

The party's leadership and electoral strength, and with it its immobility, is in a real sense part of the immobility of the whole French social, political and economic structure. The party has slowly grown to be a permanent part of the Republic with its own regional fiefs, its own bureaucracy, its own press, its own parliamentary delegation, its own clubs and its own ritual. It has become a separate political community living under the Republic. It is very doubtful that the workers and the peasants, the intellectuals and the marginal social groups will abandon it at present in favor of new adventures. The party is for them the best

[41] *XIVe Congres*, p. 62.

expression of their perennial protest against the French system—a protest that is too diffused and traditional to become revolutionary. As long as the Party expresses this protest, it will continue to be strong and to remain relatively undisturbed by doctrinal controversies.

8

Political Ideas in the
Twentieth Century

Isaiah Berlin

EDITORAL NOTE: *This is the best single statement on the ideological underpinnings of the Communist Party of the Soviet Union and of the major ideological differences between totalitarian and democratic parties. Lenin's formulation has fashioned almost everywhere the internal organization of the Communist parties. How potent the Leninist tradition remains is a matter for controversy. According to one point of view, the Leninist formulation is essential to totalitarianism and allows for no compromises with democratic procedures. Another point of view maintains, however, that the Leninist position, emphasizing elitism and internal discipline, obeyed only the needs of his time and with expanding industrialization and increased prosperity the Communist systems—almost all of them originating in underdeveloped societies—will make for greater room for intraparty democracy and individual freedoms. For the former point of view, see C. J. Friedrich and Z. Brzezinski,* Totalitarian Dictatorships, *Cambridge, Mass., 1957. For the opposite point of view, see Barrington Moore, Jr.,* Terror and Progress—USSR, *Cambridge, Mass., 1955, New York, Harper Torchbooks, 1966; I. Deutscher,* After Stalin What? *London, 1954; and at least by implication, Adam Ulam,* The Unfinished Revolution, *New York, 1963. For two excellent studies of the Soviet Communist Party and the Soviet system, see Merle Fainsod,* How Russia Is Ruled, *Cambridge, Mass., 1960, and Alfred Meyer,* The Soviet Political System, *New York, 1965.*

"Anyone desiring a quiet life has done badly to be born in the
twentieth century."—*L. Trotsky.*

I

HISTORIANS of ideas, however scrupulous and minute they may
feel it necessary to be, cannot avoid perceiving their material in terms of
some kind of pattern. To say this is not necessarily to subscribe to any
form of Hegelian dogma about the dominant role of laws and metaphysical principles in history—a view increasingly influential in our
time—according to which there is some single "explanation" of the
order and attributes of persons, things and events. Usually this consists
in the advocacy of some fundamental "category" or "principle" which
claims to act as an infallible guide both to the past and to the future,
a magic lens revealing "inner," inexorable, all-pervasive historical laws,
invisible to the naked eye of the mere recorder of events, but capable,
when understood, of giving the historian a unique sense of certainty—
certainty not only of what in fact occurred, but of the reason why it
could not have occurred otherwise, affording a secure knowledge which
the mere empirical investigator, with his collections of data, his insecure
structure of painstakingly accumulated evidence, his tentative approxi-
mations and perpetual liability to error and reassessment, can never
hope to attain.

The notion of "laws" of this kind is rightly condemned as nothing
but a metaphysical mystery; but the contrary notion of bare facts—facts
which are nothing but facts, hard, inescapable, untainted by interpretation of arrangement in man-made patterns—is equally mythological.
To comprehend and contrast and classify and arrange, to see in patterns
of lesser or greater complexity, is not a peculiar kind of thinking, it is
thinking itself. And we accuse historians of exaggeration, distortion,
ignorance, bias or departure from the facts, not because they select,
compare and set forth in a context and order which are in part, at
least, of their own choosing, in part conditioned by the circumstances
of their material and social environment or their character or purpose—
we accuse them only when the result deviates too far, contrasts too
harshly with the accepted canons of verification and interpretation
which belong to their own time and place and society. These canons
and methods and categories are those of the normal "common sense"
outlook of a given period and culture, at their best a sharpened,
highly-trained form of this outlook, which takes cognizance of all the
relevant scientific techniques available, but is itself not one of them. All

the criticisms directed against this or that writer for an excess of bias or fantasy, or too weak a sense of evidence, or too limited a perception of connections between events, are based not upon some absolute standard of truth, of strict "factuality," of a rigid adherence to a permanently fixed ideal method of "scientifically" discovering the past *"wie es eigentlich gewesen ist,"* in contrast with mere theories about it, for there is in the last analysis no meaning in the notion of "objective" criticism in this timeless sense. They rest rather on the most refined concept of accuracy and objectivity and scrupulous "fidelity to the facts" which obtain in a given society at a given period, within the subject in question.

When the great Romantic revolution in the writing of history transferred emphasis from the achievements of individuals to the growth and influence of institutions conceived in much less personal terms, the degree of "fidelity to the facts" was not thereby automatically altered. The new kind of history, the account of the development, let us say, of public and private law, or government, or literature, or social habits during some given period of time, was not necessarily less or more accurate or "objective" than earlier accounts of the acts and fate of Alcibiades or Marcus Aurelius or Calvin or Louis XIV. Thucydides or Tacitus or Voltaire was not subjective or vague or fanciful in a sense in which Ranke or Savigny or Michelet was not. The new history was merely written from what is nowadays called a "different angle." The kinds of fact the new history was intended to record were different, the emphasis was different, a shift of interest had occurred in the questions asked and consequently in the methods used. The concepts and terminology reflect an altered view of what constitutes evidence and therefore, in the end, of what are the "facts." When the "romances" of chroniclers were criticized by "scientific" historians, at least part of the implied reproach lay in the alleged discrepancies in the work of the older writers from the findings of the most admired and trusted sciences of a later period; and these were in their turn due to the change in the prevalent conceptions of the patterns of human development—to the change in the models in terms of which the past was perceived, those artistic, theological, mechanical, biological or psychological models which were reflected in the fields of inquiry, in the new questions asked and the new types of technique used, giving answers felt to be more interesting or important than those which had become outmoded.

The history of these changes of "models" is to a large degree the history of human thought. The "organic" or the Marxist methods of

investigating history certainly owed part of their vogue to the prestige
of the particular natural sciences, or the particular artistic techniques,
upon whose model they were supposedly or genuinely constructed; the
increased interest, for example, both in biology and in music from
which many basic metaphors and analogies derived, is relevant to the
historical writing of the nineteenth century, as the new interest in
physics and mathematics is to the philosophy and history of the
eighteenth; and the deflationary methods and ironical temper of the
historians who wrote after the war of 1914-18 were conspicuously influenced by—and accepted in terms of—the new psychological and
sociological techniques which had gained public confidence during this
period. The relative proportions of, say, social, economic and political
concepts in a once admired historical work throw more light upon the
general characteristics of its time and for this reason are a more reliable
index to the standards adopted, the questions asked, the respective rôles
of "facts" to "interpretation," and, in effect, to the entire social and
political outlook of an age, than the distance of the work in question
from some imaginary, fixed, unaltering ideal of absolute truth, "factual"
or "abstract." It is in terms of whether such shifts in the methods of
treating the past or the present or the future, and of the idioms and the
catchwords, the doubts and hopes, fears and exhortations which they
expressed, that the development of political ideas—the conceptual apparatus of a society and of its most gifted and articulate representatives
—can best be judged. No doubt the concepts in terms of which people
speak and think are symptoms and effects of other processes, the discovery of which is the task of this or that empirical science. But this
does not detract from their importance and paramount interest for
those who wish to know what constitutes the conscious experience of
the most characteristic men of an age or a society, whatever its causes
and whatever its fate. And we are, of course, for obvious reasons of
perspective, in a better situation to determine this in the case of past
societies than for our own. But the very sense of contrast and dis-
similarity with which the past affects us provides the only relevant
background against which the features peculiar to our own experience
stand out in sufficient relief to be adequately discerned and described.

The student of the political ideas of, for example, the mid-nineteenth
century must indeed be blind if he does not, sooner or later, become
aware of the profound differences in ideas and terminology, in the
general view of things—the ways in which the elements of experience
are conceived to be related to one another—which divide that not very
distant age from our own. He understands neither that time nor his

own if he does not perceive the contrast between what was common to Comte and Mill, Mazzini and Michelet, Herzen and Marx, on the one hand, and to Max Weber and William James, Tawney and Beard, Lytton Strachey and Wells, on the other; the continuity of the European intellectual tradition without which no historical understanding at all would be possible is, at shorter range, a succession of specific discontinuities and dissimilarities. Consequently, the remarks which follow deliberately ignore the similarities in favor of the specific differences in political outlook which characterize our own time, and as far as possible, solely our own.

II

The two great liberating political movements of the nineteenth century were, as every history book informs us, humanitarian individualism and romantic nationalism. Whatever their differences—and they were notoriously profound enough to lead to a sharp divergence and ultimate collision of these two ideals—they had this in common: they believed that the problems both of individuals and of societies could be solved if only the forces of intelligence and of virtue could be made to prevail over ignorance and wickedness. They believed, as against the pessimists and fatalists, both religious and secular, whose voices, audible indeed a good deal earlier, began to sound loudly only toward the end of the century, that all clearly understood questions could be solved by human beings with the moral and intellectual resources at their disposal. No doubt different schools of thought returned different answers to these varying problems; utilitarians said one thing, and neo-feudal romantics—Tory democrats, Bonapartists, Pan-Germans, Slavophiles—another. Liberals believed in the unlimited power of education and the power of rational morality to overcome economic misery and inequality. Socialists, on the contrary, believed that without radical alterations in the distribution and control of economic resources no amount of change of heart or mind on the part of individuals could be adequate; or, for that matter, occur at all. Conservatives and socialists believed in the power and influence of institutions and regarded them as a necessary safeguard against the chaos, injustice and cruelty caused by uncontrolled individualism; anarchists, radicals and liberals looked upon institutions as such with suspicion as being obstructive to the realization of that free (and, in the view of most such thinkers, rational) society which the will of man could both conceive and build, if it were not for the unliquidated residue of ancient abuses (or unreason) upon which the existing rulers of society—whether individuals or administrative machines—leaned so heavily, and of which so many of them indeed were typical expressions.

Arguments about the relative degree of the obligation of the individual to society and *vice versa* filled the air. It is scarcely necessary to rehearse these familiar questions, which to this day form the staple of discussion in the more conservative institutions of Western learning, to realize that however wide the disagreements about the proper answers to them, the questions themselves were common to liberals and conservatives alike. There were of course even at that time isolated irrationalists—Stirner, Kierkegaard, in certain moods Carlyle; but in the main all the parties to the great controversies, even Calvinists and ultramontane Catholics, accepted the notion of man as resembling in varying degrees one or the other of two idealized types. Either he is a creature free and naturally good, but hemmed in and frustrated by obsolete or corrupt or sinister institutions masquerading as saviors and protectors and repositories of sacred traditions; or he is a being largely, but not wholly, free, and to a high degree, but not entirely, good, and consequently unable to save himself by his own wholly unaided efforts; and therefore rightly seeking salvation within the great frameworks—states, churches, unions. For only these great edifices promote solidarity, security and sufficient strength to resist the shallow joys and dangerous, ultimately self-destructive liberties peddled by those conscienceless or self-deceived individualists who in the name of some bloodless intellectual dogma, or noble enthusiasm for an ideal unrelated to human lives, ignore or destroy the rich texture of social life, heavy with treasures from the past—blind, leaders of the blind, robbing men of their most precious resources, exposing them again to the perils of a life solitary, brutish, nasty and short. Yet there was at least one premise common to the controversy, namely the belief that the problems were real, that it took men of exceptional training and intelligence to formulate them properly, and men with exceptional grasp of the facts, willpower and capacity for coherent thought to find and apply the correct solutions.

These two great currents finally ended in exaggerated and indeed distorted forms as Communism and Fascism—the first as the treacherous heir of the liberal internationalism of the previous century, the second as the culmination and bankruptcy of the mystical patriotism which animated the national movements of the time. All movements have origins, forerunners, imperceptible beginnings: nor does the twentieth century stand divided from the nineteenth by so universal an explosion as the French Revolution, even in our day the greatest of all historical landmarks. Yet it is a profound fallacy to regard Fascism and Communism as in the main more uncompromising and violent manifestations of an earlier crisis, the culmination of a struggle fully discernible long before. The differences between the political movements of the twentieth century and the nineteenth are very sharp, but they spring from factors whose full force was not properly realized until our century was well under way. For there is a barrier which divides what is unmistakably past and done with from that which most characteristically belongs to our day. The familiarity of this barrier must not blind us to its relative novelty. One of the elements of the new outlook is the notion of unconscious and irrational influences which outweigh the forces of reason; another the notion that answers to problems exist not in rational solutions, but in the removal of the problems themselves by means other than thought and argument. The interplay between the old tradition, which saw history as the battleground between the easily identifiable forces of light and darkness, reason and obscurantism, progress and reaction; or alternatively between spiritualism and empiricism, intuition and scientific method, institutionalism and individualism—the conflict between this order and, on the other hand, the new factors violently opposed to the humane psychology of "bourgeois" civilization—is to a large extent the history of political ideas of our time.

III

And yet to a casual observer of the politics and the thought of the twentieth century it might at first seem that every idea and movement typical of our time is best understood as a natural development of tendencies already prominent in the nineteenth century. In the case of the growth of international institutions, for instance, this seems a truism. What are the Hague Court, the old League of Nations and its modern successor, the numerous prewar and postwar international agencies and conventions for political, economic, social and humanitarian purposes—what are they, if not the direct descendants of that liberal internationalism—Tennyson's "Parliament of Man"—which was the staple of all progressive thought and action in the nineteenth century, and indeed of much in the century before it? The language of the great founders of European liberalism—Condorcet, for example, or Helvétius—does not differ greatly in substance, nor indeed in form, from the most characteristic moments in the speeches of Woodrow Wilson or Thomas Masaryk. European liberalism wears the appearance of a single coherent movement, little altered during almost three centuries, founded upon relatively simple intellectual foundations, laid by Locke or Grotius or even Spinoza; stretching back to Erasmus and Montaigne, the Italian Renaissance, Seneca and the Greeks. In this movement there is a rational answer to every question. Man is, in principle at least, everywhere and in every condition, able, if he wills it, to discover and apply rational solutions to his problems. And these solutions, because they are rational, cannot clash with one another, and will ultimately form a harmonious system in which the truth will prevail, and freedom, happiness and unlimited opportunity for untrammeled self-development will be open to all.

True, the consciousness of history which grew in the nineteenth century modified the severe and simple design of the classical theory as it was conceived in the eighteenth century. Human progress was presently seen to be conditioned by factors of greater complexity than had been conceived of in the springtime of rationalist individualism: education, rationalist propaganda, were perhaps not always, nor everywhere, quite enough. Such factors as the particular and special influences by which various societies were historically shaped—some due to physical conditions, others to more elusive emotional and what were vaguely classified as "cultural" factors—were presently allowed to have greater importance than they were accorded in the over-simple scheme of Diderot or Bentham. Education, and all forms of social action, must, it was now thought, be fitted to take account of historical needs which made men and their institutions somewhat less easy to mold into the required pattern than had been too optimistically assumed in earlier and more naive times.

Nevertheless, the original program continued in its various forms to exercise an almost universal spell. This applied to the right no less than to the left. The thinkers of the right, unless they were concerned solely with obstructing the liberals and their allies, believed and acted upon the belief that, provided no excessive violence was done to slow but certain processes of "natural" development, all might yet be well; the faster must be restricted from pushing aside the slower, and in this way all would arrive in the end. This was the doctrine preached by Bonald early in the century, and it expressed the optimism of even the stoutest believers in original sin. Provided that traditional differences of outlook and social structure were protected from what conservatives were fond of describing as the "unimaginative," "artificial," "mechanical" levelling processes favored by the liberals; provided that the infinity of "intangible" or "historic" or "natural" or "providential" distinctions (which to them seemed to constitute the essence of fruitful forms of life) were preserved from being transformed into a uniform collection of homogeneous units moving at a pace dictated by some "irrelevant" or "extraneous" authority, contemptuous of prescriptive or traditional rights and habits; provided that adequate safeguards were instituted against too reckless a trampling upon the sacred past—with these guarantees, rational reforms and changes were allowed to be feasible and even desirable. Given these guarantees, conservatives no less than liberals were prepared to look upon the conscious direction of human affairs by qualified experts with a considerable degree of approval; and not merely by experts, but by a growing number of individuals and groups, drawn from, and representing, wider and wider sections of a society which was progressively becoming more and more enlightened.

This is a mood and attitude common to a wider section of opinion in the later nineteenth century in Europe, and not merely in the West but in the East too, than historians, affected by the political struggles of a later or earlier period, allow us to see. One of the results of it—in so far as it was a causal factor and not merely a symptom of the process—was the wide development of political representation in the West whereby in the end, in the succeeding century, all classes of the population began to attain to power, sooner or later, in one country or another. The nineteenth century was full of unrepresented groups engaged in the struggle for self-expression, and later for control. Its representatives counted among them heroes and martyrs, men of the moral and artistic genius whom a genuine struggle of this kind brings forth. The twentieth century, by satisfying much of the social and political hunger of the Victorian period, did indeed witness a striking improvement in the material condition of the majority of the peoples of Western Europe, due in large measure to the energetic social legislation which transformed the social order.

But one of the least predicted results of this trend (although isolated thinkers like Tocqueville, Burckhardt, Herzen, and, of course, Nietzsche, had more than an inkling of it) was a steep decline in the quality of moral idealism, and of romantic, artistic rebelliousness, which marked the early struggles of the dissatisfied social groups during their heroic period when, deeply divergent though they were, they fought together against tyrants, priests and militant philistines. Whatever the injustices and miseries of our time—and they are plainly no fewer than those of the immediate past—they are less likely to find expression in monuments of noble eloquence, because that kind of inspiration seems to spring only from the oppression or suppression of entire classes of society. There arrives a brief moment when the leaders of the most articulate, and socially and economically most developed, of these suppressed groups are lifted by the common mood and for a moment speak not for their own class or milieu alone, but in the name of all the oppressed; for a brief instant their utterance has a universal quality.

But a situation where all or nearly all the great sections of society have been, or are on the point of being, in at any rate the formal possession of power is unfavorable to that truly disinterested eloquence —disinterested partly at least because fulfillment is remote, because principles shine forth most clearly in the darkness and void, because the inner vision is still free from the confusions and obscurities, the compromises and blurred outlines of the external world inevitably forced upon it by the beginnings of practical action. No body of men which has tasted power, or is within a short distance of doing so, can avoid a certain degree of that cynicism which, like a chemical reaction, is generated by the sharp contact between the pure ideal nurtured in the wilderness and its realization in some unpredicted form which seldom conforms to the hopes or fears of earlier times. It therefore takes an exceptional effort of the imagination to discard the context of later years, to cast ourselves back into the period when the views and movements which have since triumphed and lost their glamor long ago were still capable of stirring so much vehement idealistic feeling: when, for example, nationalism was not in principle felt to be incompatible with a growing degree of internationalism, or civil liberties with a rational organization of society; when this was believed by conservatives almost as much as by their rivals, and the gap between the moderates of both sides was only that between the plea that reason must not be permitted to increase the pace of progress beyond the limits imposed by "history" and the counterplea that *"la raison a toujours raison,"* that memories and shadows were less important than the direct perception of the real world in the clear light of day. This was a time when liberals in their turn themselves began to feel the impact of historicism, and to admit the need for a certain degree of adjustment and even control of social life, perhaps by the hated state itself, if only to mitigate the inhumanity of unbridled private enterprise, to protect the liberties of the weak, to safeguard those basic human rights without which there could be neither happiness nor justice nor freedom to pursue the ends of life.

The philosophical foundations of these liberal beliefs in the mid-nineteenth century were somewhat obscure. Rights described as "natural," "inherent," absolute standards of truth and justice, were not compatible with tentative empiricism and utilitarianism; yet liberals believed in both. Nor was faith in democracy strictly consistent with belief in the inviolable rights of minorities or dissident individuals. But so long as the right-wing opposition set itself against all those principles, the contradictions could, on the whole, be allowed to lie dormant, or to form the subject of peaceful academic disputes, not exacerbated by urgent need for immediate factual application. Thus the contradictions further enhanced the role of rational criticism by which, in the end, all questions could and would one day be settled. The socialists on their part resembled the conservatives in believing in the existence of inexorable laws of history, and, like them, accused the liberals of legislating "unhistorically" for timeless abstractions—an activity for which history would not neglect to take due revenge. But they also resembled the liberals in believing in the supreme value of rational analysis, in policies founded on theoretical considerations deduced from "scientific" premises, and with them accused the conservatives of misinterpreting "the facts" to justify the miserable status quo, of condoning misery and injustice; not indeed like the liberals by ignoring history, but by misreading it in a manner consciously or unconsciously calculated to preserve their own power upon a specious moral basis. But genuinely revolutionary as some among them were, and a thoroughly new phenomenon in the Western world, the majority of them shared with the parties which they attacked the common assumption that men must be spoken and appealed to in terms of the needs and interests and ideals of which they were, or could be made to be, conscious.

Conservatives, liberals, radicals, socialists differed indeed in their interpretation of historical change. They disagreed about what were in fact the deepest needs and interests and ideals of human beings, and who held them, and how deeply or widely or for what length of time, or about their validity in this or that situation. They differed about the facts, they differed about ends and means, they seemed to themselves to a₉ree on almost nothing. But what they had in common—too obviously to be clearly realized—was the belief that their age was ridden with social and political problems which could be solved only by the conscious application of truths upon which all men endowed with adequate mental powers could agree. The Marxists did indeed question this in theory, but not in practice: even they did not seriously attack the thesis that when ends were not yet attained, and the choice of means was limited, the proper way of setting about adapting the means to the ends was by the use of all the skill and energy and intellectual and moral insight available. And while some regarded these problems as akin to those of the natural sciences, some to those of ethics or religion, while others supposed that they were altogether *sui generis* and needed altogether unique methods, they were agreed— it seemed too obvious to need stating—that the problems themselves were genuine and urgent and intelligible in more or less similar terms to all clearheaded men, that all solutions were entitled to a hearing, and that nothing was gained by ignorance or the supposition that the problem did not exist.

This set of common assumptions—they are part of what the word "enlightenment" means—were, of course, deeply rationalistic. They were denied implicitly by the whole Romantic movement, and explicitly by isolated thinkers—Carlyle, Dostoevsky, Baudelaire, Tolstoy, Nietzsche. And there were obscurer prophets—Büchner, Kierkegaard, Bakunin, Leontiev—who protested against the prevailing orthodoxy with a depth and originality which became clear only in our own time. Not that these thinkers represent any one single movement, or even an easily identifiable "trend;" but in one relevant particular they display an affinity. They denied the importance of political action based on rational considerations, and to this extent they were rightly abhorred by the supporters of respectable conservatism. They said or implied that rationalism in any form was a fallacy derived from a false analysis of the character of human beings, because the springs of human action lay in regions unthought of by the sober thinkers whose views enjoyed prestige among the serious public. But their voices were few and discordant, and their eccentric views were ascribed to psychological aberrations. Liberals, however much they admired their artistic genius, were revolted by what they conceived as a perverted view of mankind, and either ignored it or rejected it violently. Conservatives looked upon them as allies against the exaggerated rationalism and infuriating optimism of both liberals and socialists, but treated them nervously as queer visionaries, a little unhinged, not to be imitated or approached too closely. The socialists looked on them as so many deranged reactionaries, scarcely worth their powder and shot. The main currents both on the right and on the left flowed round and over these immovable, isolated rocks with their absurd appearance of seeking to arrest or deflect the central current. What were they, after all, but survivals of a darker age, or interesting misfits, sad and at times fascinating casualties of the advance of history, worthy of sympathetic insight —men of talent or even genius born out of their time, gifted poets, remarkable artists, but surely not worthy of detailed attention on the part of serious students of social and political life?

There was (it is worth saying again) a somewhat sinister element dimly recognized from its very beginning in Marxism—in the main a highly rationalistic system—which seemed hostile to this entire outlook, denying the importance of reason in their choice of ends and in effective government alike on the part of individuals or groups. But the worship of the natural sciences which Marxism shared with its liberal antagonists was unpropitious to a clearer perception of its own true nature; and so this aspect of it lay largely unrecognized until Sorel brought it to life and combined it with the Bergsonian anti-rationalism by which his thought is very strongly colored; and until Lenin, stemming from a very different tradition, translated it into an all too effective practice. But Lenin did not, and his followers to this day do not, seem aware of the degree to which it influenced their actions. Or, if aware, they did not and do not admit it. This was so when the twentieth century opened.

IV

Chronological frontiers are seldom landmarks in the history of ideas, and the current of the old century, to all appearances irresistible, seemed to flow peacefully into the new. Presently the picture began to alter. Humanitarian liberalism encountered more and more obstacles to its reforming zeal from the conscious or unconscious opposition both of governments and other centers of social power, as well as the passive resistance of established institutions and habits. It gradually found itself compelled to organize those classes of the population on whose behalf it fought into something sufficiently powerful to work effectively against the old establishment.

The history of the transformation of gradualist and Fabian tactics into the militant formations of Communism and Syndicalism, as well as the milder formations of Social Democracy and trade unionism, is a history not so much of principles as of their interplay with new material facts. In a sense Communism is doctrinaire humanitarianism driven to an extreme in the pursuit of effective offensive and defensive methods. No movement at first sight seems to differ more sharply from liberal reformism than does Marxism, yet the central doctrines—human perfectibility, the possibility of creating a perfect society by a natural means, the belief in the compatibility (indeed the inseparability) of liberty and equality—are common to both. The historical transformation may occur continuously, or in sudden revolutionary leaps, but it must proceed in accordance with an intelligible, logically connected pattern, abandonment of which is always foolish, always utopian. No one doubted that liberalism and socialism were bitterly opposed both in ends and in methods: yet at their edges they shaded off into one another. Marxism is a doctrine which, however strongly it may stress the class-conditioned nature of action and thought, nevertheless in theory sets out to appeal to reason, at least among the class destined by history to triumph—the proletariat. In the Communist view the proletariat alone can face the future without flinching, because it need not be deterred into falsification of the facts by fear of what the future may bring. And, as a corollary, this applies also to those intellectuals who have liberated themselves from the prejudices and superstitions of their economic class, and have aligned themselves with the winning side in the social struggle. To them, since they are fully rational, the privileges of democracy and of free use of all their intellectual faculties may be accorded. They are to Marxists what the enlightened *philosophes* were to the Encyclopedists: their task is to transform all those who are historically capable of it into their own liberated and rational likeness.

But in 1903 there occurred an event which marked the culmination of a process which has altered the history of our world. At the conference of the Russian Social Democratic Party held in that year, which began in Brussels and ended in London, during the discussion of what seemed at first a purely technical question—how far centralization and hierarchical discipline should govern the behavior of the party—a delegate named Posadovsky inquired whether the emphasis laid by the "hard" socialists—Lenin and his friends—upon the need for the exercise of absolute authority by the revolutionary nucleus of the party might not prove incompatible with those fundamental liberties to whose realization socialism, no less than liberalism, was officially dedicated. He asked whether the basic, minimum civil liberties—"the sacrosanctity of the person"—could be infringed and even violated if the party leaders so decided. He was answered by Plekhanov, one of the founders of Russian Marxism, and its most venerated figure, a cultivated, fastidious and morally sensitive scholar of wide outlook, who had for twenty years lived in Western Europe and was much respected by the leaders of Western socialism, the very symbol of civilized "scientific" thinking among Russian revolutionaries. Plekhanov, speaking solemnly, and with a splendid disregard for grammar, pronounced the words, *Salus revolutiae suprema lex*. Certainly, if the revolution demanded it, everything—democracy, liberty, the rights of the individual—must be sacrificed to it. If the democratic assembly elected by the Russian people after the revolution proved amenable to Marxist tactics, it would be kept in being as a Long Parliament; if not, it would be disbanded as quickly as possible. A Marxist Revolution could not be carried through by men obsessed by scrupulous regard for the principles of bourgeois liberals. Doubtless whatever was valuable in these principles, like everything else good and desirable, would ultimately be realized by the victorious working class; but during the revolutionary period preoccupation with such ideals was evidence of a lack of seriousness.

Plekhanov, who was brought up in a humane and liberal tradition, did, of course, later retreat from this position himself. The mixture of utopian faith and brutal disregard for civilized morality proved too repulsive to a man who had spent the greater part of his civilized and productive life among Western workers and their leaders. Like the vast majority of Social Democrats, like Marx and Engels themselves, he was too European to try to realize a policy which, in the words of Shigalev in Dostoevsky's *The Possessed,* "starting from unlimited liberty ends in unlimited despotism." But Lenin accepted the premises, and being logically driven to conclusions repulsive to most of his colleagues, accepted them easily and without apparent qualms. His assumptions were, perhaps, in some sense, still those of the optimistic rationalists of the eighteenth and nineteenth centuries: the coercion, violence, executions, the total suppression of individual differences, the rule of a small, virtually self-appointed minority, were necessary only in the interim period, only so long as there was a powerful enemy to be destroyed. It was necessary only in order that the majority of mankind, once it was liberated from the exploitation of fools by knaves and of weak knaves by more powerful ones, could develop—trammeled no longer by ignorance or idleness or vice, free at last to realize to their fullest extent the infinitely rich potentialities of human nature. This dream may indeed have affinities with the dreams of Diderot or St. Simon or Kropotkin, but what marked it as something relatively novel was the assumption about the means required to translate it into reality. And the assumption, although apparently concerned solely with methods, and derived from Babeuf or Blanqui or Marx or the French Communards, was very different from the practical program set forth by the most "activist" and least "evolutionary" Western socialists towards the end of the nineteenth century. The difference was crucial and marked the birth of the new age.

What Lenin demanded was unlimited power for a small body of

professional revolutionaries, trained exclusively for one purpose, and ceaselessly engaged in its pursuit by every means in their power. This was necessary because democratic methods, and the attempts to persuade and preach used by earlier reformers and rebels, were ineffective: and this in its turn was due to the fact that they rested on a false psychology, sociology and theory of history—namely the assumption that men acted as they did because of conscious beliefs which could be changed by argument. For if Marx had done anything, he had surely shown that such beliefs and ideals were mere "reflections" of the condition of the socially and economically determined classes of men, to some one of which every individual must belong. A man's beliefs, if Marx and Engels were right, flowed from the situation of his class, and could not alter—so far, at least, as the mass of men was concerned—without a change in that situation. The proper task of a revolutionary therefore was to change the "objective" situation, i.e. to prepare the class for its historical task in the overthrow of the hitherto dominant classes.

Lenin went further than this. He acted as if he believed not merely that it was useless to talk and reason with persons precluded by class interest from understanding and acting upon the truths of Marxism, but that the mass of the proletarians themselves were too benighted to grasp the role which history had called on them to play. He saw the choice as between, on the one hand, the gradual stimulation among the army of the dispossessed of a "critical spirit" (which would awaken them intellectually, but lead to a vast deal of discussion and controversy similar to that which divided and enfeebled the intellectuals), and on the other, the turning of them into a blindly obedient force held together by a military discipline and a set of perpetually ingeminated formulae (at least as powerful as the patriotic patter used by the Tsarist regime) to shut out independent thought. If the choice had to be made, then it was mere irresponsibility to stress the former in the name of some abstract principle such as democracy or enlightenment. The important thing was the creation of a state of affairs in which human resources were developed in accordance with a rational pattern. Men were moved more often by irrational than reasonable solutions. The masses were too stupid and too blind to be allowed to proceed in the direction of their own choosing. Tolstoy and the populists were profoundly mistaken; the simple agricultural laborer had no deep truths, no valuable way of life, to impart; he and the city worker and the simple soldier were fellow serfs in a condition of abject poverty and squalor, caught in a system which bred fratricidal strife among themselves; they could be saved only by being ruthlessly ordered by leaders who had acquired a capacity for knowing how to organize the liberated slaves into a rational planned system.

Lenin himself was in certain respects oddly utopian. He started with the belief that with sufficient education, and a rational economic organization, almost anyone could be brought in the end to perform almost any task efficiently. But his conclusion was in practice strangely like that of those reactionaries and Fascists who believed that man was everywhere wild, bad, stupid and unruly, and must be held in check and provided with objects of unreasoning worship. This must be done by a clear-sighted band of organizers, acting in accordance with the truths perceived by such men as Nietzsche, Pareto, or the French absolutist thinkers from De Maistre to Maurras, and indeed by Marx himself—men who by some process superior to scientific reasoning had grasped the true nature of social development, and in the light of their discovery saw the liberal theory of human progress as something unreal, thin, pathetic and absurd. Whatever his crudities and errors, on the central issue, Hobbes, not Locke, turned out to be right: men sought neither happiness nor liberty nor justice, but, above all and before all, security. Aristotle, too, was right: a great number of men were slaves by nature, and when liberated from their chains did not possess the moral and intellectual resources with which to face the prospect of responsibility, of too wide a choice between alternatives; and therefore, having lost one set of chains, inevitably searched for another or forged new chains themselves. It follows that the wise revolutionary legislator, so far from seeking to emancipate human beings from the framework without which they feel lost and desperate, will seek rather to erect a framework of his own, corresponding to the new needs of the new age brought about by natural or technological change. The value of the framework will depend upon the unquestioning faith with which its main features are accepted; otherwise it no longer possesses sufficient strength to support and contain the wayward, potentially anarchical and self-destructive creatures who seek salvation in it. The framework is that system of political, social, economic and religious institutions, those "myths," dogmas, ideals, conventional categories of thought and language, modes of feeling, scales of values, "socially approved" attitudes and habits (called by Marx "superstructure") representing "rationalizations," "sublimations" and symbolic representations which cause men to function in an organized way, prevent chaos, fulfill the function of the Hobbesian state. This is not so very remote from De Maistre's central and deliberately unprobed mystery—the supernatural authority whereby and in whose name rulers can rule and inhibit their subjects' unruly tendencies, above all the tendency to ask too many questions, to question too many established rules. Nothing can be permitted which might even a little weaken that sense of reliability and security which it is the business of the framework to provide. Only thus (in this view) can the founder of the new free society control whatever threatens to dissipate human energy or to slow down the relentless treadmill which alone prevents men from stopping to commit acts of suicidal folly, which alone protects them from too much freedom, from too little restraint, from the vacuum which mankind, no less than nature, abhors.

M. Bergson had, of course, been speaking of something not too unlike this when he had contrasted the flow of life with the forces of critical reason which cannot create or unite, but only divide, arrest, make dead, disintegrate. Freud, too, contributed to this; not in his work of genius as the greatest healer of our time, but as the originator, however innocent, of the misapplication of psychological and sociological methods by muddleheaded fools of good will and quacks and false prophets of every brand and hue. By giving currency to exaggerated versions of the view that the true reasons for a man's beliefs were most often very different from what they themselves thought them to be, being frequently caused by events and processes of which they were neither aware nor in the least anxious to be aware, these eminent thinkers helped, however unwittingly, to discredit the rationalist foundations upon which their own doctrines purported to rest. For it was but a short step from this to the view that what made men most permanently happy was not—as they themselves supposed—the discovery of solutions to the questions which perplexed them, but rather some process natural or artificial whereby the problems were made to vanish altogether. They vanished because their psychological "sources" had been diverted or dried up, leaving behind only those less exacting questions whose solutions did not demand resources beyond the patient's strength.

That this short way with the troubled and the perplexed, which underlay much right-wing thought, should be advocated from the left, was new indeed. It is this change of attitude to the function and value of the intellect that is perhaps the best indication of the great gap which divides the twentieth century from the nineteenth.

v

The central point which I wish to make is this: during all the centuries of recorded history the course of intellectual endeavor, the purpose of education, the substance of controversies about the truth or value of ideas, presupposed the existence of certain crucial questions, the answers to which were of paramount importance. How valid, it was asked, were the various claims to the best methods of discovering absolute knowledge and truth made by such great and famous disciplines as metaphysics, ethics, theology, and the sciences of nature and of man? What was the right life for men to lead, and how was it discovered? Did God exist, and could His purposes be known or even guessed at? Did the universe, and in particular human life, have a purpose? If so, whose purpose did it fulfill? How did one set about answering such questions? Were they or were they not analogous to the kind of questions to which the sciences or common sense provided satisfactory, generally accepted, replies? If not, did it make sense to ask them?

And as in metaphysics and ethics, so in politics too. The political problem was concerned with asking why any individual or individuals should obey other individuals or associations of individuals. All the classical doctrines which deal with the familiar topics of liberty and authority, sovereignty and natural rights, the ends of the state and the ends of the individual, the General Will and the rights of minorities, secularism and theocracy, functionalism and centralization—all these are but various ways of attempting to formulate methods in terms of which this fundamental question can be answered in a manner compatible with the other beliefs and the general outlook of the inquirer and his generation. Great and sometimes mortal conflicts have arisen over the proper techniques for the answering of such questions. Some sought answers in sacred books, others in direct personal revelation, some in metaphysical insight, others in the pronouncements of infallible sages or in speculative systems or in laborious empirical investigations. The questions were of vital importance for the conduct of life. There were, of course, skeptics in every generation who suggested that there were, perhaps, no final answers, that solutions hitherto provided depended on highly variable factors such as the climate in which the theorist's life was lived, or his social or economic or political condition, or those of his fellows, or his or their emotional disposition, or the kinds of intellectual interests which absorbed him or them. But such skeptics were usually treated as either frivolous and so not important, or else unduly disturbing and even dangerous; so that in times of instability they were liable to persecution. But even they—even Sextus Empiricus or Montaigne or Hume—did not actually doubt the importance of the questions themselves. What they doubted was the possibility of obtaining final and absolute solutions.

It was left to the twentieth century to do something more drastic than this. For the first time it was now asserted that the way to answer questions, particularly those recurrent issues which had perplexed and often tormented original and honest minds in every generation, was not by employing the tools of reason, still less those of the more mysterious capacities called "insight" and "intuition," but by obliterating the questions themselves. And this method consists not in removing them by rational means—by proving, for example, that they are founded on intellectual confusion or verbal muddles or ignorance of the facts—for to prove this would in its turn presuppose the need for rational methods of logical or psychological argument. Rather it consists in so treating the questioner that problems which appeared at once over-whelmingly important and utterly insoluble vanish from the questioner's consciousness like evil dreams and trouble him no more. It consists, not in developing the logical implications and elucidating the meaning, the context, or the relevance and origin of a specific problem—in seeing what it "amounts to"—but in altering the outlook which gave rise to it in the first place. Questions for whose solution no ready-made technique could easily be produced are all too easily classified as obsessions from which the patient must be cured. Thus if a man is haunted by the suspicion that, for example, full individual liberty is not compatible with coercion by the majority in a democratic state, and yet continues to hanker after both democracy and individual liberty, it may be possible by appropriate treatment to rid him of his *idée fixe,* so that it will disappear to return no more. The worried questioner of political in-stitutions is thereby relieved of his burden and freed to pursue socially useful tasks, unhampered by disturbing and distracting reflections which have been eliminated by the eradication of their cause.

The method has the bold simplicity of genius: it secures agreement on matters of political principle by removing the psychological possi-bility of alternatives, which itself depends, or is held to depend, on the older form of social organization, rendered obsolete by the revolution and the new social order. And this is how Communist and Fascist states—and all other quasi- and semi-totalitarian societies and secular and religious creeds—have in fact proceeded in the task of imposing political and ideological conformity.

For this the works of Karl Marx are not more directly to blame than the other tendencies of our time. Marx was a typical nineteenth century social theorist, in the same sense as Mill or Comte or Buckle. A policy of deliberate psychological conditioning was as alien to him as to them. He believed that many of the questions of his predecessors were quite genuine, and thought that he had solved them. He supported his solutions with arguments which he honestly supposed to conform to the best scientific and philosophical canons of his time. Whether his outlook was in fact as scientific as he claimed, or his solutions as plausible, is another question. What matters is that he recognized the genuineness of the questions he was attempting to answer and offered a theory with a claim to being scientific in the accepted sense of the term; and thereby poured much light (and darkness) on many vexed problems, and led to much fruitful (and sterile) revaluation and reinterpretation.

But the practice of Communist states and, more logically of Fascist states (since they openly deny and denounce the value of the rational question-and-answer method), is not at all the training of the critical, or solution-finding, powers of their citizens, nor yet the development in them of any capacity for special insights or intuitions regarded as likely to reveal the truth. It consists in something which any nineteenth century thinker with respect for the sciences would have regarded with genuine horror—the training of individuals incapable of being troubled by questions which, when raised and discussed, endanger the stability of the system; the building and elaboration of a strong framework of institutions, "myths," habits of life and thought intended to preserve it from sudden shocks or slow decay. This is the intellectual outlook which attends the rise of totalitarian ideologies—the substance of the hair-raising satires of George Orwell and Aldous Huxley—the state of mind in which troublesome questions appear as a form of mental perturbation, noxious to the mental health of individuals and, when too widely discussed, to the health of societies. This is an attitude which looks on all inner conflict as an evil, or at best as a form of futile self-frustration; which considers the kind of friction, the moral or emotional or intellectual collisions, the particular kind of acute spiritual discomfort which rises to a condition of agony from which great works of the human intellect and imagination, inventions, philosophies, works of art, have sprung, as being no better than purely destructive diseases—neuroses, psychoses, mental derangements, genuinely requiring psychiatric aid; above all as being dangerous deviations from that line to which individuals and societies must adhere if they are to continue in a state of well-ordered, painless, contented, self-perpetuating equilibrium.

This is a truly far-reaching conception, and something far more powerful than the pessimism or cynicism of thinkers like Plato or Machiavelli, Swift or Carlyle, who looked on the majority of mankind as unalterably stupid or incurably vicious, and therefore concerned themselves with how the world might be made safe for the exceptional, enlightened or otherwise superior minority or individual. For their view did at least concede the reality of the painful problems, and merely denied the capacity of the majority to solve them; whereas the more radical attitude looks upon intellectual perplexity as being caused either by a technical problem to be settled in terms of practical policy, or else as a neurosis to be cured, that is made to disappear, if possible without a trace. This leads to a novel conception of the truth and of disinterested ideals in general, which would hardly have been intelligible to previous centuries. To adopt it is to hold that outside the purely technical sphere (where one asks only what are the most efficient means towards this or that practical end) words like "true," or "right," or "free," and the concepts which they denote, are to be defined in terms of the only activity recognized as valuable, namely, the organization of society as a smoothly-working machine providing for the needs of such of its members as are permitted to survive. The words and ideas in such a society will reflect the outlook of the citizens, being adjusted so as to involve as little friction as possible between, and within, individuals, leaving them free to make the "optimum" use of the resources available to them.

This is indeed Dostoevsky's utilitarian nightmare. In the course of their pursuit of social welfare, humanitarian liberals, deeply outraged by cruelty, injustice and inefficiency, discover that the only sound method of preventing these evils is not by providing the widest opportunities for free intellectual or emotional development—for who can tell where this might not lead?—but by eliminating the motives for the pursuit of these perilous ends, by suppressing any tendencies likely to lead to criticism, dissatisfaction, disorderly forms of life. I shall not attempt here to trace historically how this came to pass. No doubt the story must at some stage include the fact that mere disparity in tempo and extent between technical development and social change, together with the fact that the two could not be guaranteed to harmonize—despite the optimistic promises of Adam Smith—and indeed clashed more and more often, led to increasingly destructive and apparently unavertable economic crises. These were accompanied by social, political and moral disasters which the general framework—the patterns of behavior, habits, outlook, language, that is the "ideological superstructure" of the victims—could not sustain. The result was a loss of faith in existing political activities and ideals, and a desperate desire to live in a universe which, however dull and flat, was at any rate secure against the repetition of such catastrophes. An element in this was a growing sense of the greater or lesser meaninglessness of such ancient battle-cries as liberty or equality or civilization or truth, since their application to the surrounding scene was no longer as intelligible as it had been in the nineteenth century.

Together with this development, in the majority of cases, there went a reluctance to face it. But the once hallowed phrases were not abandoned. They were used—robbed of their original value—to cover the different and sometimes diametrically opposed notions of the new morality, which in terms of the old system of values, seemed both unscrupulous and brutal. The Fascists alone did not take the trouble to pretend to retain the old symbols, and while political diehards and the representatives of the more unbridled forms of modern big business clung half cynically, half hopefully, to such terms as freedom or democracy, the Fascists rejected them outright with theatrical gestures of disdain and loathing, and poured scorn upon them as the outworn husks of ideals which had long ago rotted away. But despite the differences of policy concerning the use of specific symbols there is a substantial similarity between all the variants of the new political attitude.

Observers in the twenty-first century will doubtless see these similarities of pattern more easily than we who are involved can possibly do today. They will distinguish them as naturally and clearly from their immediate past—that *hortus inclusus* of the nineteenth century in which so many writers both of history and of journalism and of political addresses today still seem to be living—as we distinguish the growth of romantic nationalism or of naive positivism from that of enlightened despotism or of patrician republics. Still, even we who live in them can discern something novel in our own times. Even we perceive the growth of new characteristics common to widely different spheres. On the one hand, we can see the progressive and conscious subordination of political to social and economic interests. The most vivid symptoms of this subordination are the open self-identification and conscious solidarity of men as capitalists or workers; these cut across, though without destroying, national and religious loyalties. On the other, we meet with the conviction that political liberty is useless without the economic strength to use it, and consequently implied or open denial of the rival proposition that economic opportunity is of use only to politically free men. This in its turn carries with it a tacit acceptance of the proposition that the responsibilities of the state to its citizens must and will grow and not diminish, a theorem which is today taken for granted by masters and men alike, in Europe perhaps more unquestioningly than in the United States, but accepted even there to a degree which seemed utopian only thirty, let alone fifty, years ago. This great transformation, with its genuine material gains, and no less genuine growth in social equality in the least liberal societies, is accompanied by something which forms the obverse side of the medal—the elimination, or, at the very best, strong disapproval of those propensities for free inquiry and crea- tion which cannot, without losing their nature, remain as conformist and law-abiding as the twentieth century demands. A century ago Auguste Comte asked why, if there was rightly no demand for freedom to disagree in mathematics, it should be allowed and even encouraged in ethics or the social sciences. And indeed, if the creation of certain "optimum" patterns of behavior and thought and feeling in individuals or entire societies is the main goal of social and individual action, Comte's case is unanswerable. Yet it is the degree of this very right to disregard the forces of order and convention, even the publicly accepted "optimum" goals of action, that forms the glory of that bourgeois culture which reached its zenith in the nineteenth century and of which we have only now begun to witness the beginning of the end.

VI

The new attitude, resting as it does upon the policy of diminishing strife and misery by the atrophy of the faculties capable of causing them, is naturally hostile to, or at least suspicious of, disinterested curiosity (which might end anywhere), and looks upon the practice of all arts not obviously useful to society as being at best forms of social frivolity. Such occupations, when they are not a positive menace, are, in this view, an irritating and wasteful irrelevance, a trivial fiddling, a dissipa- tion or diversion of energy which is difficult enough to accumulate at all and should therefore be directed wholeheartedly and unceasingly to the task of building and maintaining the well-adjusted—sometimes called the "well-integrated"—social whole. In this state of mind it is only natural that such terms as truth or honor or obligation or beauty be- come transformed into purely offensive or defensive weapons, used by a state or a party in the struggle to create a community impervious to influences beyond its own direct control. The result can be achieved either by rigid censorship and insulation from the rest of the world—a world which remains free at least in the sense that its inhabitants con- tinue to say what they wish, in which words are relatively unorganized, with all the "dangerous" consequences thereby brought about; or else it can be achieved by extending the area of strict control until it stretches over all possible sources of anarchy, i.e. the whole of mankind. Only by one of these two expedients can a state of affairs be achieved in which human behavior can be manipulated with relative ease of technically qualified specialists—adjusters of conflicts and promoters of peace both of body and of mind, engineers and other scientific experts, psychologists, sociologists, economic and social planners and so on. Clearly this is not an intellectual climate which favors originality of judgment, moral independence or uncommon powers of insight. The entire trend of such an order is to reduce all issues to technical problems of lesser or greater complexity, in particular the problem of how to survive, get rid of maladjustments, achieve a condition in which the individual's psychological or economic capacities are harnessed to producing the maximum of unclouded social contentment; and this in its turn depends upon the suppression of whatever in him might raise doubt or assert itself against the single all-embracing, all-clarifying, all-satisfying plan.

The tendency has taken acute forms in, for example, the Soviet Union. There subordination to the central plan, and the elimination of disturbing factors, whether by education or repression, has been enacted with that capacity for believing in the literal inspiration of ideologies— in the ability and duty of human beings to translate ideas into practice fully, rigorously and immediately—to which Russian thinkers of all schools seem singularly addicted. The Soviet pattern is clear, simple and correctly deduced from "scientifically demonstrated" premises. The task of realizing it must be entrusted to technically trained believers who look on the human beings at their disposal as material which is infinitely malleable within the confines revealed by the sciences. Stalin's remark that creative artists are "engineers of human souls" is a very precise expression of this spirit. The presence of it in the various Fascist societies destroyed by the recent war, with intuition or instinct substituted for science, and cynicism for hypocrisy, are equally clear for all to see. In Western Europe this tendency has taken the milder form of a shift of emphasis away from disagreement about political principles (and from party struggles which sprang from genuine differences of moral and spiritual outlook) towards disagreements, ultimately technical, about methods—about the best ways of achieving that degree of minimum economic or social stability without which arguments concerned with fundamental principles and the ends of life are felt to be "abstract," "academic" and unrelated to the urgent needs of the hour. Hence that noticeably growing lack of interest in long-term political issues—as opposed to current day-to-day economic or social problems— on the part of the populations of the Western European continent which is occasionally deplored by shocked American and British observers who falsely ascribe it to the growth of cynicism and disenchantment with ideals.

No doubt all abandonment of old values for new must appear to the surviving adherents of the former as conscienceless disregard for morality as such. But this is a great delusion. There is all too little disbelief, whether conscienceless or apathetic, of the new values. On the contrary, they are clung to with unreasoning faith and that blind intolerance towards skepticism which springs, as often as not, from a profound inner bankruptcy, the hope against hope that here is a safe haven at least, narrow, dark, cut off, but secure. Growing numbers of human beings are prepared to purchase this sense of security even at the cost of allowing vast tracts of life to be controlled by persons who, whether consciously or not, act systematically to narrow the horizon of human activity to manageable proportions, to train human beings into more easily combinable parts—interchangeable, almost prefabricated—of a total pattern. In the face of such a strong desire to stabilize, if need be, at the lowest level—upon the floor from which you cannot fall, which cannot betray you, "let you down"—all the ancient political principles begin to vanish, feeble symbols of creeds no longer relevant to the new realities.

This process does not move at a uniform pace everywhere. In the United States perhaps, for obvious economic reasons, the nineteenth century survives far more powerfully than anywhere else. The political issues and conflicts, the topics of discussion, and the idealized personalities of democratic leaders are far more reminiscent of Victorian Europe than anything to be found on that continent now.

Woodrow Wilson was a nineteenth century liberal in a very full and unqualified sense. The New Deal and the personality of President Roosevelt excited political passions far more like those of the battles which raged round Gladstone or Lloyd George, or the anti-clerical governments at the turn of the century in France, than anything actually contemporary with it in Europe; and this great liberal enterprise, certainly the most constructive compromise between individual liberty and economic security which our own time has witnessed, corresponds more closely to the political and economic ideals of John Stuart Mill in his last, humanitarian-Socialist phase than to left-wing thought in Europe in the thirties. The controversy about international organization, about the United Nations and its subsidiaries, as well as the other postwar international institutions, like the controversies which in the years after 1918 surrounded the League of Nations, are fully intelligible in terms of nineteenth century political ideals, and therefore occupied far more attention and meant much more in America than in Europe. The United States may have disavowed President Wilson, but it continued to live in a moral atmosphere not very different from that of Wilson's time— the easily recognizable black-and-white moral world of the Victorian values. The events of 1918 preyed on the American conscience for 25 years, whereas in Europe the *exalté* atmosphere of 1918-1919 disappeared without a trace—a brief moment of illumination which in retrospect seems more American that European, the last manifestation in Europe of a great but dying tradition in a world already living, and fully conscious of living, in a new medium, too well aware of its differences from, and resentful of, its past. The break was not sudden and total, a dramatic *coup de théâtre*. Many of the seeds planted in the eighteenth or nineteenth centuries have flowered only in the twentieth: the political and ethical climate in which trade unions were founded in Germany, or England, or France did of course contain as elements the old, familiar doctrines of human rights and duties which were the common property, avowed or not, of almost all parties and views in the liberal, humanitarian, expansionist hundred years of peaceful progress.

The main current of the nineteenth century does, of course, survive into the present, and especially in America and the British Dominions; but it is not what is most characteristic of our time. For in the past there were conflicts of ideas, whereas what characterizes our time is not the struggle of one set of ideas against another but the mounting wave of hostility to all ideas as such. Since ideas are considered the source of too much disquiet, there is a tendency to suppress the conflict between liberal claims to individual political rights and the economic injustice which results from their satisfaction (which forms the substance of Socialist criticism) by the submersion of both in an authoritarian regime which removes the free area within which such conflicts can occur. What is genuinely typical of our time is a new concept of the society, the values of which derive not from the desires or the moral sense of this or that individual's view of his ultimate ends but from some factual hypothesis or metaphysical dogma about history, or race, or national character in terms of which the answers to the question what is good, right, required, desirable, fitting, can be "scientifically" deduced, or intuited, or expressed in this or that kind of behavior. There is one and only one direction in which a given aggregate of individuals is conceived to be travelling, driven thither by quasi-occult impersonal forces, such as their class structure, or their unconscious selves, or their racial origin, or the "real" social or physical roots of this or that "popular" or "group" "mythology." The direction is alterable only by tampering with the hidden cause of behavior—those who wish to tamper being, according to this view, free to determine their own direction and that of others by having an understanding of the machinery of social behavior and skill in manipulating it.

In this sinister fashion have the words of St. Simon's prophecy finally come true—words which once seemed so brave and optimistic: "The government of man will be replaced by the administration of things." The cosmic forces are conceived as omnipotent and indestructible. Hopes, fears, prayers cannot wish them out of existence; but the elite of experts can canalize them and control them to some extent. The task of these experts is to adjust human beings to these forces and to develop in them an unshakable faith in the new order, and unquestioning loyalty to it, which will anchor it securely and forever. Consequently the technical disciplines which direct natural forces and adjust men to the new order must take primacy over humane pursuits—philosophical, historical, artistic. Such pursuits, at most, will serve only to prop up and embellish the new establishment. Turgenev's naive materialist, the hero of his novel *Fathers and Sons,* the nihilist Bazarov, has finally come into his own, as St. Simon and his more pedestrian follower Comte always felt sure that he would, but for reasons very different from those which seemed plausible a century ago. Bazarov's faith rested on the claim that the dissection of frogs was more important than poetry because it led to the truth, whereas the poetry of Pushkin did not.

The reason given today is more devastating: anatomy is superior to art because it generates no independent ends of life, provides no experiences which act as independent criteria of good or evil, truth or falsehood, and which are therefore liable to clash with the orthodoxy which we have created as the only bulwark strong enough to preserve us from doubts and despairs and all the horrors of maladjustment. To be torn this way and that emotionally or intellectually is a form of *malaise.* Against it nothing will work but the elimination of alternatives so nearly in equal balance that choice between them is—or even appears —possible.

This is, of course, what the Grand Inquisitor in Dostoevsky's *Brothers Karamazov* maintained with deadly eloquence: that what men dreaded most was freedom of choice, to be left alone to grope their way in the dark; and the Church by lifting the responsibility from their shoulders made them willing, grateful and happy slaves. The Grand Inquisitor stood for the dogmatic organization of the life of the spirit: Bazarov for its theoretical opposite—free scientific inquiry, the facing

of the "hard" facts, the acceptance of the truth however brutal. But by
an irony of history (not unforeseen by Dostoevsky) they have formed
a pact, they are allies, and today are almost indistinguishable. Buridan's
ass, we are told, unable to choose between two equidistant bundles of
hay, starved to death. Against this fate the only remedy is blind obedience and faith. Whether the refuge is a dogmatic religion or a dogmatic natural science matters relatively little: for without such obedience and faith there is no confidence and no hope, no optimistic, "constructive," "positive" form of life.

VII

At this point it might be said that the situation I have described is not
altogether new. Has not every authoritarian institution, every irra-
tionalist movement, been engaged upon something of this kind—the
artificial stilling of doubts, the attempt either to discredit uncom-
fortable questions or to educate men not to ask them? Was this not
the practice of the great organized churches, indeed of every institution from the national state to small sectarian establishments? Was this
not the attitude of the enemies of reason from the earliest mystery cults
to the romanticism, anarchistic nihilism or surrealism of the last century
and a half? Why should our age be specially accused of addiction to the
particular tendency which formed the central theme of the social
doctrines of Plato, or of the sect of the medieval Assassins, or of much
Eastern thought and mysticism?

But there are two great differences which separate the political characteristics of our age from their origins in the past. In the first place,
the reactionaries or romantics of previous periods, however much they
might have advocated the superior wisdom of institutional authority or
the revealed word over that of individual reason, did not in their
moments of wildest unreason minimize the importance of the questions
to be answered. On the contrary they maintained that so crucial was
it to obtain the correct answer that only hallowed institutions, or inspired leaders, or mystical revelation, or divine grace could vouchsafe
a solution of sufficient depth and universality. No doubt a hierarchy of
the relative importance of questions underlies any established social
system—a hierarchy the authority of which is itself not intended to be
open to question. Moreover, the obscurity of some among the answers
offered has in every age concealed their lack of truth or their irrelevance
to the questions which they purported to solve. And perhaps much
hypocrisy has traditionally been necessary to secure their success. But

hypocrisy is very different from cynicism or blindness. Even the censors of opinion and the enemies of the truth felt compelled to pay formal homage to the vital importance of obtaining true answers to the great problems by the best available means. If their practice belied this, at least there was something to be belied: traitors and heretics often keep alive the memory—and the authority—of the beliefs which they are intent on betraying.

The second difference consists in the fact that in the past such attempts to becloud the nature of the issues were associated specifically with the avowed enemies of reason and individual freedom. The alignment of forces has been clear at any rate since the Renaissance; progress and reaction, however much these words have been abused, are not empty concepts. On one side stood the supporters of authority, unreasoning faith, suspicious of, or openly opposed to, the uncontrolled pursuit of truth or the free realization of individual ideals. On the other, whatever their differences, were those supporters of free inquiry and self-expression who looked upon Voltaire and Lessing, Mill and Darwin and Ibsen as their prophets. Their common quality—perhaps their only common quality—was some degree of devotion to the ideals of the Renaissance and a hatred of all that was associated, whether justly or not, with the Middle Ages—darkness, suppression, the stifling of all heterodoxy, the hatred of the flesh and of gaiety and of the love of natural beauty. There were of course many who cannot be classified so simply or so crudely; but until our own day the lines were drawn sharply enough to determine clearly the position of the men who most deeply influenced their age. A combination of devotion to scientific principles with "obscurantist" social theory seemed altogether unthinkable. Today the tendency to circumscribe and confine and limit, to determine the range of what may be asked and what may not, to what may be believed and what may not, is no longer a distinguishing mark of the "reactionaries." On the contrary, it comes as powerfully from the heirs of the radicals, the rationalists, the "progressives," of the nineteenth century as from the descendants of their enemies. There is a persecution not only of science, but by science and in its name; and this is a nightmare scarcely foreseen by the most Cassandra-like prophets of either camp.

We are often told that the present is an age of cynicism and despair, of crumbling values and the dissolution of the fixed standards and landmarks of our civilization. But this is neither true nor even plausible. So far from showing the loose texture of a collapsing order, the world is today stiff with rigid rules and codes and ardent, irrational religions.

So far from evincing the toleration which springs from cynical disregard of the ancient sanctions, it treats heterodoxy as the supreme danger.

Whether in the East or West, the danger has not been greater since the ages of faith. Conformities are called for much more eagerly today than yesterday; loyalties are tested far more severely; skeptics and liberals and individuals with a taste for private life and their own inner standards of behavior, if they do not take care to identify themselves with an organized faith, are objects of fear or derision and targets of persecution for either side, execrated or despised by all the embattled parties in the great ideological wars of our time. And although this is less acute in societies traditionally averse to extremes—Great Britain, say, or Switzerland—this makes little difference to the general pattern. In the world today individual stupidity and wickedness are forgiven more easily than failure to be identified with a recognized party or attitude, to achieve an approved political or economic or intellectual status. In earlier periods, when more than one authority ruled human life, a man might escape the pressure of the state by taking refuge in the fortress of the opposition—of an organized church or a dissident feudal establishment. The mere fact of conflict between authorities allowed room for a narrow and shifting, but still never entirely non-existent, no-man's-land, where private lives might still precariously be lived, because neither side dared to go too far for fear of too greatly strengthening the other. Today the very virtues of the paternalistic state, its genuine anxiety to reduce destitution and disease and inequality, to penetrate all the neglected nooks and crannies of life which may stand in need of its justice and its bounty—its very success in those beneficent activities—has narrowed the area within which the individual may commit blunders, has curtailed his liberties in the interest (the very real interest) of his welfare or of his sanity, his health, his security, his freedom from want and fear. His area of choice has grown smaller not in the name of some opposing principle—as in the Dark Ages or during the rise of the nationalities—but in order to create a situation in which the very possibility of opposed principles, with all their unlimited capacity to cause mental stress and danger and destructive collisions, is eliminated in favor of a simpler and better regulated life, a robust faith in an efficiently working order, untroubled by agonizing moral conflict.

Yet this is not a gratuitous development: the social and economic situation in which we are placed, the failure to harmonize the effects of technical progress with the forces of political and economic organization inherited from an earlier phase, do call for a greater measure of social control to prevent chaos and destitution, no less fatal to the development of human faculties than blind conformity. And certainly it is morally unthinkable that we give up our social gains and meditate for an instant the possibility of a return to ancient injustice and inequality and hopeless misery. The progress of technological skill makes it rational and indeed imperative to plan, and anxiety for the success of a particular planned society naturally inclines the planners to seek insulation from dangerous, because incalculable, forces which may jeopardize the plan. And this is a powerful incentive to "autarky" and "socialism in one country" whether imposed by conservatives, or New Dealers, or isolationists, or Social Democrats, or indeed imperialists. And this in its turn generates artificial barriers and increasingly restricts the planners' own resources. In extreme cases it leads to repression of the discontented and a perpetual tightening of discipline, until it absorbs more and more of the time and ingenuity of those who originally conceived it only as a means to a minimum of efficiency. Presently it grows to be a hideous end in itself, since its realization spells ruin to the system now caught in a vicious circle of repression in order to survive and of survival mainly to repress. So the remedy grows to be worse than the disease, and takes the form of those orthodoxies which rest on the simple puritanical faith of individuals who never knew or have forgotten what *douceur de vivre,* free self-expression, the infinite variety of persons and of the relationships between them, and the right of free choice, difficult to endure but more intolerable to surrender, can ever have been like.

The dilemma is logically insoluble: we cannot sacrifice either freedom or a minimum standard of welfare. The way out must therefore lie in some logically untidy, flexible, and even ambiguous compromise: every situation calls for its own specific policy, since out of the crooked timber of humanity, as Kant once remarked, no straight thing was ever made. What the age calls for is not (as we are so often told) more faith or stronger leadership or more rational organization. Rather is it the opposite—less Messianic ardor, more enlightened skepticism, more toleration of idiosyncrasies, more frequent ad hoc and ephemeral arrangements, more room for the attainment of their personal ends by individuals and by minorities whose tastes and beliefs find (whether rightly or wrongly must not matter) little response among the majority. What is required is a less mechanical, less fervent application of general principles, however rational or righteous, a more cautious and less self-confident application of accepted, scientifically tested, general solutions in unexamined individual cases. We must not submit to authority because it is infallible but only for strictly and openly utilitarian reasons, as a necessary evil. Since no solution can be guaranteed against error, no disposition is final. And therefore a loose texture and a measure of inefficiency and even muddle, even a degree of indulgence in idle talk, idle curiosity, aimless pursuit of this or that without authorization—"conspicuous waste" itself—may allow more spontaneous, individual variation (for which the individual must in the end assume full responsibility), and will always be worth far more than the neatest and most delicately fashioned imposed pattern. Above all, it must be realized that the kinds of problems which this or that method of education or system of scientific or religious or social organization of life is guaranteed to solve are *eo facto* not the central questions of human life. They are not, and never have been, the fundamental issues which embody the changing outlook and the most intense preoccupation of their time and generation. It is from absorbed preoccupation with these fundamental issues and these alone, unplanned and at times without technical equipment, more often than not without conscious hope of success, still less of the approbation of the official auditor, that the best moments come in the lives of individuals and peoples.

Political Modernization:
The Single-Party System

RUPERT EMERSON

EDITORIAL NOTE: *Single party systems were hailed by many as the midwives of political modernization, the founders of authority, and the vehicles for political participation in the new nations. As Rupert Emerson points out—and his concluding remarks written in 1963 have retrospectively the character of a prophecy—they have been unable to do so and he explains some of the reasons. The reader should consult the publication edited by Joseph La Palombara and Myron Weiner,* Political Parties and Political Development, *Princeton, 1966. Also see Ruth Schachter Morgenthau,* Political Parties in French-Speaking West Africa, *Oxford, 1964.*

I

THE problem of modernization, be it political or otherwise, arises from the fact that a few of the world's societies have in the last centuries forged ahead to achieve riches and power which enabled them to overrun most of the rest of the world, establishing their imperial domination. To counter this power by coming to a level of equality with it and to secure their share of the more ample life which had now become possible, other peoples found themselves confronted by the necessity of rebuilding their societies on the model of those who had both stolen a lead and often the other peoples' countries as well. The most decisive push in this direction came as an unintended by-product of imperialism and more particularly of colonial rule.

It is startling to remember that the entire range of the last great forward surge of Western imperialism and its demise are embraced within the lifetime of anyone who has now reached the age of eighty or beyond. A conventional date for the beginning of this wave of imperialism is the Berlin Conference of 1884-85 which formally opened the scramble for Africa. Its end is marked by no such specific event but it follows close after World War II, although the forces working to overturn Western imperialism were obviously gathering in the inter-war decades. The opening phases of the anti-colonial drive are marked by the independence in Asia of the Philippines and India, and in Africa of Morocco and Tunisia, the Sudan and Ghana, promptly followed by the extraordinary liberating sweep of 1960.

Save for scattered and isolated colonial dots on the map and the gravely threatening mass of Southern Africa which remains white-dominated, the colonial era has come to an end with amazing suddenness and finality. Despite the warnings in some quarters against the threat of neocolonialism, a recrudescence of colonialism in anything even remotely reminiscent of its familiar guise is profoundly unlikely. It is indicative of the change which has taken place that it has become one of the major preoccupations of the United Nations, now largely in the hands of the new countries, to see that every vestige of colonialism vanishes. Where in the very recent past imperial power was a proud symbol of greatness and strength it has now been translated into evidence of sin which must be immediately eradicated. Disinterested observers are inclined, however, to the view that, while exceptions must be made on both sides and the weighting of the scales is difficult, territories under Western colonial rule, for all its evils and shortcomings, have made a more effective advance toward modernization than have comparable countries which somehow managed to evade becoming dependencies.

An examination of the problems of political modernization requires no elaborate survey of the early stages of Western imperialism, but two or three points may be singled out which have a significant bearing on the main theme. An essential ingredient of the contemporary problem is that with the rarest of exceptions training for self-government on modern lines is a very recent matter. It is, of course, true that some of the contacts of the European powers with southern Asia, from which empires later developed, date back to the beginning of the seventeenth century or even earlier. The connections of the British with India, of the Dutch with Indonesia, and of the Spanish with the Philippines were old-established by the time the partitioning of Africa got under way. In that part of the world the renewed burst of imperialism which characterized the three or four decades preceding World War I was largely an extension or consolidation of earlier imperial activities and acquisitions, involving both a rounding out of territorial holdings and an intensification and rationalization of European rule and economic exploitation. The modern colonial system which set the stage for a takeover by the presently independent governments was in good part a product of this more recent phase, even though some of the colonial relationships date much further back.

In Africa even in those very limited areas in which the full extent of the conventional figure of eighty years is relevant the period of Western overlordship or tutelage is still brief. Actually in the great bulk of Africa, south of the Sahara, Western administration penetrated beyond occasional and hesitant footholds on the coast only at a considerably later time than the Berlin Conference, and in many rural areas it had had only a minimal impact even by the time of independence. Throughout Africa, as in Indonesia and elsewhere under colonial auspices, only a handful of people participated significantly in the management of their countries although the numbers increased in the last years of colonialism, and only when independence was almost in sight was substantial responsibility vested in the people of the country.

It would, of course, be ridiculous to lump all the colonial regimes together and assume that they all produced similar results. The colonial policy and administrative practice of the different powers varied greatly, and the same power operated in quite different fashions in different circumstances, is, for example, in territories where there was or was not a sizable body of white settlers. The range of difference is reflected in such summary observations as that the Americans assumed from the outset that the Philippines should move toward self-government, the British in due course eased the entry of Indians into the Indian Civil Service and expanded their political participation particularly at the local and provincial level, the French in principle moved to assimilate their colonial subjects into French culture and a single far-flung French Republic, and the Belgians held all power in their own hands while cautiously raising the general Congolese level of education and economic employment.

If the period of effective colonial tutelage was brief, the time which has elapsed since independence is almost inconsequential in terms of any effort to assess the probable course of political evolution in the new countries. Colonial rule, whether it be seen as oppression and exploitation or as benevolent introduction to the modern world, is a shattering experience, and it will be many years before the peoples exposed to it can be expected to find their own solid footing. The processes of adaptation to a radically different style of life which were started under imperialist and other pressures must now be taken over by the people and turned to their own purposes. Both independence and development bring new forces into play which seem inevitably destined to bring about basic readjustments of the balance between generations, interests, and classes. Externally the new countries must somehow fit themselves into a world whose own foundations have been shaken by wars and revolutions and by an unceasing flow of revolutionary scientific discoveries which are fundamentally changing the relation of men to each other and to their environment. The transition from the pre-colonial traditional societies through the decades or centuries of alien-imposed colonial rule to a fully achieved and stable independence is more likely than not to be a painful and turbulent one. On the face of it, it is more realistic to expect drastic and seemingly erratic changes of direction than straightforward advance along the lines laid out by the first post-colonial generation.

The currently fashionable adjective used to describe the new countries is "emerging," but whether the term is "backward," "underdeveloped," "developing," or some other such, the implication is the same. The peoples are assumed to be emerging both from the colonial regimes to which they have been subjected and from the social systems in which they have traditionally lived; and what they are emerging into is the modernity whose content and pattern have been shaped in Western Europe in the last two or three centuries. The bearing of the now discarded term "backward"—nicer words are constantly introduced to cover harsh realities—was that the peoples so described had lingered far behind the "advanced" peoples who had set in motion the dominant civilization of the nineteenth and twentieth centuries. To "develop" or "emerge" is to join the ranks of those in the West who have achieved a hitherto undreamt of power over both man and nature, an unparalleled prosperity, and, for a time, the imperial leadership of mankind at large. For a time—a time which may perhaps reach well beyond the era of Western imperial domination—the standards by which all men were judged were those which reflected the civilization brought into being in a small corner of Western Europe and carried abroad by its migrant sons.

The West is often accused of attempting, in parochial arrogance, not only to force its own values and systems down the throats of other peoples but also to label as inferior all those who fail to adopt these values and systems for themselves. No doubt there is justice in such a charge. Certainly the imperial supremacy which the West established over so vast a segment of the world invited the bitter resentment which colonialism has evoked, and discrimination on the basis of race and color has been a constant feature in one or another guise.

The West can be attacked for its arrogance but the story has other sides as well. The most significant consideration is that the revolution which the West brought to men's affairs did in fact furnish an unprecedented power and made possible a material well-being which no other society had been able to approach. It is arguable that once such forces had been loosed in the world they were irresistible and that no people which wanted to lead an independent life could expect to survive unless it took over key elements of this revolution as its own. I have contended elsewhere that future analysts may find the most lasting consequence of colonialism to have been the spread of the new-style Western civilization accompanied by all its virtues and vices.[1]

At all events, whatever the validity of these propositions, it is the "backward" peoples themselves, or their leaders speaking for them, who are producing the most convincing demonstration of the assumption that to "emerge" is to adopt the characteristic features which distinguish the West from other and earlier civilizations. What makes "modernization" modern is the ability to live, to think, to produce, to organize, in substantially the same fashion as the Western countries whose imperial hold has now been almost totally broken. With the rarest of exceptions the men who have thrust themselves forward as the governing elites of the Asian and African states have explicitly aimed at coming to terms of equality with the West by taking over its science, its techniques, its institutions. Certainly these elites have also demonstrated their pride in the inherited culture of their people and have made clear their desire to preserve and promote it; but the greater emphasis is on modernization as defined by the Western model. To this end foreign aid and technical assistance are eagerly sought through international and bilateral channels. It is obviously desirable that the modernization should be adapted as closely as possible to the local scene and its particular cultural inheritance, but the point of importance is far less the special elements of adaptation than the attainment of equality with the West—or, better yet, superiority to it—through utilization of the West's own concepts and instruments. In passing it might be noted that it has so far been a losing stern chase since the pace of development in the emerging countries has been constantly outstripped

[1] See my *From Empire to Nation*. Cambridge, Massachusetts: Harvard University Press, 1960.

by the continuing advance of the West, even apart from the constant danger that any material gains which are secured will be devoured by the multiplication of population, most notably in Asia.

Political modernization has been sought no less than economic and other forms of development, and is certainly of no less importance. Indeed, it has become increasingly apparent that the existence of an effective political and administrative system is a prior condition for the attainment of economic development. It is, however, somewhat more difficult to determine precisely what is meant by political modernization and to make an objective assessment of it than in the case of other types of modernization.[2] Presumably the easiest of all to identify and to measure is economic development for which a number of objective quantifiable criteria are readily available, such as the gross national product, per capita income, the type and quantity of agricultural and industrial production, the rate of economic growth, the number of workers drawn into wage employment, etc. In the field of transport and communications or of hygiene and medical care similar sets of statistics likewise yield good evidence as to the progress which is being made, and advances in education are shown in the number of schools, teachers, and pupils at different levels in the educational system.

The assessment of political development is a more problematical matter for a variety of reasons. One major point of confusion is that the "advanced" Western standard against which development is to be measured is itself dubious and controversial. If the problem is approached in terms of political structure, there is surely no particular model which can be set up as representing an agreed ideal or a necessary, or even a peculiarly favorable, precondition for economic and social development. Indisputably advanced countries have, even in the present century, experimented with more or less every form of government that is likely to appear in the new states, short of the improbable event that the latter revert to feudalism or an outright tribalism. In the last decades the name of democracy has been most frequently invoked as representing the most desirable mode of government, but democracy has developed so many variants and been used to cover so large a multitude of sins as to become almost meaningless unless it is closely defined.

The advanced West has known one-party, two-party, and multiparty democracies; it has known monarchies and dictatorships, including the modern inventions of fascism and communism; and it has tried out

---

[2] Robert E. Ward has made a brief and suggestive inquiry into the meaning of political modernization in the opening pages of his Political Modernization and Political Culture in Japan. *World Politics* (July 1963), 569-596.

such hybrid forms as de Gaulle's Fifth Republic which has presumably been influential in promoting the vogue of strong presidential regimes in ex-French Africa. The available evidence appears to indicate that a variety of radically different governmental forms are compatible with, or may positively promote, economic and other types of development. Great Britain, Germany, Italy, Switzerland, the United States, Japan, and the Soviet Union are all to be counted in the ranks of the advanced. It would be a quite arbitrary matter to pick out one among the strikingly divergent political systems which they have evolved as the model by which the degree of modernization of the emerging countries should be judged. We have, indeed, no reason whatsoever to assume that some of the new countries may not devise other and radically different forms of government, perhaps more closely related to their indigenous tradition, which will prove to be equally effective instruments for development.

A further complication is that in almost every instance the new countries come to independence already endowed with constitutions which must be characterized as specifically "modern" and are usually closely akin to the political system of the imperial power from which they have just separated. Thus, all the colonial territories which have moved to independence have either started their new life with Constitutions designed for them by the colonial power, usually in some measure of agreement with the nationalist leaders, or have devised Constitutions drawn essentially from Western models as soon as they have become free or shortly thereafter. This is not to contend that, say, the 1945 Constitution of Indonesia, re-introduced by Sukarno, or the post-independence Constitutions of Ghana and Tanganyika have no elements of novelty in them or are uninfluenced by local tradition, but the general proposition still holds that the new countries have drawn almost exclusively on Western constitutional models, perhaps making an eclectic combination of forms. Constitutionally speaking, therefore, political modernization has been achieved before or coincidentally with the end of colonial status.

In such circumstances the significant element is likely to be the way in which the constitutional structure is actually utilized, the political style in which public affairs are managed. In the emerging countries no less than in the advanced what is important is not the elegance of the constitutional or legal facade, but the reality of political behavior which lies behind it. As the West well knows, the gap between formal governmental institutions and actual political operations may be immense; and it is a gap which is likely to be larger in the new than in the older established states because of the heavy borrowing by the former of alien and still unfamiliar political forms, developed elsewhere in different climes and circumstances. To dig beneath the outward forms and discover where power actually rests and how it is manipulated is by no means always easy. It will be a substantial time before the newly independent countries break away from the impact of their former colonial regimes and from the temptation—perhaps one should say, the necessity —to copy the West as furnishing in its manifold guises the only authentic models of what modernization means. It is more plausible than not that in due course these countries will develop political institutions which are more specifically their own, unless the determinist position is accepted that their development along modern economic lines will necessarily bring them the same kind of political institutions as have accompanied economic development in the West.

Although the constitutional foundations associated with modernity are too varied to permit any simple identification, five characteristic features of any modern political system can be summarily stated: 1) Political leadership must be so organized as to make reasonably firm and swift decisions possible. 2) There must be a rationalized and reasonably noncorrupt civil service whose members are selected primarily on the basis of merit and ability and who can be counted on, in the ordinary course of events, to obey orders. 3) The government's financial affairs must be regularized and separated from the private financial affairs of those who are in political or administrative control. 4) There must be a judiciary and courts of law which administer some reasonable approximation of even-handed justice. 5) The writ of the government must run, in principle at least, throughout the entire country, even though at any given moment there may be substantial pockets of resistance or noncompliance.

The most trustworthy indices of the success of any political system in achieving modernization are to be found in the results for the society of which it is in charge. The maintenance of law and order internally and the preservation of the state's identity and integrity externally are the minimum and indispensable requirements. Assuming that these requirements are met, if the economy is advancing and the standard of living improving, if public health is making headway and education is spreading, it is a reasonable presumption that the government is doing its job well.

The responsibilities and aspirations of the governments of the emerging countries are as extensive as are the difficulties by which they are confronted. They are charged with, or have taken upon themselves, the immense task of bringing their people as speedily as possible to the level of the advanced, despite the fact that they are at best only meagerly equipped with the tools needed for the task. Since the transition to independence has generally taken place peacefully, they have usually inherited the colonial administrative systems as going concerns, although European civil servants have often left in substantial numbers as the nationalists took over. The functioning of the ex-colonial regimes has been grievously impaired only in the surprisingly rare instances of bitter and protracted revolutionary war, as in Indonesia, Vietnam, and Algeria, or where the parting was marked by a fit of bad temper as in the French reaction to Guinea's vote of "No" in the referendum on the de Gaulle constitution of 1958. Even where the colonial governmental machinery is inherited intact, however, it was the creation of the imperial authorities and is therefore unlikely to meet the new national demands satisfactorily. Although the colonial governments had come to reach well beyond the provision of the minimum services of law and order, the new governments have universally taken on a large array of broader functions which may be lumped under the general headings of economic development and the promotion of social welfare, plus entry into the wholly new field of international representation and action.

The purposes and scope of a colonial regime, manned in all its commanding heights by expatriate officials, are inevitably different from and more limited than those of a national government, and particularly a national government which takes over in a first surge of enthusiasm for its new-found power and responsibilities. Since the leaders in the new countries are virtually all men who have a substantial familiarity with the progressive programs and practices of the West, they set off from the assumption that it is their responsibility to see that their people are furnished with social welfare facilities of a type comparable with those existent elsewhere, even though the social and economic foundations of the societies which they govern have not begun to approach the level of the advanced societies which are taken as the model. Thus, to pick a single example, it is assumed, despite the heavy costs of many kinds, that universal education should be provided in the earlier grades and secondary and higher education greatly expanded. In aspiration at least, the new countries set as their more or less immediate goal the achievement of the whole apparatus of the advanced states which, in glaring contrast to themselves, are already equipped with highly developed economies and administrations.

Of particular moment is that fact that universally the new countries look to the government to carry the main burden of economic development. The general absence of a supply of indigenous entrepreneurs, the lack of capital or at least its unavailability for productive and developmental purposes, and the scarcity of private groupings and associations which might carry some of the burden all contribute to the belief that the government should play the major role. Deriving in good part from the experience of capitalism under the colonial regimes—seen as represented by alien concerns exploiting the local populace—there is a fear and suspicion of private enterprise, which is bolstered by wide acceptance of the theory that imperialism is an inevitable product of capitalism. In almost every country the view is dominant that socialism is the appropriate label for the kind of social-economic system which is desired. Socialism in this sense has no necessary connection with Marxism, and far less with the specific Marxist variant of Communism, but is rather a general term to cover a system adapted to local conditions and traditions, in which there will be a cooperative pulling together rather than an unleashing of the antisocial forces of privtae profit-making. In the large it may be said that the community is valued more than the individual. To put it in the simplest terms, socialism is a good word, and capitalism a bad one. In order to arrive at the socialist society and the planning which is incident to it, the government must take over the direction of economic life—but the extent to which the government actually intervenes varies greatly from state to state.

It is one of the ironies of the situation that the modernizing role of governments has undergone a decided expansion just at the time when the trained and "modernized" manpower available to them has been sharply reduced through the removal of at least some of the alien civil servants who have staffed the colonial regimes. Or, alternatively, where the expatriates have in fact stayed on, the new governments are left in the anomalous position of having to rely on this alien contingent, often in key posts, at a time of maximum national self-assertion. This has been peculiarly the case in most of the former French African territories which have remained so closely tied to France through the continued presence of French personnel and through financial and economic reliance on France as to open them to the charge of having secured only an outward show of independence.

A partial and temporary answer to the lack of expertise can be found in the utilization of externally supplied technical assistance and similar devices, but this is no answer for the long haul. In many countries great efforts are being made to train and recruit the administrators, but it is inevitably a slow and costly process, entailing much loss and inefficiency on the way. At the same time every country has been plagued by the problem of trying to keep the official payroll clear of the multitude of people who feel that they are entitled to a place on it, either because of family connections or their education or merely because it is their country, no longer under alien rule and now obligated to take care of its own. These are the growing pains of new states and must be borne with, but they do not ease the already extraordinarily difficult processes of modernization and development.

The difficulties are, of course, compounded by the fact that nowhere are adequate revenues available to the governments to meet the costs of the expansive programs which they would like to introduce. The vicious circle of poverty perpetuating poverty, where riches multiply wealth, is an inescapable limiting factor. Again, foreign aid from a variety of donors or lenders can somewhat ease the situation but the basic reliance must be on home resources, particularly when private foreign enterprise and investment are likely to be eyed with suspicion, despite official pronouncements of welcome to the foreign investor. The full mobilization of home resources is often made very difficult, or for immediate purposes impossible, by the ability of the well-to-do to evade taxation, not infrequently on the assumption which has cropped up in many other parts of the world that their prosperity, far from imposing obligations on them, entitles them to special privileges.

A major cause of difficulty and even of potential disaster for the emerging countries is that they so often rest upon the unstable foundation of populations which are internally divided. Only rarely does one find in these countries the kind of homogeneity and national solidarity with which at least wishful thinking endows the modern state. As Edward Shils has put it:

> In almost every aspect of their social structures, the societies on which the new states must be based are characterized by a "gap." It is the gap between the educated and the uneducated, between the townsman and the villager, between the cosmopolitan or national and the local, between the modern and the traditional, between the rulers and the ruled. It is the gap between a small group of active, aspiring, relatively well-off, educated, and influential persons in the big towns, and an inert or indifferent, impoverished, uneducated, and relatively powerless peasantry.[3]

An even more dangerous threat to unity and stability appears when to this list are added the gaps which derive from the inclusion within a

[3] EDWARD SHILS, *Political Development in the New States*. 's-Gravenhage: Mouton & Co., 1962, p. 30.

single political system of different tribal, caste, religious, and linguistic communities.

To seek to enlist the active participation of the people in creating a viable state and setting the processes of development in motion becomes a hazardous enterprise when substantial segments of the population are perhaps only dubiously aware of the existence of the new state and its government and certainly are moved by no overriding loyalty to them. The ability of the government to make its writ run throughout the entire territory may be decisively challenged, and even the continued unity of the state placed in jeopardy. To give a single example, the government of Burma has never been able since winning independence in 1947 to have unhampered access to, and establish its control over, all parts of the country. The disorders which tribalism has inflicted on the Congo need no elaboration.

The most evident lack is the failure to have achieved a feeling of national identity in some deeper sense of belonging together and sharing a common destiny than can be expected to flow from the superimposed fact of common membership in a recently constructed state. A few Asian and African countries, such as Japan and divided Korea and Vietnam, match up passably well to the ideal type of the nation which can be abstracted from the experience of a small number of West European peoples, but many can claim virtually nothing more than the tenuous roots with which a brief encounter with colonialism has endowed them. A cursory glance at their history furnishes the reason why this should be so, but an understanding of how they arrived where they are does not change the fact that they can often be given no more than a courtesy title of nationhood. Much is heard of nationalism and of the nationalist leaders who carry on the anti-colonial struggle, but for the most part the nations themselves are at the best only beginning to be shaped.

Africa south of the Sahara is a classic example of this situation since the multiplicity of states into which it is being divided are almost all colonial inventions, designed with cavalier disregard for the tribes and peoples which compose them. Even at the time when independence came, substantial parts of tropical Africa might have been given a different political shape, as most notably in the maintenance of the two big French federations of West and Equatorial Africa instead of "balkanization" into a dozen political entities. The magnitude and vigor of the drive for pan-African solutions indicate the lack of satisfaction with the present political division of the continent. In Asia, although Indonesia and the Philippines can claim a somewhat greater antiquity as political entities than their African counterparts, their boundaries are those which were established by the colonial powers. Even India had known little, if any, unity before the British *raj* enforced it, while Pakistan was barely dreamed of before the 1930's.

Where there has been no significant prior unity of a national variety the fact of organizing a nationalist movement and carrying on a revolutionary struggle has a significant effect in stimulating the spread of national awareness and loyalty. In a number of recent instances, however, the imperial authorities have been so ready to relinquish their hold that they have granted independence well before there was any effective and organized demand for it, much less an irresistible revolutionary drive. Although future legends may require a different and more heroic version, independence has in fact often been peacefully conceded on the basis of an agreed timetable and program. One of the results is that many of the ex-colonial peoples have not undergone such national welding together as might have come to them from the experience of concerting their forces to wage political and perhaps military warfare against the colonialists. The contemporary campaign against the dangers of neo-colonialism can be traced in part to the need to rouse a sense of nationalist fervor in peoples who were able to find an easy path to freedom, or to re-arouse it for those whose memory of the anti-colonial struggle is fading.

Where the population of a country is relatively homogeneous a nationalist movement or the attainment or near approach of independence will ordinarily have a unifying effect, but where the population is diverse the effect may be to call attention to differences and points of incompatibility. With the coming of independence it becomes increasingly impossible to evade the question, which perhaps hardly came to the surface under alien imperial rule, as to who will wield power in the new dispensation. In the interest of which nationality, tribe, or religious community will the new state function? The issue is perhaps most unmistakably clear where white settlers are involved, as in Algeria, Southern Rhodesia, or, at its most terrifying, in South Africa, in all of which independence for the native majority or the white minority means the subordination of the other. In India as independence neared, a large segment of the Muslim minority found intolerable the thought of Hindu domination, and in Cylon the aftermath of freedom was the clash of Sinhalese and Tamils. The transition to independence of Ghana was threatened by the reluctance of the Ashanti to accept rule by other tribes, and Kenya's independence has been delayed by the fears of the lesser tribes for their future under Kikuyu and Luo supremacy. British Guiana's political advance has been plagued by the feud which increasing self-government has stirred up between those of African and of Indian descent. Other parts of the British West Indies have, however, been able to take self-government and independence in their stride, and the extraordinary example of Malaya, whose interracial alliance between Malays, Chinese, and Indians may still prove too good to last, establishes that the ending of colonial rule need not aggravate tensions even when racial diversity is great.

The emerging countries are all of them in one or another stage of transition from a past which can be determined with considerable accuracy to a future of which only dim outlines can be discerned. Some clues as to what lies ahead of them can perhaps be derived from an examination of their political evolution to date, and particularly of their experience with democracy, to which almost all have expressed their devotion but in fashions which many democrats may feel inclined to repudiate as wholly unacceptable.

II

Before the current wave of colonial emancipation got under way it appears to have been widely taken for granted by both the colonial-nationalists and their backers in the imperial centers and elsewhere that the societies which were about to be liberated would surely give full expression to democracy. This reflected not only a general belief in progress but more specifically an optimistic faith that underdogs who achieved the freedom to which they were entitled could be counted on to run their societies in accord with the dictates of freedom. To doubt this proposition and its corollaries was to open up the entire foundations of liberal anti-colonialism to skeptical or hostile reexamination. The main opponents of such a view were indeed those who were convinced opponents of the whole swing toward colonial independence and took for granted the contrary proposition that only trouble lay ahead of peoples who were so obviously incompetent to manage their own affairs. At the extreme, the European who saw the African as having just come down from the trees was not likely to be impressed by his ability to rule himself on acceptable modern lines.

For the others, however, it was something of an article of faith both that democracy in its Western guise represented the highest form of political life and that the peoples who were achieving freedom would be satisfied with nothing less than the best. The imperial authorities were assailed because they had failed to live up to the democratic convictions of the mother countries in their dealings with the dependent peoples, imposing on them instead autocratic and bureaucratic rule. One of the principal criteria of political advance in the colonies was the grant of an increasing measure of democratic participation in the governmental process through elective councils and legislatures whose enhanced control over the executive began to break the exclusive hold of the expatriate officials. It was a logical presumption that with the coming of independence full power would be vested in the representatives of the people, elected on the basis of universal suffrage. The nationalists based themselves on their claim to speak for their own people as against the alien colonial masters, and had become familiar with democracy and its values in the course of their Western-style education at home or abroad. It may also have played a role that the spokesmen for the imperial powers made it clear that a democratic form of government could be managed only by a mature and advanced people; "natives" were not to be trusted with such a complex and delicate instrument. For the colonial peoples it became therefore a matter of pride and prestige to demonstrate that they as well as their erstwhile colonial rulers could make democracy work.

As has been seen, when the nationalist heirs of the colonial regimes took over, they operated for the most part under constitutions which were either a continuation of the colonial structure, modified to meet the requirements of an independent state, or had been hammered out in agreement with the imperial authorities prior to independence. In other instances, such as those of India and Indonesia, new constitutions were drafted by a constitutional convention or the political leaders. With only trivial exceptions the political systems under which the new states started their lives were quite evidently drawn from Western democratic models and were assumed to set the countries for which they were designed on a political path strictly comparable to that of the formerly dominant Western powers.

The optimistic faith with which the emerging countries started on their new careers has not been justified by the results as far as the maintenance of democratic rule is concerned; but it may be that the standards and expectations set for them and which their leaders set for themselves were improper and ill-designed. At all events in country after country, with or without drastic constitutional revision, the original democratic presuppositions have given way to quite different systems of centralized and authoritarian control in military or civilian hands. The countries which have maintained an acceptably Western style of democratic constitutionalism are a small minority of those which have come to independence since World War II; and the earlier example of the twenty Latin-American republics does not lend much encouragement. Certainly in terms of sheer size, and perhaps in accomplishment as well, India heads the list despite those critics who point to the unbroken dominance of the Congress, the hold of the caste system, and other anomalies and shortcomings. In neighboring Southeast Asia both the Philippines and Malaya have maintained a respectable record of democratic performance. In the Middle East, Israel and Lebanon, balanced uneasily on its confessional division, would be the leading candidates. Among all the African states Nigeria has the best claim to have preserved a measure of multiparty constitutional democracy but the disturbances in the Western Region and the treason trials involving major opposition leaders have somewhat tarnished the Nigerian record. The occasional claims of Southern Rhodesia and South Africa to represent oases of parliamentary democracy in a continent overrun by authoritarian leaders and elites must be disallowed in view of their failure to give political expression to the bulk of the people of their countries.

I have deliberately expressed doubt as to the correctness of the standards and expectations which have been set and have referred to "an acceptably Western style" of democracy. What is involved is obviously a central and inescapable issue as to the meaning and structure of democracy. The alternative approach of discarding the concept of democracy itself and shifting to the assumption that some other social-political form than democracy is more effective and desirable has as yet made only slight headway. In the 1930's, when the Fascist regimes appeared to be making a great splash in the world, it was possible to share their scorn for democracy, but the presently available alternatives to democracy are not attractive; and Communism, of course, puts itself forward as embodying the true democracy in contrast to the oppressive rule of the bourgeoisie which masquerades as democracy in non-Communist societies. As a random sample of an opposing position, one J. Chuks Obi wrote that while it is fashionable to regard democracy as a panacea for all social and economic ills,

> There is a real sense in which economic development demands leadership and direction from as *few* as possible. The astonishingly rapid transformation of Russia did not owe its achievements to a well-packed House of Assembly. British capitalism and industrial leader-

ship in the 19th century was not founded on government for the people and by the people. One cannot help thinking that when Dr. Sukarno advocated a "guided democracy" for Indonesia he had an eye on Nigeria where over 1,000 legislators for a population of about 33 millions (real text-book democracy) is proving an expensive luxury.[4]

As a matter of history a case can unquestionably be made for such a position, but in terms of present-day politics it is a position which finds few takers; and it is to be noted that Sukarno spoke of guided *democracy*.

The cardinal political assumption remains that the people rule, and that the governmental system runs on their behalf. Therefore democracy must figure in the title of the system; but what is democracy? Two major conceptions come immediately to mind, one deriving from the parliamentary systems of the West, and the other, also with Western origins but less reputable ones, which has found more favor in the emerging countries. Both share the great common ground of resting on a doctrine of popular sovereignty and on the acceptance, at least in principle, of universal suffrage. Although the differences run significantly deeper than this somewhat mechanical version of them would indicate, the breaking point comes where the Western liberal system requires the existence of two or more political parties, forming a government and an opposition, while Asian and African leaders have been moving more and more explicitly toward a single-party system, for which an impressive body of theoretical justification is being advanced.

The Western view sets off from the assumption that unless a variety of opinions, programs, and persons can be presented to the electorate for their approval or disapproval, the people are not in a position to make an informed choice between the alternatives which are open to them. Without full freedom for an opposition to canvass every possibility and to speak its mind, the sins and errors of the government cannot be brought to light, and, of even greater importance, nor can what may be wiser measures secure an adequate hearing. Only by establishing institutional safeguards for criticism and innovation, it is contended, it is contended, is it possible to ensure that all viewpoints have been heard and that all means of achieving the public good have been explored. The opposition must therefore be free to organize and to publicize its views, to offer its candidates for election on the same terms as the governing party, and to take over the government if it wins public favor. The distinguished British authority, Sir Ivor Jennings, has put it succinctly:

[4] *West Africa* (March 29, 1958), 304.

"If there is no opposition, there is no democracy," [5] and the Governor-General of Nigeria, Nnamdi Azikiwe, has made the same point slightly more elaborately:

> Unless an opposition exists—as a "shadow cabinet" capable of replacing the government—democracy becomes a sham. . . . Failure to tolerate the existence of an opposition party would be disastrous to the existence of democracy. It is the easiest invitation to dictatorship.[6]

However strong the case may be for this version of democracy, an overwhelming majority of Asian and African states have in the last few years moved away from it to embrace more authoritarian military or one-party, and usually one-man, regimes. By far the greatest of them, of course, is China which discarded the one-party authoritarianism of Chiang Kai-shek for the totalitarianism of Mao and the Communists, but the Communist pattern has so far been followed only in neighboring North Korea and North Vietnam, and in distant Cuba, although it has obviously had a significant influence elsewhere. The military have taken over in the Republic of Korea, Burma, Thailand, Pakistan, Egypt and from time to time other Arab countries, and the Sudan. In most of the rest of the Afro-Asian countries one-party political systems have been established, either *de facto* or through official outlawry of other parties. In a few instances parties have either never played a role, as in Ethiopia or Saudi Arabia, or have been reduced to insignificance, as in Egypt under Nasser or Indonesia under Sukarno, with the exception of the Communists in the latter case.

In order to make room for a more extensive survey of the justifications which the Asian and African leaders have themselves brought forward for the one-party system, only a brief listing will be attempted here of the major elements, for the most part already suggested in the preceding pages, which are usually regarded as responsible for the turn away from the liberal Western pattern. It might be added that while most external observers would agree on the items to be included in such a list they would be likely to disagree as to the weighting to be given them.

The easiest starting point is no doubt the gap which exists between the new elite which has become the heir to political power and the mass of the people in the emerging countries. The former have a substantial Western-style education, not infrequently including advanced degrees,

[5] *Cabinet Government*. Cambridge: Cambridge University Press, 1937, p. 15.
[6] Cited by SUSAN and PETER RITNER, Africa's Constitutional Malarky. *The New Leader* (June 10, 1963), 20.

are literate in at least one Western language which often serves as the *lingua franca* for the country, and are well acquainted with Western forms of government. The masses, on the other hand, are still illiterate, live close to the subsistence line, and have had no occasion to become familiar with any higher level of government than that which impinges on them locally, be it of a traditional variety or some modernized version brought in by the colonial or central authorities. These things are changing: education in many countries is spreading greatly, standards of living are slowly improving, universal suffrage in principle brings political activity to every corner of the country, and expanding governmental functions impinge more and more even upon the remote villages; but the gap between elite and mass remains great, though more intermediate groupings are coming into being. The usual meagerness and inadequacy of the network of mass communications also hinder the narrowing of the gap between governing elite and governed mass. It is typical that a highly educated and influential Pakistani intellectual should have told me the other day that at the most ten per cent of the people of his country have any measure of political awareness and play any continuing political role.

The existence of the many other gaps which break up the homogeneity of the societies renders presently impossible the achievement of that basic consensus which most theorists of liberal democracy see as essential to its flourishing or even to its survival. The danger exists, not as an abstract threat for the future but as an inescapable present reality, that these gaps are likely to mean that any opposition party or movement of consequence bases itself on a tribal or other racial, linguistic, religious, or regional grouping which at least implicitly, if not quite openly, threatens the national unity which it is the goal of the dominant leaders to consolidate or bring into being. Given the lack of political experience of a modern type, the opposition is likely to conceive itself as the all-out enemy of the governing group and perhaps of the state itself rather than to grasp the subtle and sophisticated idea of becoming His Majesty's loyal opposition. It has frequently been said that in Ghana the word for "opposition" is "enemy."

A different order of considerations involves the ease with which the parliamentary system can be converted into an instrument for one-party rule. So long as the generally accepted political morality includes the assumption that two or more parties competing for power according to an implicitly agreed set of rules are an essential part of the political game democracy in the Western sense finds expression in the parliamentary forum. The entire situation changes if the emphasis is placed on the right of the majority not only to constitute the government, but also to take all power to itself without regard for the minority. From the assumption that the majority rules with a firm hand and that the minority is no more than a tolerated nuisance, it is a relatively small step to seeing it as only a nuisance, no longer to be tolerated. In such circumstances opposition parties can be outlawed or by one or another device absorbed within the ruling 'national' party; and what set out to be a parliamentary government on the Western model takes on a totally different hue. A convenient device for bringing the opposition into line is the provision adopted by several of the French-speaking African states that the entire country forms a single electoral constituency, and that the party whose national list secures the highest vote takes all the seats in the parliament. What emerges is executive predominance centered on the national leader.

As the leaders of the new countries themselves see it, it is only plausible to assume that their awareness of the gap between them and the masses is one of the key features of the situation. Their goal is to construct modern countries, and it would be obviously absurd to rely on the unmodern masses to undertake and guide their own transformation. The masses must be carried along in the process, but the controlling hand must be that of the contingent in the society which has itself achieved modernity. Contemporary democratic presuppositions make it unfashionable and perhaps politically unfeasible to come out openly with elitist doctrines but they occasionally make a more or less overt appearance. In a period less committed to full-scale democracy, Sun Yat-sen, as one of the first of those to confront the dilemmas involved in modernizing a society which very reluctantly abandoned its traditional ways, spoke out openly for a period of tutelage during which the people at large would be educated to assume their new democratic responsibilities. In his *San Min Chu I* he referred repeatedly to the inequality of men in ability and held the majority of the people to be without vision. Those of us who have a broader vision, he held, must guide the people into the right way and escape the confusions into which Western democracy has fallen.

The phrase which has come to be most widely used to designate this kind of tutelage is Sukarno's "guided democracy" which combines the conviction of the day that democracy is in order with the conviction that some people are more equal than others. In his first address as President of the United States of Indonesia, in December, 1949, Sukarno denied that democracy was anything new for Indonesia, but insisted that it differed from the democracy of others:

Eastern democracy—more clearly Indonesian democracy that has
descended to us from generation to generation, is *democracy accompanied by leadership: democracy with leadership!* That is Eastern democracy, Indonesian democracy. *The leader carries a great
responsibility,* the leader must know how to lead, the leader must
lead.[7]

Although Sukarno has always related his political speculations and
institutional proposals very closely to the Indonesian scene and its tradition many of the key propositions which he has emphasized turn up
with regularity in a number of the other new countries. The heart of
the matter is his repudiation of the notion of an opposition and of a
majority which is automatically entitled to override a minority even
though its margin of victory may be only a single vote. Democracy, if
properly guided, has his blessing, but not the Western liberal version
of it which he has derided as "free-flight democracy." The idea of an
opposition he has lumped with liberalism and capitalism as alien to the
Indonesian experience and outlook, serving to divide the community
against itself rather than to unite. In his view, what Indonesian tradition
renders desirable and feasible is the gathering together in the top
councils of government of people representing as far as possible every
viewpoint and every phase of the country's life. Their function is not
to define the opposing positions more sharply and come to a vote in
which one faction outnumbers the other, but to continue the discussion
until all have collaborated in reaching a decision which all accept.
Omnipresent in the background is Sukarno himself, prepared to take
the decision which represents the popular will if agreement fails to
emerge from the deliberations.

Time and again in a number of African countries surprisingly similar
declarations of political principle have been made, denouncing the
Western liberal-parliamentary conception of the opposition and insisting
that African tradition calls for the slow ironing out of disagreement
until the sense of the meeting has been arrived at. Thus in presenting
the case for a one-party state in Ghana in 1962 Minister of Defence
Kofi Baako told the National Assembly that the multiparty system was
unfitting to Ghana where tradition called for a council of elders, approved by the people and with a chief to lead them. He continued:

There is no question of a deliberate division of that group, one side
saying "I am opposing" and another side saying "I am governing."

[7] Cited by GERALD S. MARYANOV, *Decentralization in Indonesia as a Political Problem.*
Southeast Asia Program, Cornell University, 1958, pp. 49-50.

All of them in fact govern and they govern by consultation and by deliberation.[8]

A different kind of objection to the multi-party system which has frequently been advanced in Africa, as, for example, by Sékou Touré in Guinea and Julius Nyerere in Tanganyika, is the contention that political parties developed in the West in response to the need of different classes to protect and promote their conflicting interests, whereas since Africa has produced no corresponding class differentiation it has no need of a multiplicity of parties. (There is here an interesting parallel to the Soviet claim that since the U.S.S.R. has arrived at a monolithic pattern of society without exploiting classes and other intermediate groupings, it requires only a single all-embracing party; but, on the other hand, Communist theorists are by no means prepared to accept the view that African societies are classless.)

A further step in the direction of the one-party system is made when the nationalist movements are brought into the argument. European and American parties, Nyerere has asserted, came into being as the result of internal social and economic divisions, one party arising to challenge the monopoly of political power of some aristocratic or capitalist group. In Africa, on the other hand, the function of parties was to challenge the external threat posed by the alien rulers: under such circumstances the parties represented not factions and divisions within the country, but "the interests and aspirations of the whole nation. . . . A Tanganyikan who helped the imperialists was regarded as a traitor to his country, not as a believer in 'Two-Party' democracy!" [9]

This introduction of the nationalist movements has served the one-party advocates well. With a heavy admixture of sarcasm they have confronted their Western and domestic critics with the question as to whether their countries, having achieved a nationalist consolidation of political forces against the colonial authorities, must now deliberately break down the unity which has been gained in order to satisfy the doctrinaire insistence of Western-style democrats on the existence of more than one party.

At this point the controversy is likely to swing back to what was suggested earlier as the fundamental distinction between the Western

[8] *Ghana Today,* June 6, 1962. He continued on to contend that only the mistakes a government made justified an opposition; therefore, to say that an opposition is necessary for democracy implies that a government must make mistakes to allow the opposition to stay; which has the effect of destroying democracy.

[9] *Democracy and the Party System,* pp. 14-15. (This is a pamphlet written by Nyerere, and published, without date, by the Tanganyika Standard Limited, Dar es Salaam.)

liberal approach to democracy and the variant approach which has spread so widely in other parts of the world. It is a characteristic difference that Western spokesmen are likely to stress the protection which their conception offers to minorities and to individuals, enabling diversity to flourish and encouraging the growth of a pluralistic society, while the emphasis in the new countries falls rather on the need for unity and a strong government which can take hold of the immensely difficult and urgent problems confronting it. It is felt that if the government has the popular approval of the mass it should be free to go about its business unhampered by checks and balances or other niceties of liberal constitutionalism. Madeira Keita of Mali has said of democracy that "in its naively original sense" it is "the exercise of public authority in conformity with the will of the masses." [10] In a cruder and more activist version of much the same proposition Castro protested in 1961 that the Cuban people had been deluded by a false democracy for sixty years:

> Speak to the people of elections and they will answer you that what interests them now is that the revolution advance rapidly and that no time be lost.
>
> For the first time the people hold power. For the first time it is the people who govern. It matters very little whether the formalities are observed. What counts is the essence of democracy, that is, that the people and public opinion determine the destiny of the country. We have need of all our time to push the revolution ahead, to develop our economy, to defend ourselves against imperialism. [11]

In Castro's statement there is at least a hint of what is probably the most frequent comment about the Western parliamentary system in general and the multi-party system in particular: These are luxuries which we cannot now afford; perhaps later on when we have caught up with the advanced countries we will be able to afford them. As the months and years have gone by, however, the tendency has been to postpone to a more and more remote future the time when such luxuries might prove desirable and to elaborate increasingly on the virtues inherent in the one-party system.

[10] *The Ideologies of the Developing Nations,* PAUL E. SIGMUND, ed. New York: Praeger, 1963, p. 176. A more radical version was put forward by Sékou Touré: ". . . if the dictatorship exerted by the government is the direct emanation of the whole of the people, dictatorship is of a democratic nature and the State is a democratic State, democracy being the exercise, by the people, of National Sovereignty." *Towards Full Re-Africanization.* Paris, Présence Africaine, 1959, p. 28.

[11] JEAN LACOUTURE and JEAN BAUMIER, *Le poids du tiers monde.* Paris: Arthaud, 1962, p. 172. *The New York Times Book Review,* July 21, 1963, carries on its front page a picture of a wall in Guayaquil, Ecuador, on which is crudely scrawled: "130 años de elecciones—130 años de MISERIA."

The most urgent task here and now is almost certain to be seen not as the protection of individual and minority liberties but the realization in broad strokes of what is taken to be the community will—or perhaps what the elite feel it should be. The first order of business is not the creation of an opposition which can criticize but the establishment of a strong and vigorous government which can govern. Since so many of the emerging countries are in greater or less degree recent and artificial constructs whose inner solidarity rests on unstable foundations it is easy to comprehend why the leaders give priority to the consolidation of national unity through the prompt and decisive action of an effective government. Without such a government neither development nor a defense against disintegration or a return of colonialism is possible.

While it is evidently not necessarily the case that two or more parties should prejudice or disrupt the incipient national unity, it is reasonable to expect that they will not promote unity to the same extent as a single party, dedicated to that purpose; and national unity is regarded as a more real and desirable good than a pluralistic political freedom. The risks of disintegration which attach to a multi-party system are, of course, greatly enhanced where party loyalties and voting patterns are determined on the basis of particularistic racial, tribal, or other ethnic groups, as is so often the case in the Asian and African states. Furthermore, at least in principle, the one-party system avoids the dispersion of effort which an opposition involves and makes it possible to enlist all the limited expertise and leadership which is available for a combined attack upon the national problems. In practice, however, the solidarity of the ranks of the national leaders is gravely impaired in many countries by the substantial number of distinguished figures or potential contributors to national well-being who are held in preventive detention, are otherwise jailed, or have vanished into exile.

The apologists for the one-party state are not unlikely to play both sides of the street; that is, to assert that the single party can appropriately exist without violating democratic precepts because it is essentially a continuation of the national unity won in the anti-colonial struggle, and at the same time, perhaps less overtly, to plead the necessity of having a single party if the break-up of the society is to be prevented. The latter argument is bolstered by the charge that the imperialists and other external enemies foster the rise and activity of opposition parties in order to undermine the solidarity of the state which has so recently come to independence. Although the situation varies from country to country, it is in general more realistic to see the trend toward the authoritarian one-party system as deriving from the lack of national unity rather than as the expression of it. It is evidently the case in most instances that the single governing party is the same nationalist movement which won independence or is the direct descendant thereof, but one essential justification for the centralization of political control is that national unity is so tenuous as not to be trusted to operate without the firmest of guidance from the top. The single party is an instrument to achieve the national solidarity which is otherwise conspicuous by its absence, and often it is the principal instrument available for that purpose.

One salient feature of the single-party system as it has functioned in practice is that in most instances the capstone of the structure has been the single charismatic leader. Indeed, it is often not going too far to see the ruling party as in fact the vehicle, or even an emanation, of the central figure who dominates the entire political landscape. At the present day their names have become household words and need no lengthy recitation: Gandhi and then Nehru, Sukarno, Chiang and then Mao, Bourguiba, Nkrumah, Sékou Touré, Houphouet-Boigny, Banda, Nyerere, to name only a few. A forthright expression of what is involved was made by the governing party in the Congo (Brazzaville) which contended that,

> While in Europe the rules of parliamentary behaviour are based on a relative or absolute majority. . . . parliamentary democracy in Africa is based on unanimity. One can truthfully say that an African state which is incapable of giving its undivided support to a unanimously acknowledged leader is, and will remain, a land deeply divided against itself, and to all intents and purposes ungovernable within the framework of the new institutions.[12]

This emergence of the strong heroic figure in new countries at a troubled time is nothing new in the historical record; it has of late been pointed out by several writers that what might be castigated as an abuse in the presently emerging countries found its close parallel in the unmeasured adulation of George Washington in the early days of the United States. The need of a visible symbol, and more than a symbol, of national identity and striving is very great. For the politically unsophisticated the whole paraphernalia of parliaments and cabinets, ministers and civil service hierarchies are remote, unreal, and confusing, while a single figure, visible in the flesh and constantly paraded before

---

[12] Cited by CARL G. ROSBERG, JR., Democracy and the New African States, in *African Affairs, Number Two*. St. Antony's Papers, Number 15, ed. by Kenneth Kirkwood. London, Chatto & Windus, 1963, p. 30.

the public as the savior of his people, has an unmistakable and dramatic reality.

In constitutional terms the consequence has been a marked shift away from the European parliamentary pattern and toward the presidential system. After decades of finding few imitators the American constitution has again come into its own as a model for the new countries, although what has been taken over from it is far more the central national figure of the president than the host of checks and balances and countervailing institutions which plague the life of the American President. No occupant of the White House would recognize himself in the not overly exaggerated portrayal by a Tunisian newspaper of the "absolute supremacy" which Bourguiba has conquered for himself; "Everything converges toward the holder of power who, alone, exists, decides, and in expressing himself expresses the country and incarnates it." [13]

What has been sought is a direct and evident concentration of power in the hands of a single national leader. The division of power which at least appears to exist where a President is ceremonial head of state while a Prime Minister, surrounded by a Cabinet and responsible to a parliamentary majority, actually controls the government has proved intolerable to countries which yearn for a simpler and more straightforward version of their new-found sovereignty. Considerations of the same sort have played a small role in persuading several of the newer members of the Commonwealth to become republics. Although nationalist pressures have been the most important, it has also been contended that the people find it difficult to comprehend an independence in which the Queen is still sovereign and in which her representative, the Governor-General, co-exists with the Prime Minister.

The swing to authoritarian single-party regimes has inevitably produced much controversy as to the extent to which political freedom has been impaired and whether and on what grounds such impairment can be justified. The extreme position, rarely stated in blunt terms and to be found most frequently among those who have undergone substantial exposure to Marxist thought, lays all its emphasis on the community as an integrated whole—Sékou Touré has spoken of Africa as being essentially *communaucratique*—whose general will, if guided by the right hands, must always be right. The mere fact that a minority opposes makes it immediately suspect and opens it to the charge of being a tool of the neo-colonialists.

[13] Cited from *Afrique-Action,* October 7, 1961, by Clement Moore in an unpublished Ph.D. dissertation, Harvard University, 1963.

On more pragmatic grounds, the accusation that the new states have abused the liberty of their people is met, particularly when it comes from Western critics, both by citing the abuses of colonialism and by pointing out that all countries have greatly tightened up the apparatus of control in time of war or other crises. The crisis deriving from the anti-colonial revolution and the setting in motion of an independent government and the drive for development are held amply to justify the restrictions of private liberty which have been imposed.

As a means of reconciling the demands of political freedom with those of one-party authoritarianism some reigning parties have adopted the familiar Communist device of democratic centralism which calls for full freedom of discussion at all levels as decisions are being reached and for unquestioning observance once they are made. This is a mode of procedure which has the advantage of being easily squared with the assumption of Sukarno and many others that the kind of democracy traditionally characteristic of Asian and African countries is a confrontation of all opinions in free discussion which ultimately achieves an agreed version of the community's will. As a statement of intent it is admirable and, if wholly lived up to, it could meet virtually all requirements, but the abyss which separates theory from practice is likely to be peculiarly great in this sphere. The formal promise of full freedom to oppose the leader and to challenge the desires of the party hierachy is all too likely in reality to lead to political retaliation against the dissident faction. To make the voice of the village heard at the top is a difficult matter under any circumstances; the single party headed by a charismatic leader does not gladly suffer criticism; and within the single-party state it is hard to parallel the institutional safeguards which protect dissident opinion in a country where two or more parties are accepted features of the political scene. In a message celebrating the 14th anniversary of the founding of his Convention People's Party in June, 1963, Nkrumah declared that if innerparty democracy and self-criticism is practiced "it will follow that all decisions of the party are decisions of the entire membership" and party democracy will be fully achieved.[14] But the dissidents and minorities are far from having had an easy time in Ghana.

Of other justifications of the one-party system, only two need be cited. Tom Mboya has recently argued that the political experience of the new countries of Asia and Africa demonstrates that the party system is not a necessary part of democracy, and he concludes that "what is necessary is the freedom to form parties. It is not necessary that more than one

[14] *West Africa*, June 22, 1963, p. 703.

should in fact exist and function effectively."[15] To this he adds the further proposition, in one sense undeniable and in another highly debatable, that a sovereign people may decide to forego their right to form parties and decree irrevocably that the country shall in the future have only one party.

Nyerere, who has also backed the idea that what is important is the freedom to form opposition parties, has been pleased to develop an argument to the effect that legislators and others within a single party have in fact a greater measure of freedom than do political figures within a two or multi-party system. The gist of this proposition is that where an opposition exists, the members of each party must be held to a strict party discipline in order to deny any opening to the rival. Within the single party, on the other hand, all are free to express their own opinions until the party line has been shaped, with the backbenchers contributing as much as the leaders. As Nyerere's thinking has evolved he has become an increasingly firm supporter of the single party concept and of the practical merger of party and government. With the expectation of shocking the political theorists who identify democracy with opposing parties, he has laid it down that,

> where there is *one* party, and that party is identified with the *nation as a whole*, the foundations of democracy are firmer than they can ever be where you have two or more parties, each representing only a section of the community.[16]

The issues involved are relatively simple and straightforward. The single-party system, or the military rule which has been imposed in several countries, has evident virtues where the people are sharply divided among themselves and unity is a first requisite, where a new political, social, and economic society must be brought into being, and where the hardships and disciplines of development must take priority over private preferences. It is obvious that no single and all-embracing answer can be given, but the other side of the situation must have more attention than the leaders of the new countries are inclined to give it. Even assuming that the nationalist movements are led and manned by disinterested patriots and that in the first rounds the parties and governments which take over after independence sincerely strive to embody the will of the people, how likely are they to drift away to holding power for its own sake and for the fruits it yields them, giving only the necessary bread and circuses and plebiscitary celebrations to the popu-

[15] The Party System in Africa. *Foreign Affairs* (July 1963), p. 653.
[16] *Democracy and the Party System, op. cit.,* p. 7.

lace? Can the leadership in fact be trusted to welcome those who criticize and would like to replace it, and can the people be expected to be aware of the issues and alternatives when the media of mass information and the main nongovernmental organizations of society, such as those of the workers, farmers, women, and youth, have been taken over as instruments of the single-party government? The single party and the charismatic leader have not generally been marked by tolerance, nor is it a very distinctive freedom to be able to vote for a single slate of candidates. But there is little in the way of available evidence to indicate that the people at large in the new countries are seriously disaffected by the turn their political systems have taken.

Let me conclude with a comment, a question, and a prophecy.

Economic development is more likely to bring into being the conditions which are requisite for the successful working of a democratic system than any other combination of forces and factors which may be brought into play.

But is there any reason for confidence that the kind of conditions which surrounded democracy in a few countries at a given time in history will produce democracy elsewhere at a different time; or are the people of many countries going to be prepared to let their political affairs be run for them by essentially self-selected elites, shaken up from time to time by revolutionary outbursts?

For the foreseeable future, as the armed forces of the new countries grow, the taking over of governments by the military will be a more and more frequent occurrence. Although Ayub Khan has endowed Pakistan with basic democracies, for the military regimes as for the one-party one-man governments the return to liberal parliamentary democracy of the Western type is on the whole less rather than more likely to come to pass.

Sources and Acknowledgments

AVERY LEISERSON, "The Place of Parties in the Study of Politics," reprinted by permission of *The American Political Science Review,* LI, No. 4 (December 1957), 943-54. Avery Leiserson is Professor of Politics at Vanderbilt University. He is the author of *Parties and Politics: An Institutional and Behavioral Approach* (1958), and numerous other works.

SEYMOUR MARTIN LIPSET, "Party Systems and the Representation of Social Groups," reprinted by permission of *The European Journal of Sociology,* I, No. 1 (1960), 3-8. Seymour Martin Lipset is Professor of Social Relations and Government at Harvard University. He is the author of *The First New Nation* (1963), *Political Man* (1960), and numerous other works.

JAMES B. CHRISTOPH, "Consensus and Cleavage in British Political Ideology," reprinted by permission from *The American Political Science Review,* LIX, No. 3 (September 1965). James B. Christoph is Professor of Political Science at Ohio State University. He is editor and co-author of *Cases in Comparative Politics,* and a number of other publications.

RICHARD ROSE, "Parties, Factions, and Tendencies in Britain," reprinted by permission from *Political Studies,* XII, No. 1 (February 1964), 33-46. This is a revised form of a paper originally presented to the American Political Science Association in Washington, D.C., in September 1962. Richard Rose is Professor of Politics at Manchester University, England. He is the author of *Politics in England: An Interpretation* (1965), and editor of *British Politics* (1966), among a number of other publications.

LEON D. EPSTEIN, "Political Parties in Western Democratic Systems," delivered at a conference commemorating the 50th anniversary of the Department of Government, Indiana University, November 5-7, 1964, prior to publication in a modified form in Edward H. Buehrig, ed.,

Essays in Political Science, University of Indiana Press, 1966. Reprinted here by permission. Leon D. Epstein is Professor of Politics and Dean of the College of Letters and Science of the University of Wisconsin. He is the author of *British Politics in the Suez Crisis* and of *Politics in Wisconsin,* among numerous other works.

HENRY W. EHRMANN, "Direct Democracy in France," reprinted by permission from *The American Political Science Review,* LVII, No. 4 (December 1963). Henry W. Ehrmann is Professor of Government at Dartmouth College. He is the author of *French Business* and editor of *Interest Groups on Four Continents,* among numerous other works.

ROY C. MACRIDIS, "The Immobility of the French Communist Party," reprinted by permission from *The Journal of Politics* (November 1959), 613-634. Roy C. Macridis is Professor of Politics at Brandeis University. He is the author of *The Study of Comparative Government,* and co-author of *The De Gaulle Republic—Quest for Unity,* among numerous other publications.

ISAIAH BERLIN, "Political Ideas in the Twentieth Century," reprinted by special permission from *Foreign Affairs* (April 1950). Copyright by the Council of Foreign Relations, Inc., New York. Isaiah Berlin is Professor of Philosophy at All Souls College, Oxford University. He is the author of *Karl Marx: His Life and Environment,* and *The Hedgehog and the Fox,* among numerous other publications.

RUPERT EMERSON, "Political Modernization: The Single-Party System," reprinted by permission from *Monograph Series in World Affairs,* The Social Science Foundation and Department of International Relations, University of Denver, No. 1. Rupert Emerson is Professor of Government at Harvard University. He is the author of *From Empire to Nation* (1960) and co-author of *Politics of Awakening in Africa,* among numerous other works.

hARPER ⚜ ɈORChBOOKS

HUMANITIES AND SOCIAL SCIENCES

American Studies: General

HENRY STEELE COMMAGER, Ed.: The Struggle for Racial Equality TB/1300
CARL N. DEGLER, Ed.: Pivotal Interpretations of American History TB/1240, TB/1241
A. S. EISENSTADT, Ed.: The Craft of American History Vol. I TB/1255; Vol. II TB/1256
CHARLOTTE P. GILMAN: Women and Economics § TB/3073
JOHN HIGHAM, Ed.: The Reconstruction of American History △ TB/1068
LEONARD W. LEVY, Ed.: American Constitutional Law TB/1285
LEONARD W. LEVY, Ed.: Judicial Review and the Supreme Court TB/1296
LEONARD W. LEVY: The Law of the Commonwealth and Chief Justice Shaw TB/1309
ARNOLD ROSE: The Negro in America TB/3048

American Studies: Colonial

CHARLES GIBSON: Spain in America † TB/3077
LAWRENCE HENRY GIPSON: The Coming of the Revolution: 1763-1775. † Illus. TB/3007
PERRY MILLER & T. H. JOHNSON, Eds.: The Puritans: A Sourcebook Vol. I TB/1093; Vol. II TB/1094
EDMUND S. MORGAN, Ed.: The Diary of Michael Wigglesworth, 1653-1657 TB/1228
EDMUND S. MORGAN: The Puritan Family TB/1227
RICHARD B. MORRIS: Government and Labor in Early America TB/1244
JOHN P. ROCHE: Origins of American Political Thought: Selected Readings TB/1301
JOHN SMITH: Captain John Smith's America: Selections from His Writings TB/3078

American Studies: From the Revolution to 1860

RAY A. BILLINGTON: The Far Western Frontier: 1830-1860. † Illus. TB/3012
GEORGE DANGERFIELD: The Awakening of American Nationalism: 1815-1828. † Illus. TB/3061
WILLIAM W. FREEHLING, Ed.: The Nullification Era: A Documentary Record ‡ TB/3079
RICHARD B. MORRIS, Ed.: The Era of the American Revolution TB/1180
A. F. TYLER: Freedom's Ferment TB/1074

American Studies: Since the Civil War

MAX BELOFF, Ed.: The Debate on the American Revolution, 1761-1783: A Sourcebook △ TB/1225
W. R. BROCK: An American Crisis: Congress and Reconstruction, 1865-67 ○ △ TB/1283
EDMUND BURKE: On the American Revolution. † Edited by Elliot Robert Barkan TB/3068

WHITNEY R. CROSS: The Burned-Over District: The Social and Intellectual History of Enthusiastic Religion in Western New York, 1800-1850 TB/1242
FRANCIS GRIERSON: The Valley of Shadows TB/1246
SIDNEY HOOK: Reason, Social Myths, and Democracy TB/1237
WILLIAM E. LEUCHTENBURG: Franklin D. Roosevelt and the New Deal: 1932-1940. † Illus. TB/3025
ARTHUR S. LINK: Woodrow Wilson and the Progressive Era: 1910-1917. † Illus. TB/3023
JAMES MADISON: The Forging of American Federalism. Edited by Saul K. Padover TB/1226
ROBERT GREEN MC CLOSKEY: American Conservatism in the Age of Enterprise: 1865-1910 TB/1137
ARTHUR MANN: Yankee Reformers in the Urban Age TB/1247
R. B. NYE: Midwestern Progressive Politics TB/1202
FRANCIS S. PHILBRICK: The Rise of the West, 1754-1830. † Illus. TB/3067
WILLIAM PRESTON, JR.: Aliens and Dissenters TB/1287
JACOB RIIS: The Making of an American ‡ TB/3070
PHILIP SELZNICK: TVA and the Grass Roots TB/1230
TIMOTHY L. SMITH: Revivalism and Social Reform: American Protestantism on the Eve of the Civil War TB/1229
IDA M. TARBELL: The History of the Standard Oil Company: Briefer Version ‡ TB/3071
GEORGE B. TINDALL, Ed.: A Populist Reader ‡ TB/3069
ALBION W. TOURGÉE: A Fool's Errand TB/3074
VERNON LANE WHARTON: The Negro in Mississippi: 1865-1890 TB/1178

Anthropology

JACQUES BARZUN: Race: A Study in Superstition. Revised Edition TB/1172
JOSEPH B. CASAGRANDE, Ed.: In the Company of Man: Portraits of Anthropological Informants. TB/3047
DAVID LANDY: Tropical Childhood ¶ TB/1235
EDWARD BURNETT TYLOR: The Origins of Culture. Part I of "Primitive Culture." § Intro. by Paul Radin TB/33
EDWARD BURNETT TYLOR: Religion in Primitive Culture. Part II of "Primitive Culture" § TB/34

Art and Art History

EMILE MÂLE: The Gothic Image: Religious Art in France of the Thirteenth Century. § △ 190 illus. TB/44
ERICH NEUMANN: The Archetypal World of Henry Moore. △ 107 illus. TB/2020
DORA & ERWIN PANOFSKY: Pandora's Box TB/2021

Business, Economics & Economic History

GILBERT BURCK & EDITORS OF FORTUNE: The Computer Age: And Its Potential for Management TB/1179

---

† The New American Nation Series, edited by Henry Steele Commager and Richard B. Morris.
‡ American Perspectives series, edited by Bernard Wishy and William E. Leuchtenburg.
* The Rise of Modern Europe series, edited by William L. Langer.
** History of Europe series, edited by J. H. Plumb.
¶ Researches in the Social, Cultural and Behavioral Sciences, edited by Benjamin Nelson.
§ The Library of Religion and Culture, edited by Benjamin Nelson.
Σ Harper Modern Science Series, edited by James R. Newman.
○ Not for sale in Canada.
△ Not for sale in the U. K.

1

3